Lord Byron at Harrow School

Paul Elledge

Lord Byron at Harrow School

Speaking Out, Talking Back, Acting Up, Bowing Out

The Johns Hopkins University Press
Baltimore and London

© 2000 The Johns Hopkins University Press
All rights reserved. Published 2000
Printed in the United States of America on acid-free paper
9 8 7 6 5 4 3 2 1

The Johns Hopkins University Press
2715 North Charles Street
Baltimore, Maryland 21218-4363
www.press.jhu.edu

Library of Congress Cataloging-in-Publication Data will be found at the end of this book.
A catalog record for this book is available from the British Library.

ISBN 0-8018-6343-0

for
Gordon Peerman and Ben Curtis
physicians to the soul

Contents

Acknowledgments ix
Abbreviations xiii

    Prologue 1

1 : Tutor and Tenant 16
2 : Virgilian King: *5 July 1804* 44

    First Interval 64

3 : William Henry West Betty 85
4 : Villain: *6 June 1805* 98

    Second Interval 135

5 : Shakespearean King: *4 July 1805* 140

    Epilogue: *"The Sixth of June"* 165

Notes 169
Selected Bibliography 207
Index 217

Illustrations follow page 134.

Acknowledgments

This project originated in a gift. Upon my relieved surrender of the department chair several years back, my Vanderbilt colleagues in English expressed themselves with the generous offering of a well-preserved, handsomely bound 1833 copy of Thomas Moore's two-volume *The Letters and Journals of Lord Byron, with Notices of His Life*. Rereading that text after many years, I found my subject. I thanked my friends then, not knowing the extent of their largesse; I thank them again here, now that I do. Other gifts have followed.

I gratefully acknowledge Dean of Research Russell Hamilton and the Vanderbilt University Research Council for the awards of two consecutive summer grants and support for a one-term research leave of absence, along with travel funds and assistance with the costs of permission to reproduce illustrations.

Vanderbilt University librarians Dale Manning, Paula Covington, and Anne Rueland have, like Auntie Mame, opened doors—a.k.a. electronic "files"—for me that I never dreamed existed, and escorted me through them with capital forbearance. Interlibrary loan officers Jim Toplon and Marilyn Pilley once again proved efficient in locating and prompt in delivering materials essential to my research.

Among British librarians, my first thanks must go to Mrs. Rita Gibbs, archivist at Harrow School, for good-spirited diligence, tenacity, and resourceful digging in conditions that would break the spirit of a saint. Her assistance to me in the Archive Room, and thereafter by e-mail and telephone, her mediation with other parties, and her success at arranging an interview, against all odds, with boys of the school having Speech Day experience were invaluable to my project.

Mrs. Gibbs's immediate predecessor, Alasdair Hawkyard, introduced me to the Harrow School archives, usefully guided a tour of the grounds, and offered experienced counsel. Peter D. Hunter, Vaughan Librarian and English master at the school, kindly advised me on the fine Harrow collection of materials related to Lord Byron. And N. R.

Bomford, former headmaster of Harrow, cordially granted me a ticket to the 1996 Speech Day ceremonies.

Among other British archivists, I particularly thank Simon May at St. Paul's School for informative correspondence and conversation, and memorably warm hospitality; Peter Holmes at Westminster School for a full and illuminating historical account of speechmaking at the institution; and James B. Lawson of the Shrewsbury School for tireless, exceptionally resourceful research far beyond the call of responsible librarianship, and for the exciting discoveries that it produced. I was also fortunate in receiving gracious welcome and generous research assistance from Mrs. P. Hatfield at Eton College, Geoffrey Brown at the Merchant Taylors' School, James Sabben-Clare, headmaster at Winchester College, and Mrs. Shirley Corke at Charterhouse.

With courteous expedition, the staffs of the British Library and especially of the London Theatre Museum provided access to an abundance of material unavailable elsewhere, and comfortable space for perusing it. And the curators of the Myer Davis Collection at the University of Pennsylvania supplied copies of manuscript material.

Charles E. Robinson, executive director of the Byron Society of America, patiently answered a battery of inquiries, or connected me with others who did so, among them Peter Cochran, Michael Rees, Melissa Bakewell (on Augusta Leigh), Annette Peach (on Byron portraiture), and the late Leslie A. Marchand, first authority and honored patriarch of Byron scholarship. For the ready magnanimity of these colaborers in the vineyard, I am most grateful.

Benita Eisler, author of a recent, full-scale Byron biography, shared information with me from the John Murray archives, closed during the years of my research while another author completes her biography of the poet for his publishers. Carl Miller of London agreeably furnished a manuscript copy of his produced but not yet published play "Master Betty: A Gothic Tale."

My Johns Hopkins editors Maura Burnett, Marie Blanchard, and Barbara B. Lamb performed their redemptive magic on my text with enviable skill and subtle tact.

I have benefited from the technological tutelage and clerical services of Carolyn Levinson and Janis May, and particularly from those of Sara Corbitt, who processed, corrected, copied, packaged, stayed late, and endured my obsessive tinkering with remarkable tolerance and unfailing good cheer. Paul Burch efficiently manned the fax and FedEx desk. And Tom Haddox rendered meticulous assistance with the index and proofs.

My Vanderbilt colleague Mark Schoenfield insistently—and occasionally to my impatient exasperation—turned routine queries into opportunities for spacious, newly angled interrogation of my subject, to the immeasurable enrichment of my thinking about it. Ken Collins and Rod Downey read versions of the manuscript, Collins with the exacting eye of a scholar and stylist, Downey with the instinct and experience of a dramatist, and both contributed many valuable comments. Roy Gottfried's wit supplied distance and refreshment, and his otherwise tiresome conservatism prudently checked my radical imagination. Richard Mallette offered e-mail commiseration and encouragement through the rough patches, shared satisfaction in the smooth, and continued to model for me the searching, disciplined mind of a true intellectual, and the artistry of friendship well maintained.

And then there is Peter Manning. Always—mercifully—there is Peter, for a grateful multitude of us the selfless master-reader nonpareil of Romantic texts and of texts about Romantic texts. So smart and stimulating was his review of an early version of my manuscript, and so compelling his recommendations for revision and elaboration, that I have shamelessly pilfered the substance and, sometimes, the very language of his critique. For Peter's sturdy, steadying companionship through my own Harrovian pilgrimage, I could not feel more generously blessed or profoundly indebted.

Abbreviations

BLJ
: Leslie A. Marchand, ed., *Byron's Letters and Journals.* 13 vols. Cambridge, Mass.: Belknap Press, Harvard University Press, 1973–94.

CPW
: Jerome J. McGann, ed., *The Complete Poetical Works of Lord Byron.* 7 vols. Oxford: Clarendon Press, 1980–93.

DJ
: Byron's *Don Juan,* in *CPW,* vol. 5.

Marchand
: Leslie A. Marchand, *Byron: A Biography.* 3 vols. New York: Alfred A. Knopf, 1957.

Moore
: Thomas Moore, *The Letters and Journals of Lord Byron, with Notices of His Life.* 2 vols. Paris: Baudry's European Library, 1833.

Playfair
: Giles Playfair, *The Prodigy: A Study of the Strange Life of Master Betty.* London: Secker and Warburg, 1967.

Prothero
: Rowland E. Prothero, *The Works of Lord Byron: Letters and Journals.* 6 vols. London: John Murray, 1898–1902.

Tyerman
: C. J. Tyerman, "Byron's Harrow," *Byron Journal* 17 (1989), 17–39.

Lord Byron at Harrow School

Prologue

ICONOCLAST, MAVERICK, DEPRESSIVE, SCAMP: young Lord Byron nevertheless earned respectable distinction with recitations on three public Speech Days at Harrow School. For his 5 July 1804 "*Debut* as *an orator,*" as he called it in sweaty anticipation (*BLJ* 1:48)—his language prescient of the public, performative career launched on that occasion—the sixteen-year-old chose the part of Drances in a colloquy from book 11 of the *Aeneid,* but later switched with a schoolmate to take the role of King Latinus, presumably to avoid the embarrassment that a reference to Drances's "flying feet" might have caused the club-footed boy. For a solo performance on 6 June 1805, he selected a speech by Zanga the Moor, villain of Edward Young's *The Revenge*. And a month later, on 4 July, near the end of his Harrow career, Byron declaimed King Lear's impassioned address to the storm (*Lear* 3.2.1–9, 14–24). These facts about the boy's recitations have been known since Thomas Moore retailed them in 1830. But I want here to look closely behind and beyond the particular forensic moments, to their historical contexts and biographical circumstances and ramifications, to persons and events prominent on Byron's physical and psychic landscapes at the time—as rehearsed and disguised in his letters and early poetry—in order to argue that his Speech Day performances encoded and reflected a host of anxieties, conflicts, rivalries, and ambitions which they also helped him to manage.[1]

His selection of texts for declaiming—the discourse of two kings and a show-stealing, scene-chewing villain—participates in a larger pattern of deliberate self-fashioning that began at least as early as Byron's Harrow years and evolved into the elaborate mode and vogue of self-representation that partially, with his hefty patronage, helped to define the era. To discern his initial experiments with identity formation, to watch his auditions, his inaugural performances of "Byron"—in the provincial run, so to speak, before his London premiere—to track the emergence of these constructs from a confluence of wondrous adolescent energies is to understand anew why and how enduringly certain events and relationships wrote themselves into the text that Byron famously became. It is also to marvel at his adroit manipulation of circumstances to maximum personal advantage before a public already assumed to be interested, if perhaps unfairly biased, and ripe for his enthrallment. Byron's Speech Day representations before the school—of self, of self as other, of other as self—were critical, complexly cathected episodes for him, charged with connections to his mother and half sister, his headmasters and tutors, his Harrow intimates and rivals, his Newstead tenant, his lameness, his London theatrical spectatorship. With the Harrow Speech Day events as my focus, I imagine in the story below what it feels like to be a noble but poor and fatherless boy, hobbled, hungry for affirmation and love but wary of trusting offers of either, arrogantly but vulnerably rejecting any gesture resembling condescension, hypersensitively alert and coiled to respond to even nuanced scorn, actual or assumed. As a narrative about self-creation and self-representation, this is also a story of keeping and telling secrets, of repressions, hints, evasions, equivocations, deceptions, and embellishments in the unfolding of which we watch the apprentice autobiographer learn, test, and perform his craft. It is the story of young Byron making his own separate peace by making, through assorted traumatic wars, his own separate self.

In the run-ups to the three Speech Days, in the recitations themselves, and in their aftermaths appear a number of the psychobiographical tensions that Byron's poems will later enact: the ritualized partings and extravagant farewells; the rhythms of approach and withdrawal, advance and retreat; the exploitation of inexhaustible resources for self-dramatization in chronically, compulsively repeated situations; the restless longings for partnership, completion, home; the prickly defensiveness, the daring aggression, the brooding rumination and frisky highjinks. His Harrow declamations, however, are less causal than illustrative, not so much determining as demonstrative: they amount to auditions or trials of performative and autotherapeutic strategies, subsequently refined and polished in the mature verse. Methodologically, I am less interested in detecting clues—although I do on occasion snoop—than in textual analysis: I read the relationship between actual inscribed texts—speeches, letters, conversations, recitations, dramas, poems, journals, reviews, newspapers—and the text of Byron's life that intertextualizes them. But it is just as important also to read Byron's reading of and response to dramatizations of other texts and to the bodies performing them, particularly, in the pages below, his unacknowledged projection onto and uneasy psychological rivalry with William Henry West Betty, the thirteen-year-old sensation of the 1804–5 London theatrical season. From examination of this interaction may develop not only fuller understanding of Byron's psychology but opportunities for wider reflection of a historical order on how the self can be constructed in response to models advanced by the culture. A narrative history including Byron's 1804–5 theatrical patronage, in other words, may provide a sense of why William Betty became such a phenomenon and of the uses to which he might be put in wartime England, where models of masculinity were unstable and transitory, when journalism had sufficiently matured, even beyond Dryden's hacks, to produce and sustain notoriety.

Essentially cultural, Byron's model of self-creation entails a gradual testing and accumulation of roles, a defining of identity through performance and astute appropriation of opportunity. Byron becomes "Byron" in part by first, through imaginatively driven acts of speech, becoming Zanga, Lear, Penruddock, and other dramatis personae. His self-fashioning does not so much seek a goal known in advance as cast forward, searchingly, acting to open up, assimilate, or resist an ever shifting, unfolding futurity. Analysis of such a process may reasonably depart from the emphasis on infantile experience in Freudian psychology and paradigms derived from it, to focus rather upon moments of intense self-consciousness, when an embattled or apprehensive or troubled self arrives at self-definition in awareness of and reaction to particular pressures and anxieties. The liberation of Byron from neurotic repetition by his own inherited and rewritten texts enables perception of his *successful* adolescence, achieved both because of and despite the hardships and handicaps accompanying it. Conventionally, adolescence provides a second chance, an opportunity for dissolving or at any rate loosening the fixations in which the child is trapped by dependence upon its parents; adolescence offers space, opening, and incentive for new identity formation. During his Harrow years Byron, with a nearly infallible instinct for identifying apt occasions and designing performances suitably matched to their singularity, attempts a reversal of fortune by participation in such events as Speech Day. This argument does not undervalue biographical narratives (like Byron's own of his hero's childhood in the first canto of *Don Juan*) that stress the overbearing mother or, say, the wound of the lameness, but rather shifts attention to the epigenetic processes of the poet's adolescence, to the environment that variously allows and opportunistically encourages Byron to become "Byron." The beginning of that famous transformation—or realization—is not the voyage and tour of 1809–11 but enrollment at Harrow School, where Byronic imagination, means, and will ally to speak out, talk back, act up—to make a scene, to enact a life already at harrow.

SPEECH DAY AT HARROW SCHOOL originated as a deliberately tamer substitute for the long-standing and much-beloved annual archery contests—colorfully climaxed with conferral of the Silver Arrow award—discontinued by new headmaster William Heath in 1772 as disruptive, expensive, and potentially dangerous, particularly because a draw for London thugs.[2] But the history of declamations at the school goes back nearly one hundred years, to 1674, when John Dennis carried the title of "Orator" and boys regularly recited the *Contio Latina*, a retrospective on the year, before the governors' annual council.[3] Dramatic performances at the school, staged by boys and possibly framed by a larger academic and social occasion, claim even earlier provenance: a brief article by B. P. Lascelles in the *Harrovian* of November 1905 announces the acquisition by the Vaughan Library at Harrow School of a 1697 printing of "Sophonisba, or Hannibal's Overthrow. A tragedy acted at the Theatre-Royal by their Majesties' Sevants. Written by Nathaniel Lee, Gent.," first published in 1677 and reissued after Lee's death. Attached to the title page of this document, two manuscript pages contain, respectively, twenty-eight scripted lines of "rhyming heroics" titled "A Prologue spoken by Sophonisba, as it was acted by the Scholars of Harrow, made by Mr. Bags, spoken by Charles Bressey," and twenty-five scripted lines titled "The Epilogue made by Mr. Reuse, spoken by Capell Billingsley." Lacelles identifies these two pages as "the first known record of Harrow theatricals" and deduces 1697–98 as the probable date of the school's production; records from 1697 to 1703 identify seven of the cast members as "Orators." Extracurricular dramatic activity turns up again eleven years before Dr. Heath's formal institution of the Speech Day tradition, which still survives. Lord Teignmouth's *Life of William Jones* recalls from approximately 1757 boys' plans to produce *The Tempest,* and three years later Jones wrote from Harrow to his sister, "I am to speak Antony's speech in Shakespeare . . . and am this week to make a declamation."[4] And Richard Brinsley Sheridan's biographer positions his subject in the Speech Day spotlight before one existed, for the boy left Harrow in 1768: "Having on Speech Day to deliver a Greek oration in the character of a military chief, he [Sheridan] ordered for himself an English general's uniform in which he spoke it."[5] Although only half of the *Sophonisba* cast had achieved "Orator" status by the date of the Harrow production, those seven, including the male and female leads in the play, brought public speaking experience to the stage and so established a historical connection between oratory and theater at Harrow, and confirm that speeches of some order by which boys earned honors and titles were a part of school life long before they were clustered and institutionalized in 1772.[6]

After observing Edmund Burke in action, James Boswell wrote: "It was like the exhibition of a favourite actor."[7] So, too, in lesser measure, speaking and acting trod the Harrow boards in tandem. If close relationship between these two arts seems obvious, even inevitable, noticing it at play in British public schools will document the prominence of performativity as an institutional constituent of them. At Eton, for example, "the best speeches and declamations in the Upper School were those delivered by the members of the different dramatic companies."[8] And at Merchant Taylors': "The plays which are now a regular feature of Speech Day or Election Day, seem to have been gradually developed from the speeches and epigrams which were the original feature of the day."[9] Annually at Shrewsbury, in a Michaelmas parallel to the Hillary speeches, Shakespeare and, usually, a farce, were staged for guests, trustees, and neighborhood "gentlemen" in space refitted as a theater for the occasion, but after 1882 these dramatizations were advanced to Speech Day. St. Paul's moved in the opposite direction, eventually decoupling dramatic presentations from its Apposition Day schedule of speeches. But the most obvious and compelling evidence of linkage between oratory and theater in the public school consciousness appears in the speech "bills" or programs themselves, where virtually from the beginning of speech day events at most institutions, recitation lists include excerpts from classical, Renaissance, and occasionally contemporaneous drama along with formal "orations," parliamentary speeches, and passages of nondramatic poetry. Where "performances" of speeches are reviewed, the rhetoric of evaluation is inevitably theatrical.

Inasmuch as the general contour and constitution of Harrow Speech Day seems to have remained relatively stable across the years, it may be well here to provide a profile of the typical nineteenth-century event, understanding that particular components have come and gone as taste, space, talent, curriculum, ceremonial and pedagogical objectives, and headmasterly whim may have dictated:

> Speech Day is a holiday . . . the place . . . is thrown open for most of the day to the wandering parent. . . . From ten onward, the band of the school corps discourses on the lawn. . . . About eleven the advance-guard of parents and guests arrives. Half an hour later they are on us in force. At that hour the Speech-room doors open and the guests are marshaled to their proper doors . . . according to the color of their tickets. By twelve every seat is filled, and the speeches begin before an audience a thousand strong, but there is always room for a few more, some dozens of boys who have not been able to secure tickets are sifted in until every available inch of sitting or standing room is occupied. Of the speeches themselves, little need be said. Monologues in many tongues, samples of prize compositions, and dramatic scenes in Greek, English, French, or German follow in quick succession, interspersed with a presentation of prizes and medals. . . .
>
> Then follows the time-honoured practice of "cheering on the steps." As the guests file down the steps from the Speech-room, the head [boy] of the school, standing (on a box) in the open space overlooking the street, calls to the crowd of boys and guests assembled below for "three cheers for the Pannonian Ambassador" [or other dignitary] when His Excellency is descending the steps. The celebrity lifts his hat in response to the cheers. . . . [T]he head of the school is prompted by some one who "knows who's who," and some slight diplomacy has to be exercised in delaying the exit of celebrity number two until the cheers for celebrity number one have died away. Then lunch for boys and guests in the [masters'] houses. Salmon and claret cup are essential.
>
> In the afternoon a military band . . . perform on the terrace. . . . At half-past four a house-singing in the Speech-room, a concert composed entirely of school songs, accompanied by the school orchestra: a performance as popular as the speeches itself.[10]

Thus then, and largely now, at Harrow. In 1996, the festivities began at 10:30 A.M. with "Bill," a roll-call, to which the formally clad boys (some in colorfully mutinous waistcoats) individually responded by passing in front of the headmaster, tipping their signature straw boaters, before a packed and milling schoolyard crowd of peers, parents, and guests. Then the crush for seats in the speech room, the seven declamations—one in French—the headmaster's address, and the parade of scholars across the stage to receive academic prizes (books). Thereafter, a bagpipe band provided music on the forecourt, and, later in the afternoon, a concert band on the terrace and a chamber ensemble in the chapel. Cricket, basketball, climbing, water polo, and track events as well as art, photography, and technological exhibitions continued on offer throughout the day. At 4:15, house masters were "at home" for tea, and at 5:15 the fortunate chosen were admitted to "Churchill Songs," the hugely popular vocal concert by the boys, warmly blessed in Churchill's day by his frequent attendance. That the celebration should climax with an event named for an alumnus who not only loved it but whose fame ultimately rested upon his rhetorical and oratorical power is a forceful reminder of the elocutionary genesis and centerpiece of the day.

But festivals of various forms, including speeches, recitations, declamations, and dramatizations by one or more schoolboys, were already an event at other public schools when Dr. Heath replaced arrows with utterance at Harrow in 1772. Since shortly after its 1611 establishment, Charterhouse, for example, has commemorated the anniversary of the death of Thomas Sutton on 12 December, then and now called Founder's Day, with a dinner for former pupils, at which the current head boy, named the Orator, delivers an encomium, originally in Latin, in honor of the founder. Since 1561, excepting only the years of the Civil War and the two World Wars (1914–18 and 1939–45), the dean of Christ Church, Oxford, and the master of Trinity College, Cambridge, have traveled to Westminster School for (until recently) "election" of boys to colleges at their respective institutions and the succeeding dinner party where recitations, usually of timely and often of irreverent epigrams, make up part of the postprandial entertainment.[11] Winchester College has paused for "Medal Speaking"—"a very esoteric, low-key affair"—every year since 1761 (excepting only 1791–96), when prizes for Latin and English composition and declamation are awarded, by royalty from 1797 onward, and designated boys perform their recitations before guests and academically outfitted dons: "It is a simple, dignified, and pleasing ceremony—and not overlong."[12] Eton College's Fourth of June, technically commemorating the birthday of George III, is only the latest incarnation of a tradition dating back to the ancient Montem—the great day of visitation by the outside world to an Eton *en fete*—and conflates with it the old ceremonies of Election Saturday, which always featured speeches and sometimes other performances by the boys.[13]

Similarly, Merchant Taylors' School continues a speech day tradition originally celebrated on the Feast of St. Barnabas, 11 June (now on

7 : Prologue

a Saturday in late May or early June), for which survive the Latin and English texts of speeches from the early eighteenth century onwards: headmaster James Townley, upon his election in 1761, instituted periodic "repetitions" (recitations) during the school year of "passages from the Bible in Hebrew, and from English, Latin and Greek writers."[14] Apposition Day at St. Paul's School recalls the founder Dean John Collet's stipulation that the High Master's job performance be annually evaluated by "apposers" who tested both masters and boys by putting academic questions to them; upon proof of the High Master's satisfactory execution of responsibility, the celebration of his reappointment normally included speeches, and, in the nineteenth century, Latin and Greek plays, usually Aristophanes and Plautus—and sometimes French and English titles as well (Molière, Shakespeare, and Sheridan). And so on. Among schools without speech days when Harrow inaugurated its version, many would soon stage them. Dr. Samuel Butler, for example, headmaster at Shrewsbury (1798–1836), instituted and nurtured an annual Speech Day from 1821, although for unknown reasons it disappeared a decade after his retirement. But most schools continued the practice, and still do, with customs, embellishments, and grace notes unique to each evolving over the years. It is in any event clear that with his initiation of Speech Day at Harrow. Dr. Heath recovered and expanded a rhetorical exercise from the school's past, and at the same time appropriated an oratorical and theatrical custom well established and respected at rival institutions, and he may thereby have improved Harrow's own competitiveness for matriculating boys.

Fashions change, of course, if notoriously at slower pace in British public schools than outside them; but something of the tone and the pedagogically disciplined and purposive nature of the generic speech day of the period may be gathered from the following excerpted account of Eton's Fourth of June as staged in the third quarter of the nineteenth century. It was, we are told, that "ordeal" requiring sixth form students to

> don knee breeches, wherein to spout their speeches to the Provost, Head Master and the assembled multitude in upper school. . . . [Frank Tarver] was the mentor in matters dramatic, and indeed it would not have been a bad thing if the whole school had partaken of his teaching in rhetoric and elocution. How many Etonians have been pitchforked into the world, to fill important positions in which the art of speech-making is essential,

without a notion of how to stand and face an audience, how to manage the voice, or how to emphasize a phrase with an appropriate gesture? Even the art of reading aloud is neglected, and I have heard the noblest passage of Scripture so murdered by parsons at the lectern that it is wellnigh impossible to follow even with an open Bible, and this from the lack of a few simple lessons in elocution. There are few men who have never had the occasion to make a speech in public, and seeing that oratory is seldom a matter of instinct or heredity at least in England, why should not a simple training in elocution be a necessary part of public school training? . . . When we assembled in the Upper School to see the great impassive swells in the Sixth Form, clad in dress coats and knee-breeches, declaiming fragments of the classics before an array of dignitaries with the fervent gesticulations and vivacity of old stagers, we recognized with astonishment the work of Frank Tarver. When some quiet, studious little colleger who was only known as a "sap," cast aside his shyness, and, with but an occasional halt, gave us a dim idea of the humor of a Dogberry or a Sneer, we were amazed, and cheered accordingly.[15]

    This tribute to the tutor is equally a pitch for the retention of his subject in the curriculum, and it is based upon the practical benefits of his art to the postgraduate parliamentary or clerical careers of Etonians. But a pronounced theatrical emphasis seasons the promotion, an awareness of the entertainment factor in effective declamation and of the performative credentials required of participants in Speech Day successes. Frank Tarver is "dramatic" mentor; he teaches posture, body language, voice management, oral interpretation, complementary gesture, stage-presence, and mobility, impersonation amounting to identification with roles; the occasion inspires amazement and huzzahs! Whatever named, the structures hosting speech days, under the pressure of that event, become for the nonce a theater packed with patrons expecting to be entertained by actors trained in the performance of roles. And this remains so even when proof of *elocutionary* skill—that is, speechmaking—is the institutional *raison d'être* for the occasion.

    Ostensibly it was at Harrow, but Speech Day as theater, showtime, and excuse for roistering is clear in the following report of one boy, written home, of Prince Albert's 1851 attendance:

> A distant roar was heard from the end of the town. Great excitement. [Headmaster] Vaughan and bishops range themselves in front, masters and governors on each side. The cheering gets nearer, sound of horses heard,

up dash policeman on horse, these outriders in red, and here he is in a carriage and four with a large white hat on. He dismounts—immense sensation! Masters preceded by white wands began walking two by two before. Cheering from the street is taken up by cheering from the Yard [of the school]. The Prince, attended by the M. of Abercorn and two others, advances, bowing low, presents two fingers to Dr. Vaughan and is bowed up the steps; enthusiasm reaches its highest pitch; he is in the Speech-room, where the cheering is immense. Then the Yard cheers again, for he has taken his seat, the cheers taken up in the town and wafted away gradually till there is comparative silence. I followed the procession as close as I could and got a pretty good standing place in Speechroom. The speeches were much admired, Edward's [Edward Thomas Hoare?] and [Edward] Bloomfield's perhaps as much as any. When they were over the whole School assembled in the yard to cheer the notabilities, such as P. Albert, M. of Abercorn, two arch-bishops, five bishops, Sydy Herbert, Gladstone, Chevalier Bunsen . . .[16]

—and, one is tempted to add, a partridge in a pear tree! On this occasion, and for this boy, speeches are apparently upstaged by the pageantry of the royal visitation, and then marginalized to one-sentence notice, and the cheering effectively drowns them out. Earlier, we heard Lascelles suggest that "little" need be said of the speeches, and my own account of the 1996 Speech Day syntactically depreciates their status. And yet nobody, in the schoolboy's account just quoted, in town or gown, ignores them: they focus the event, center the gravity of its entertainment, give it a name. They are favorably reviewed, remembered as vehicles for friends' achievements. Nothing would have happened without them. At Shrewsbury, "the chief incidents of Speech day," rank ordered, "were, then as now, the delivery of speeches, the distribution of prizes, and a luncheon to conclude."[17] In cinematic language, speeches may or may not be the featured attraction on the occasion they signify, but they produce it. And they both reflect and augment its performative value.

Even at dress rehearsal, the encoded point of the exercise can be discerned. Here is the *Eton Chronicle*'s review of "Speeches" for 13 May 1863, almost certainly auditions for the June festival:

> Wood spoke with his usual clever and telling delivery, the above comic speech [Dean Swift's on his own death], keeping the audience in a constant state of laughter, and receiving at the end enthusiastic applause. Tinne *ma*[jor] had the wind pretty completely taken out of his sails by

Wood's brilliant performance; but, with the exception of one slight hesitation, spoke as if he understood his speech [the first Phillipic of Demonsthenes] which, it being in Greek, was no easy undertaking. We hope a good Greek speech will be spoken on the 5th of June ["Fourth of June" celebrations were for various reasons, weather first among them, sometimes moved to neighboring days], as tending to exhibit greater mastery of the part, and display in "Elocution," a point lost sight of almost every where but Eton; "Speeches" at other schools having slightly lapsed into "acting" and "dress." Follet spoke [from Shakespeare's *Richard II*] with clearer intonation, and altogether more pleasing effect and delivery than we have hitherto seen in him.

And from the same source, about another audition six days later (where, incidentally, a recitation from Byron's *Childe Harold's Pilgrimage* began the program): "They all spoke well, especially Freemantle [as Evander from the *Aeneid,* book 2]. We are afraid an Eton audience do not appreciate any but English Speeches; but this Latin address was excellently sustained throughout. Bridges [as Shakespeare's 'Henry,' presumably V?] created a favourable sensation; his action was peculiarly suited to the words, and his coolness was admirable."

Eton prides itself here on having preserved the elocutionary integrity of its speech day tradition, but Wood wins first mention for his entertainment value; for all his superior intonation, Follett pleases for what is "seen" in him; and less Bridges's words than his fitting of "action" to them with a "coolness" of demeanor earns him kudos. Moreover, that the *Eton Chronicle* editors were disappointed in their wish for "a good Greek speech" on the fifth of June to affirm the elocutionary rationale of the affair may also witness its subordination to dramatic principle (the *Chronicle* of 11 June 1863 lists no Greek speeches among the twenty-two delivered on the fifth). In any case, costumes do not actors make, nor their absence acting deter. With the performative passion abroad in the land—Mr. Yates in Austen's *Mansfield Park* speaks of the widespread "itch for acting"—its captivation of even so conservative a citadel as Eton College is not surprising.[18] For the country was stagestruck. On stage and off, for actors and audiences, theater had become the national intoxicant.

FOR TOO LONG having virtually dismissed nineteenth-century British theater as the embarrassing poor relation of high Romantic art, the critical industry over the last decade has diligently rehabilitated "Romantic theatricality" to such an extent that Romanticism as spectacle, spectatorship, and spectacular self-construction now threatens to overwhelm scholarly discourse on the culture. So pronounced and widespread is the impact of dramatic consciousness now seen to have been upon early-nineteenth-century sensibilities that a major spokesperson for the view has persuasively advanced "theatrical modes of self-representation" as the very foundation of Romanticism.[19] Overcompensation plays its role, of course, in the discovery, recovery, and interpretation of a neglected dimension of nineteenth-century life, and, unchecked, might produce the theater that ate the era—a monstrous cultural construct in which all behaviors and creations appear "performative." And yet such a claim, historically contextualized, seems not much exaggerated.

Bracketed on one side by a French Revolution played, perceived, imagined, and represented as theatrical event, and on the other by fierce ideological battles oratorically staged and waged in Parliament by troupers thoroughly aware of the show expected of them by an international audience—both scenes daily "reviewed" by a dramatically disposed press that also augmented the entertainment value of current events with caricaturing cartoons—and hosted by an ego-driven "Regency" (beginning before and extending beyond the prince's stewardship, necessarily born of the king's madness) addicted to aggressive self-indulgence and shameless self-promotion, the period still reads like an ever-complicating melodrama of heroes, villains, knaves, and fools, all in starring roles. Within this larger frame, subplots proliferate, local eruptions replicating and corroborating the enclosing spectacles—intrigues, trials, executions, riots, mobs, conflagrations, massacres, assaults on individuals and institutions. And their stimuli, energies, and patterns spill over and filter down into socioeconomic transactions and domestic relations through all classes to create what Pascoe judiciously names the theatricality of everyday life.[20] But the shape of dailiness is itself heavily determined by the professional show-business saturation of a culture patronized by an enthusiastic royalty—playhouses, panoramas, pantomimes, puppet shows, and the like—and the amateur offshoots that it spawned, particularly the private theatricals where even the dramatically challenged could and did entreat the thespian muse. Thus steeped, Romantic lives imitated the arts that reflected, hyperbolized, and entertained them; Romantic lives developed as self-conscious inventions from obsessively viewed paradigms, flowered as staged affairs for display and observation. From the collaboration of extraordinary historical events, the pressures and anxieties of mimesis and self-construction, and a culturally coerced melodramatic heightening emerged not merely a distinction of personhood within and across classes; the same forces produced from the debris of liberating catastrophe those figures whose giant stature gave the age its "heroic" nomenclature.

Of these Byron was one. But whereas most of the canonical Romantic writers have wanted champions to disclose their participation in the theatrical spirit of the age, and women writers have most abundantly benefited from a critical revival largely inspired by their own dramatic modes of self-representation, Lord Byron's theatrical imperative has never been in doubt. The melancholy posturing on the Harrow churchyard gravestone, the self-publicized swimming rivalry with Leander, the flaunting of "lordship" in a misbegotten preface, the wickedly mysterious skulking of the personae behind the oriental tales, the grandstanding as profligate, the embrace of the Greeks, the parading of the wounded heart in early verse, and the mature broadsides against every sacred cow—all bear witness to a gift and a taste perhaps usefully encapsulated in an image from 1816 of Byron and Shelley daily living and acting on one side of Lake Geneva under the shocked telescopic gaze of British tourists from the other side, with, one suspects, for all of his complaints to the contrary, his lordship rather relishing the notoriety. I gratefully accept and affirm recent reconceptualizations of Romanticism developed from understandings of the performative imagination and of the Romantic self possessing, possessed by, and enacting it. Such reformulations themselves, so far from disputing, authorize Byronic conceptions of persons and poetry as alternately improvised and crafted performances on the cultural stage where, as Edmund Burke argued, theatricality defined the natural in British public and private life. That Byron imagined his career as poet—and the poetry that acted it out—as a species of dramatic performance for public delectation seems to me incontestable. Led backward from that commonplace, I am rather concerned here with how the young Byron's introduction into performance at Harrow tutored and invigorated the act that he immediately, upon sampling acclaim, became and remains. In short, I study below the constitutive importance of Byron's schoolboy performances in their institutional setting, for their impact on his psychological, social, and poetic development and the early verse reflective of it, and their situatedness within the cultural repertoire he would have experienced in and near the precincts of Harrow School before leaving for Cambridge in 1805.

Chapter 1 tracks Byron's relationships with two men, each slightly older than himself, the same age, and bearing the same first name: Henry Drury, his first Harrow tutor, and Henry, Lord Grey de Ruthyn, his Newstead Abbey tenant. With both individuals, Byron's associations were stressfully vexed, and in representations to relatives milked for all the melodramatic worth the boy could wrench from them; carefully read, his record reveals a proud, angry, frightened, hypersensitive, bewildered young man, bent on avenging perceived injustices, talking back against abuse, and doubtfully searching for an identity to assume or become, or a vehicle for exploring his options. Chapter 2 observes him trying out one option, as declaimer for his headmaster and then as public performer in his first Speech Day appearance, and surveys elocutionary instruction and practice at Harrow and other public schools. The first Interval, a complementary break from the Harrow scene, resumes the psychobiographical account with perspectives on fallout from Byron's transactions with his mother, his beloved Mary Ann Chaworth, his earlier companion Mary Duff, his half sister Augusta Leigh, his school fellow George, Lord Delawarr, and Lord Grey, and its implications for his oratorical and performative future. William Betty, the phenomenal child actor who for two seasons captivated Britain's theatrical consciousness, focuses my third chapter, where I propose the significant histrionic and personal influence of Master Betty and his roles upon a curious if resistant Byron just as he prepared for his second Speech Day performance. Chapter 4 analyzes in detail the textual foundation of that performance, and hypothesizes a number of reasons for Byron's success—and his need to succeed—as the villain Zanga. The second Interval investigates his participation in private theatricals. Administrative instabilities at Harrow and their effect upon the increasingly confident and emboldened young actor ripple through chapters 4 and 5, the latter of which views Byron's Lear in the context of local and national politics and the boy's pending departure from the school. My epilogue discovers a trace of Byron's Speech Day experience in his first *Don Juan* canto, inscribed fourteen years after the event. Throughout, I have sought to read the boy for the sake of reading the poetry, to determine how the eloquence and performative mobility of young Byron write themselves into and elucidate the textualized verses which are our reason for reading him at all. And if my attention remains largely on the early poetry, I believe that at least some observations will find other applications beyond it.

Much of what follows is unapologetically inferential criticism. But it tries always to remain faithful to the historical record, and sensible in using it as a basis for extrapolation: I mean to historicize and interpret with a mutually constraining prudence. Perhaps more important, my study seeks to honor the chronic implicitness of Lord Byron himself, however complex and various its configurations—a presence, a stamp, a signature identifiable in his every project. Byron never shrank from leaving his mark. It was part—arguably the most vital part—of his act. Mine plots its provenance and earliest significations.

1 : Tutor and Tenant

EVEN THOUGH AWARDING no oratorical prizes, Harrow School Speech Day nevertheless retained into Byron's time its competitive edge as a showcase for exceptional skills, and it offered opportunities for claiming or affirming reputation and earning popularity.[1] At the beginning, the ten prestigious school monitors (or preceptors)—positions of honor and responsibility—spoke on each of three Speech Days, with selected boys from the sixth form reciting in rotation on one of the three. In 1804, Byron shared the platform with seventeen others—five, including himself, in ensembles—and as a monitor in 1805 with fifteen and seventeen boys at the two festivals (some, again, grouped) (Prothero 1:27–29). Texts from Greek and Latin orators, poets, and dramatists, Shakespeare, and Gray formed the standard fare, with other native authors gaining ground, among them on the three days that Byron spoke Collins, Hume, Milton, and Addison.[2] Two selections appear on both lists for 1805 (May of that year saw no Speech Day), although not those that Byron performed: he had no textual challengers. Of the three texts from which Byron recited, the *Aeneid* had historically enjoyed by far the most frequent representation on Speech Day programs (at Harrow and other public schools), particularly the colloquy from book 11, perhaps because the Harrow curriculum included Aeneas's story, perhaps because corporate performance taxed nerves less than individual recitation. Since 1792, the passage from book 11 had appeared on Speech Day bills seven times before Byron's selection of it (and thrice since his matriculation), but on only the first and second occasions—before he arrived at Harrow—did it include the role he ultimately took; otherwise, two boys recited the lines of Drances and Turnus, with King Latinus, Byron's part, elided. In other words, prior to performing it, Byron had not seen his chosen role dramatized at Harrow Speech Day: for his generation of schoolmates, he created the part and may for a time have "owned" it. For of the three additional appearances of the Virgil passage on Speech Bills through the decade, only one, in May 1807, includes

Latinus, a possible comment on the superiority of a performance remembered by younger boys subsequently selecting lines for recitation. This spotty history of Latinus's representation in the Harrow event has some bearing on Byron's enactment of the part, and I will return to it. As for his other choices: at previous Speech Day ceremonies, Byron may have heard lines from *King Lear*—possibly the speech to the storm—performed (by Cuthbert Ellison, a monitor and later Head of School) on 7 May 1801, during his initial Harrow term, and again (by the Honorable Frederick Gough Calthorpe) on 3 May 1804, a year before he spoke it. But Zanga had appeared only once on the Harrow program (by Henry Hinxman), on 3 June 1802, with Byron presumably present, although Young's play had remained popular throughout the kingdom since its 1722 premiere.[3] I do not at all suppose his witnessing performances of these parts to be Byron's sole or even chief reason for choosing them. On the contrary, I believe his most powerful motivations quite otherwise. But he may have been incited to consider the roles by observing good or bad—and therefore in both cases challenging—enactments of them on the Harrow Speech Day programs.

Byron entered Harrow at thirteen in April 1801, rather late in the day to begin public school, for the youngest pupil at the time was six, and many entered before reaching ten (Tyerman, 29). The population of the school when Byron arrived was probably above 300 (it had reached 350 in 1803 [22]). But as Mayne has indicated,[4] the lad brought with him more disadvantages than a lame foot, however sufficient his physical impairment to invite the cruelties of his mates. His meager social connections did no honor to his title; his impoverished status would have been known by staff and boys, and was probably discussed openly, hurtfully;[5] he may still have spoken in a strong Scotch dialect; his scholastic deficiency was so apparent that Dr. Joseph Drury, the headmaster, kept him back for individual tutelage before permitting him to join peers in the form room, burdened with the "new boy" tag. And he was, as he confessed to Pryse Gordon many years later, "a complete spoiled child," with "screams and tears . . . at command."[6] He arrived, in short, with monumental handicaps against ready acceptance by his fellows; and, thus stigmatized, and as he believed persecuted, he "*hated*" the place for two and one-half years.[7]

Contributing to his unhappiness was dissatisfaction with Henry Drury, the headmaster's son, who was one of four assistant masters and Byron's first tutor, in whose house he boarded. Tensions between pupil

17 : Tutor and Tenant

and tutor had reached such a pitch that the boy refused to return to Harrow and Henry's instruction after the Christmas 1802 holidays, and a tutorial change was effected. Dr. Drury put forward the administrative view of the estrangement in a 4 February 1803 letter to John Hanson, the Byrons' solicitor:

> The reason why Lord Byron wishes for this change [in tutorial assignment] arises from the repeated complaints of Mr. Henry Drury respecting his Inattention to Business, and his propensity to make others laugh and disregard their Employments as much as himself. On this subject I have had many very serious conversations with him [Byron, that is, not Henry], and though Mr. H.D. had repeatedly requested me to withdraw him from his Tuition, yet, relying on my own remonstrances and arguments to rectify his Error, and on his own reflection to confirm him in what is right, I was unwilling to accede to my son's wishes. Lord Byron has now made the request himself; I am glad it has been made, as he thereby imposes on himself an additional responsibility, and encourages me to hope that by this change he intends to lay aside all that negligence and those Childish Practices which were the cause of former complaints. (Prothero 8:12–13n)

The habitual rowdiness and delinquency indicated by "very many serious conversations" of a disciplinary sort, not to mention evidence of the performative character already entertaining appreciative audiences, elicit a measure of sympathy for the beleaguered tutor and his appeals for relief. But in some degree confuting Byron's later suspicion of victimization by familial solidarity, Dr. Drury "repeatedly" denies his son, with faith and pride in his own counsel, and on pedagogical principle. For the satisfaction he takes in rationalizing the outcome of his denials suggests that the inducement of Byron's request for reassignment was their aim, no matter how inconvenient for Henry and potentially harmful to his boys. At the same time, however, and although the letter no doubt means to inform Hanson and through him Mrs. Byron of the boy's disorderly conduct, its sketch of Henry as master does not flatter him. Unquestionably he was provoked; but Henry's recurring complaints to his father, his apparent supervisory inadequacies, and his quick-fix remedy of transfer (or expulsion) give some credence to Byron's later characterization of his tutor as hostile, irrational, and irresponsible, and suggest not merely a bad match but Henry's unwillingness or impotence to make it better. Dr. Drury may in fact know that, for his letter inadvertently hints that denying Henry's request disciplined the junior master to improved tutelage.[8]

But if the spoiled, willful Byron's general indifference to set lessons with a taxing and unsympathetic taskmaster underlay his alienation from Henry, the tutor may also have focused for him anger displaced from taunting schoolmates beyond the reach of Byron's avenging pugilistic skills (he boasted of winning all playing field fights but one), or from grief and frustration over his cousin Margaret Parker's death in the fall of 1802,[9] or from assorted other adolescent miseries, including resistance to any authority opposing his own, or from an exaggerated sense of his own consequence as a "lord" improperly honored by commoners on the faculty. Byron's transfer to the charge of Mr. Benjamin Evans, another assistant master, in February 1803 provided momentary respite[10]—and no doubt fueled the boy's proud obduracy—but resentments simmered through the winter until in late April a perceived insult from his former tutor sent Byron railing to his mother (as Henry had fled to his father), whose own tumultuous temper his letter to her probably mirrors. We lack Henry's side of this story; Byron's is of the uniquely accused boy insulted, abused, and victimized by a mean-spirited opportunist venting anger wholly disproportionate to the offense, and publicly humiliating the young lord in a manner unbefitting his rank. The letter smokes with indignation:

> Mr. Henry Drury has behaved himself to me in a manner I neither *can* nor *will bear.* He has seized now an opportunity of Showing his resentment towards me.[11] Today in church I was talking to a boy who was sitting next to me, *that* perhaps was not right, but hear what followed. After church he spoke not a word to me but took this boy to his pupil room, where he abused me in a most violent manner, called me *blackguard* said he *would* and could have me expelled from the School, and bade me thank his *charity* that *prevented* him, this was the message he sent me, to which I shall return no answer, but submit my case to *you* and those you may think *fit* to consult. (*BLJ* 1:41–42)

In light of the particular if belated retaliation that I shall argue Byron offers to such perceived abuse, I stress here the role of speech in his inscribed response: the boy suffers for having spoken; he endures Henry's silence, then the insulting discourse first denied his hearing and now mediated through the agency of the classmate in what is itself a performance, a mimesis or acting-out of the tutor's reprimand commissioned by Henry himself. Byron then answers Henry's initial silence with his own, deferring the matter to the conversations of others but not, as we shall see, forgetting it. Meanwhile, he bills the incident to his mother as Henry's "Showing his resentment towards me"—another enactment or staging of an intense emotional state which Mrs. Byron, as audience, is advised to "hear." Byron's irreverent talk is punished by two performances of speech acts aimed at a specific audience expected to understand them. However petulant both principals in this episode, it provides the boy with a model of how performative art can represent and affect reality, transmit messages, assault, and injure. It would be a mistake to locate the genesis of Byron's theatricality in this bitter moment, but the incident and its reporting illustrate his sensitivity to the rhetoric of abuse elaborately enacted. (Indeed, the elaborateness is itself arresting. What possible reason, other than Henry's fear of confronting Byron, could have moved him to mediate his reproof through the presumably innocent classmate, unless embarrassing publicity of Byron's misbehavior was his object?)[12]

In submitting his "case" to Mrs. Byron (and promoting its transmission to the lawyers) rather than answering Henry directly, Byron is of course replicating the offense of mediated communication charged against Henry, although to be sure his subordinate position complicates the parallel, as does Henry's filial relation to the headmaster, a kinship likely to redound to his discredit. And so Byron acknowledges later in the letter: "Is this usage fit for any body [?] had I *stole* or behaved in the most *abominable* way to him his language could not have been more outrageous, what must the other boys think of me to hear such a message ordered to be delivered to me by a *master* [?] [that is, ordered by a master to be delivered to me] better him take away my life than ruin my *character*" (*BLJ* 1:42). High dudgeon indeed from this fifteen-year-old keenly aware of himself as an unpopular boy of rank now maligned by an assistant master to a classmate! If Henry did in fact dispatch his insult by messenger, and in anything like the reported language—although one can imagine the boy, especially if already disposed against Drury, embellishing the terms of rebuke—the chastening does appear extraordinary, even bizarre, unworthy of a tutor. Henry Drury is seemingly engaged in self-serving malice, deliberately spreading infamy about a mischievous boy perhaps often still irritating to him, now beyond the reach of his supervisory rod. Even allowing for exaggeration in Byron's account, he appears justified in objecting to vilification if not slander. The breathless insistence, the tumbling rhetoric and repetitions bespeak overwrought emotion. But the stagy flourish with which my quotation ends nevertheless witnesses reasonable, understandable concern for reputation, for image, among schoolmates. For in effect, Henry has proclaimed him a disreputable boy.

In long-range impact, this experience offered Byron a potent lesson in the power of language to hurt, defame, and enrage: Henry, in an authorial and performative mode, with speech to a selected audience, has avenged himself on an enemy. If perhaps not born in this event, the satiric Byron is surely nourished by it. But in the shorter term, we need to ask why Byron, just now, should object to Henry's characterization, when he appears to have worked—if he worked at anything during his early Harrow experience—to earn a reputation for fighting and troublemaking.[13] Why not welcome Henry's authoritative assistance in blackening his image? But to do so surrenders or at least shares control of production of the image: it permits Henry's participation in the creation of Byron the Wicked Schoolboy; and for every increase of the master's power in that operation, the boy's shrinks. Again, he is less concerned with the offense—he twice admits in the letter his misbehavior in church—and with the disproportion of Drury's language to the mischief, than with the appropriation of power and the affront of indirect accusation, what he may have thought the skulking insult that stifled contradiction and redress. He protests ungentlemanly conduct—a trenchant irony, given the priority assigned to refined behavior at Harrow by its headmaster; his is the rage of injured aristocratic pride, of usurped privilege in self-creation, and together with an endemic adolescent hyperdrama such rage must have made Byron the *enfant terrible par excellence* at the school.

"My conscience," he goes on, "acquits me of ever *meriting* expulsion at this school I have been *idle* and I certainly ought not to talk in church, But I have never done a mean action at this school to him or any *one*. If I had done anything so *heinous* why should he allow me to stay at the School, why should he himself be so *criminal* as to overlook faults, which merit the appellation of Blackguard" [?] (*BLJ* 1:42). It takes one to suspect one, Byron writes, returning the charge of criminality and yet exonerating both himself and Henry, for the second cannot be guilty if the first is not. By the same token, however, if Henry is to be legitimately indicted, Byron must also be guilty of graver offense than misconduct at worship. But more important are the implications of the word *blackguard* in early-nineteenth-century society. By that time, when applied to an individual rather than a group, it approximated its modern meaning, "one of the idle criminal class; a 'tough': hence, a low worthless character addicted to or ready for crime; an open scoundrel" (*OED*, def. 6). But the word had not entirely lost its collective eighteenth-century sense of the devil's bodyguards or attendants, or any group "of black dress, race, or character, or the underworld."[14] And the sociological implications of its etymology bear upon Drury's use and Byron's grasp of the word. With reference to a group of persons, it had originally identified "the lowest menials of a royal or noble household, who had charge of pots and pans and other kitchen utensils . . . the scullions and kitchen-knaves" (*OED*, def. A1). And well into the eighteenth century the word continued to suggest the socially excluded or marginal, the unwashed, the unacceptable, the have-nots: "the rabble . . . the vagabond, loafing, or criminal class . . . the vagrant children of great towns," and particularly those who earned their bread by polishing boots, blacking shoes on the street. Since 1683, says John Farmer's *Slang and Its Analogues* (vol. 1), "the word seems to have become more and more depraved," until signifying "a low, worthless fellow, one open to and ready for any villainy."

What may have particularly infuriated Byron in Henry's epithet, then, was its contempt of rank and privilege. Not only does Henry fail to honor his lordship with direct address; he associates the aristocrat with what Byron himself, like Nietzsche after him, later called "the herd" in distancing himself from it. Henry links the young nobleman with a mendicancy that almost certainly reminded the boy of the discrepancy between his title and his wealth; and so far from recognizing his rank, the epithet in its historical resonances relocates the lad below stairs. In the Harrow context, it identifies him with those ruffians whose shenanigans occasioned the substitution of Speech Day for the time-honored archery competitions. And if Byron knew the etymological associations of the term with boots, it would have been felt to target as well the impairment so frequently and painfully subjected to "correction" by bootlike contraptions prescribed by doctors to be strapped onto his lame foot, and in any event to focus attention on the disability.[15]

Obsessively, unstoppably Byron continues: "If he had it in his power to have [me] expelled, he would long ago have *done* it, as it is he has done *worse,* if I am to be treated to this manner, I will not stay at this *school*" (*BLJ* 1:42). Petulant and tetchy, Byron not only disempowers

Drury as *master* by appropriating to himself the option of leaving Harrow; simultaneously, his statement empowers Henry linguistically by assessing defamation as a greater evil than expulsion. And it quietly assumes a proper standard of "treatment" and Mrs. Byron's sympathy with it, as violated by Henry. Then, in this sentence we reach the crux: "I write you that I will not as yet appeal to Dr. Drury, his son's influence is more than mine and *Justice* would be *refused* me" (*BLJ* 1:42). Mixed up with all of Byron's other motives is envy of Henry Drury—envy of sonship, of his presumed favoritism in Dr. Drury's eyes (although the evidence is ambiguous), of his "influence" in that quarter. Behind this complaint lies a fantasized familial structure, with Dr. Drury as the ideal father misled by the wicked sibling to disfavor the younger one: the father who can be set right only by the mother's appeal on behalf of the maligned son. Moore (*Life,* 1:38) quotes from one of Byron's "manuscript journals": "Dr. Drury, whom I plagued sufficiently, was the best, the kindest (and yet strict, too) friend I ever had—and I look upon him still as a father" [1:38]).[16] More poignantly but to the same point are these lines from "Childish Recollections," Byron's "parting song" (1:372)[17] to Harrow:

> Ah! sure some stronger impulse vibrates here [at Harrow School],
> Which whispers friendship will be doubly dear
> To one, who thus for kindred hearts must roam,
> And seek abroad, the love denied at home:
> Those hearts, dear Ida [Harrow], have I found in thee,
> A home, a world, a paradise to me.
> Stern Death, forbade my orphan youth to share,
> The tender guidance of a Father's care;
> Can Rank, or ev'n a Guardian's name supply,
> The Love, which glistens in a Father's eye?
> For this, can Wealth, or Title's sound atone,
> Made, by a Parent's early loss, my own?
> What Brother springs a Brother's love to seek?
> What Sister's gentle kiss has prest my cheek?
> For me, how dull the vacant moments rise,
> To no fond bosom link'd by kindred ties.
> . . . .
> Thus, must I cling to some endearing hand,
> And none more dear, than Ida's social band. (ll. 213–42)[18]

These lines are written either late in 1806 or when Byron revised and expanded the poem early in 1807 (*CPW* 1:382), after he has known paternal vacancy filled and the longing for brotherhood satisfied. Their evidence of his valuing Harrow as a haven at least partially substitutive of home and its normal stewards and relatives is fundamental to understanding his expectations and disappointments, his anxieties and quarrels and passions while on the site, particularly with respect to authorities and classmates.[19] Earlier, however, in the letter to his mother about the competitive "sibling," he is less benign: "I told you when I *left* you at Bath that he would seize every means & opportunity of Revenge, not for [my] leaving him so much as the mortification he suffered Because *I* begged you to let me leave him" (*BLJ* 1:42). Once again, less the deed than the word about the deed, the word threatening or desiring the deed, constitutes the principal offending instrument; and once again a statement that parallels and indicts Byron's and Henry's indirect complaints. By pointing to his fulfilled prophecy Byron also claims judgment superior to his mother's and ratchets up a notch the pressure on her to take steps lest additional injury occur. By drawing his mother actively into the fray, the boy tries to realize the imagined family structure driving his fantasy. The wounded son appeals to the father for justice through the favoring mother, who is thus set against the rival sibling.

Stirred to new anger by the cabalistic word, Byron recycles an old defense: "If I had been the Blackguard he talks of, why did he not of his own accord refuse to keep me as his *pupil* [?]" In the absence of such responsible behavior, that is, the boy cannot be guilty unless Henry is unworthy of the tutorial office. Byronic logic traps the teacher: if Henry tells the truth, he has been negligent; if he lies, he libels. It is a clever if by now tiresome whine. But Byron is not yet done: "you know Dr. Drury's first letter in it were these words, 'My Son and Lord Byron have had some disagreements, but I hope that his future behavior will render a change of tutors unnecessary'" (*BLJ* 1:42). Byron must come by this information through his mother, whose own indiscretion is now turned back on her in advocacy of her son's position. By privileging Byron with the confidence from the Harrow headmaster, Mrs. Byron invites her son to think himself partner in the (possibly continuing) conversation with Dr. Drury. The disruptive appeal to the father/authority in the boy's letter, then, attempts to soften and dilute blackguardism into "disagreement" by authoritatively renaming the offense, and registers the headmaster's faith in Byron's potential to reform, indeed credits him with it. But it also recognizes that change may be necessary. Byron adroitly situates the quotation to suggest that Henry's behavior, not his own, necessitated the change and might require other steps that Mrs. Byron could now promote, against the other "parent" who has nevertheless forwarded the notion of change.

There is yet more: "Last time I was here [at Harrow] but a short time and though he endeavored, he could find nothing to abuse me in, amongst other things I forgot to tell you he said he had a great mind [to] expel the boy for speaking to me and that if he ever again spoke to me he would expel him" (BLJ 1:42). To point to Henry's failure to *discover* faults isn't quite to claim innocence of them, but Byron's statement subtly attributes negligence to the junior master. And by widening the range of the tutor's pollution and abuse to include Byron's partner in the church mischief, the young lord increases the pressure upon his guardians to save the school from Henry's bungling, while suggesting Byron's own greater value to it than either the tutor or the classmate could command. At the same time, however, these lines shed dark luster upon Byron as a sinister agent whose association imperils an academic career: it grants him exactly the decadent stature that Byron's early heroes seemed to incarnate, that his reading public relished, and that Robert Southey, a decade later, would identify as Byron's Satanic own.

Additionally diluting the claims of innocence in conceding the partial justice of Henry's accusation, as though to impress Mrs. Byron with his sweet reasonableness, Byron writes: "Let him explain his meaning, he abused me but he neither did nor can mention anything bad of me further than what every Boy else in the School has done[.] I fear him not but let [him] explain his meaning 'tis all I ask" (BLJ 1:42). Having just conferred upon himself distinction in the practice of wicked arts, Byron quickly backtracks and distributes schoolboy mischief equably at Harrow, thus restoring himself to the community of (delinquent) boys. Interestingly, however, he reduces his own complaint against Henry to one request: explain. This brilliant—and acutely ironic—shot targets a deficiency the obverse of an asset, the dysfunctioning tutorial gift. Henry has spoken unintelligibly; he has failed to "explain" himself, and is so charged by the person in the best position to judge his practice of explanation and enlightenment. Linguistically, Henry fails, and is exposed in that failure by successful linguistic play. The pupil trumps his teacher's rhetorical skill. With this deft stroke of "student evaluation,"

Byron establishes additional grounds for affirming to his own and the offending party's parents the "necessary" change of tutors.[20]

The bravado of Byron's "I fear him not" pales a little against the reiterated request for maternal intervention with the headmaster, as the family fantasy reemerges: "I beg you will write to Dr. Drury to let him know what I have said, he has behaved to me as also Mr. Evans very kindly. If you do not take note of this I will leave the School myself, but I am sure *you* will not see me *ill treated* better that I should suffer anything than this" (*BLJ* 1:42). Despite Dr. Drury's supposed favoritism toward his biological son in judicial matters, the surrogate son still has a chance; better, he has already experienced two masters' favor—Byron thus tilts administrative and faculty bias toward himself—and Mrs. Byron's influence as negotiator weights Byron's words with maternal authority, as though he did not trust his own. The aim here is to marshal the "parental" forces to Byron's side in the quarrel, with Evans called as another powerful witness to the young lord's merits. Byron's threat to leave bares the teeth shown already in his prolonged absence of the previous spring; and it claims rights, as we have seen, that preempt Henry's to expel him. Whether Byron intends irony in his certainty of Mrs. Byron's support is undeterminable; however, to modern readers the statement resonates with the mother's physical and verbal abuse of the boy far surpassing anything of which Henry is accused, but in private and without mediation. Exactly what worse suffering Byron with his theatrical gesture expects or imagines is not easily conceived since his Harrow experiences so far have been largely disagreeable and his life outside the school reasonably happy. It is a self-important rhetorical flourish, a punchy exit line, strictly consistent with the performative quality of a letter that both enacts and critiques Henry Drury's also mediated and creatively theatricalized message.

But if finished with what we might call the logical portion of his letter—the rational argument for assistance in a noble cause—Byron has yet to exhaust his emotional appeals. In a display of concern for his mother's fatigue—which assumes her concentration on his words and projects his own weariness from writing (and probably from reliving) onto her—Byron engages in a soapsudsy, emotional blackmail almost certainly learned at home: "I believe you will be tired by this time," he writes, "of reading my letter but If you love me you will now show it. Pray write me immediately" (*BLJ* 1:43): demonstrated affection is the boy's demand, but the understood connection between inscription and enactment, writing and performing, points to their near equivalency in the unfolding Byronic career. Or if the referent for his final "it" is "my letter," he still calls upon his mother to participate in a confrontational little drama of his composition, with the maternal parent defending her favorite, to the paternal figure, against abuse by the elder sibling in a transaction designed either to jettison or discredit him. Mrs. Byron does in fact prove her love by "showing" the letter. The brashness of the conditional in the quoted sentence ("If . . .") and of the imperative ("Pray write . . .") bespeak as much anxiety as confidence; but their boldness softens in a postscript which (1) sends love and good health from Hargreaves Hanson, a Harrow school friend and the son of Byron's solicitor; (2) remarkably for the schoolboy, declares no "want of money," in what looks like a manipulative trade-off for the mother's persuasive intercession with Dr. Drury, more crucial now than cash; and (3) invokes God's blessing on Mrs. Byron—twice! The signing is Byron's usual one for these months, a proper but chilly, "your affectionate Son." Incidentally, the next of Byron's extant letters, for 23–30 June 1803, thanks Mrs. Byron for money, announces his promotion to a "higher form," and claims that "Dr. Drury and I get on very well." Since February, he has been the pupil of Mr. Evans.

From Mrs. Byron, this letter of 5 May 1803 passed to Hanson and thence to Dr. Drury, who on 15 May responded to the attorney with a surprising confession and an apology on behalf of his son: "The Perusal of the inclosed has allowed me to inquire into the whole Matter, and to relieve your young friend's [Byron's] Mind from any uneasy impression it might have sustained from a hasty word I fairly confess. I am sorry it was ever uttered; but certainly it was never intended to make so deep a wound as his letter intimates" (Prothero 1:13n). Well, then, was only a shallow wound "intended"? Do the first and second clauses of the opening sentence mean that Drury (or Henry) has apologized to Byron, as they appear to do? Although not unthinkable, such an event would surely have been extraordinary, and impressed itself indelibly upon the boy's memory, not to mention inflating his already exaggerated sense of self-importance. The regretted word is of course "blackguard," the apologetic withdrawal of which would not only legitimate Byron's anger over its unjust use but also psychologically prime him for and authorize his intensified rage when Henry's uncle Mark Drury applies the same epithet to him a year later (see below).

Tactful and diplomatic, even in parts formulaic, the remainder of

Dr. Drury's letter to the lawyer Hanson seems both sensitive and sincere in its concern for the disorderly boy: "I may truly say, without any parade of words, that I am deeply interested in Lord Byron's welfare. He possesses, as his letter proves, a mind that feels, and that can discriminate reasonably on points in which it conceived itself injured [the circumlocution nearly states that the injury in question is illusory]. When I look forward to the exercise of his Talents hereafter, and his supplying the Deficiencies of fortune by the exertion of his abilities and by application, I feel particularly hurt to see him idle, and negligent, and apparently indifferent to the great object to be pursued. This event, and the conversations which have passed between us relative to it, will probably awaken in his mind a greater degree of emulation, and make him studious of acquiring Distinction among his Schoolfellows, as well as of securing to himself the affectionate regard of his Instructors" (Prothero 1:13n). Drury's "probably" is more hopeful than confident of success and regard, but his faith was of course rewarded, even before Byron left Harrow. On only one point would the paragraph have displeased Byron, had he seen it. His "Deficiencies of fortune" embarrassed him at the school, as did the pensioner status that they imposed upon him. This evidence that his relative poverty figured in Drury's thinking as a(nother) handicap for which he must compensate—indeed, as an ineradicable part of his Harrow identity—would have confirmed Byron's suspicions of economic prejudice practiced or nurtured against him among the faculty. But "Deficiencies of fortune" may point beyond specifically economic issues to the larger traditional opposition of Talents and Fortune. In that perspective, Byron's fatherlessness and clubfoot are signs of Fortune's mistreatment, indeed of her fickleness in afflicting whom she has also blessed. Had he read Dr. Drury's letter, Byron would have found pious condescension if not class snobbery in the conjunction of "Talents" with "exertion" and "application," as though the headmaster were recommending middle-class values to the apprentice who must rise by labor, unendowed by the gift of Fortune. Such counsel scarcely relegates Byron to "blackguard" status, but it assumes (or hopes for) receptivity to a ripe earnestness that the young lord would in future never show, and perhaps betrays a fundamental misunderstanding of the boy by his teacher, unless Drury dissembles for the parent's sake.

BACK IN JANUARY 1803, Henry Edward Yelverton, Lord Grey de Ruthyn, age twenty-three, applied for the permanent lease on Newstead Abbey, which he signed in April before taking possession of the property by 2 July and leaving immediately, with plans to return in October. Much of this eventful summer Byron spent at Newstead and its neighboring estate Annesley Hall, where he (re)discovered Mary Ann Chaworth, age eighteen, viewed anew with bedazzled fifteen-year-old eyes and aroused libido. We need not rehearse the story of Byron's frustrated passion for the betrothed Mary. But it is important in this context to remember that his desperate infatuation became his first reason for postponing return to Harrow in the fall; others developed, and he did not resume school until January 1804, after his sixteenth birthday. Meanwhile, Lord Grey had taken up residence at Newstead and declared it hospitable to Byron, who promptly became a frequent guest, providing the (slightly) older man with agreeable and probably admiring companionship for moonlit hunting expeditions and other diversions. Of the relationship between lessor and lessee there is no known record; but it seems fair to assume from the complaints of Owen Mealey, the gardener, about the boy's constant demands for service that Byron permitted no one on the estate to forget his title and ownership, although he may have found his pride and expectations reinforced by Grey's alleged tendency to mistreat his own social inferiors. Byron remained at Newstead through Christmas, but between 28 December and his birthday (22 January 1804), some act or word from Lord Grey sent the boy spinning in disgusted recoil against him, and by the end of January he had returned to Harrow.

Two months later, he began correspondence with his half sister Augusta Leigh. The two had probably first met during the Christmas holidays of 1801 (Marchand so speculates: 1:13), and Augusta had written to her brother several times.[21] He finally responded, apologetically, on 22 March 1804, attributing his silence "to a shyness naturally inherent to my Disposition" (*BLJ* 1:44). In what purports to be compensation for his slackness as a correspondent and a suitable return for Augusta's "kindness," Byron proposes that she hereafter "consider me not only as *a Brother* but as your warmest and most affectionate *Friend,* and if ever Circumstances should require it as your *protector.* Recollect, My Dearest Sister, that you are *the nearest relation* I have in *the world both by the ties of Blood and Affection,* If there is anything in which I can serve you; you have only to mention it; Trust to your Brother, and be assured he will never betray your confidence" (*BLJ* 1:44).

This is a remarkable expression of love and loyalty to a relative barely known. I do not impute insincerity to it but suspect that its ardor has more to do with Byron's own feelings of abandonment and betrayal, and even his need to feel protected, than with an as yet experientially grounded emotion for his half sister. Not much earlier, he had felt the sting of Henry Drury's accusation, against which he was wholly unprotected before a student body almost certainly informed of the charge through the drumbeats of gossip, which as we saw may have been Henry's purpose in mediating the reprimand. Rejection by one's tutor—especially by one's former tutor, since reassignment might then be supposed the tutor's wish—because the relationship is personal and privileged, amounts to major betrayal. Furthermore, the incident estranging Byron from Grey, an apparently agreeable companion of several weeks, badly shocked the boy—he will return to it repeatedly in correspondence with Augusta, once assured of her confidence (a probable reason for pledging his own in this first letter)—and fundamentally interrogated, for the already relationally equivocal Byron, the very nature of friendship and fidelity and trustworthiness. At this same time, his suit of Mary Ann Chaworth had foundered on the rock of her engagement. And finally, Byron's relations with his mother were rapidly deteriorating. His first letter to Augusta understandably expresses great yearning, a lonely desire for relationship. It seeks first to bind Augusta in steadfast association as kin and friend, without possibility of betrayal on his side. It then goes on, confidentially (?), to declare friendship for Augusta's future husband and his own then "Brother." Next, he asks to be remembered to Lord Sidney Osborne (who may "have forgot me by this time") and to "poor old [Joe] Murray [the Newstead servant], tell him we will see that something is to be done for him, *for while I live he shall never be abandoned In his old Age*" (BLJ 1:45). Marchand points out that Byron was "always solicitous" for Murray's welfare (BLJ 1:45n), but one wonders what might have prompted this urgent reassurance, unless written out of raw, painful experience and vibrant fear of his own additional abandonment.

With two minor exceptions, there is nothing in his letter except its rings on the changes of the friendship theme (greetings for the mother, a postscript reminding Augusta of a promised gift—this, too, a token of his steadfastness). But in the earliest instance of sibling conspiracy—a patent effort to bond more intimately with his sister—Byron hopes that his absent mother will not interrupt this communication or "peruse my epistle, there is one part of it which would produce from her a panegyric on a *friend of yours* not at all agreeable to me, and I fancy, *not particularly delightful to you*" (*BLJ* 1:44–45). The identity of this friend is unknown but the intent of the reference is clear: if Byron disapproves and Augusta is herself lukewarm, and the mother approves of this "friend," then Augusta is well-advised to cut the individual, especially because she has the infinitely superior friend in her brother. The hint of jealousy, however, is less important than the aim of conspiratorial exclusion, which tightly binds the siblings. "Do not forget to love me," Byron concludes, remaining "more than words [can] express, your ever sincere, affectionate Brother and Friend" (*BLJ* 1:45).

Four days later, obedient to Augusta's "injunction" to promptness, he writes again, lamenting (a little stiffly) their long separation but gratified that "fortune has now sufficiently atoned by discovering to me a relation whom I love, a Friend in whom I can confide . . . and I hope you will never think your Brother unworthy of your affection and Friendship" (*BLJ* 1:45). The sentiments, the yearning, the hopes all echo those of the first letter, and appear to suggest the absence of other trusted confidants, of reliable mates, in his boyhood circles. This will soon change, but for the moment, with a genteel decorum, he sounds starved for the affection of a friend, and for an occasion to be one. December conceals a cause: indeed, the correspondence with Augusta provides Byron the opportunity of replacing the friend by whose estrangement he has come to require another, safer one; above all, he needs to speak to a friend, confidentially, of what has made him so urgently need one. But he can only hint. And yet that he hints *this soon* into the correspondence, and to a relative little known, measures the pressure exerted on him by the Grey event: "I am as you may imagine a little dull here [at Southwell, with Mrs. Byron], not being on terms of even intimacy with Lord Grey I avoid Newstead, and my resources of amusement are Books, and writing to my Augusta, which wherever I am, will always constitute my Greatest pleasure" (*BLJ* 1:45–6). The phrase "of even intimacy" is tantalizing. Read as equivalent to "even of intimacy," it identifies a stage along a relational continuum, with other phases before and beyond itself. Given his history with Grey, Byron cannot mean that he has not yet reached "even" the level of "intimacy" with his tenant (see the *OED* on *intimacy* as familiarity, close association or acquaintance); he rather means that having gone (far?) beyond that phase, he has now retreated far below it. In the circumstances, "I am not even intimate with him" means that I have been, and have given it up.

The phrase acknowledges a prior "intimacy" of more than "close acquaintance." It may inadvertently betray a consciousness or recollection or anxiety or fantasy about Grey warmer than the relational protocol and temperature of "close familiarity" indicates.²²

But the locution "of even intimacy" may also and perhaps primarily mean "of *equal* intimacy" and thus reflect again Byron's hypersensitivity to issues of status and wealth. One can imagine a casual remark by Grey implying a gap between the dashing lord wealthy enough to rent and the impecunious lord forced to lease—a gap in social and economic equality or "evenness." Lacking articulation or implication, that difference nevertheless would have been implicit, perhaps conscious, in all Byron-Grey association on the Newstead estate, and might have provoked Byron's compensatory behavior noted above—a show of lordly responsibility to some (Joe Murray) and of baronial power over others (Owen Mealey).²³

In any event, Lord Grey has now displaced the young nobleman from his own estate for the second time, first as tenant, then as traitor. Potentially filling the vacuum of Grey's absence, books and Augusta offer amusement—these, we might believe, approximately equivalent substitutes for the diversions formerly provided by Newstead and Grey; and the possible parallel invests Grey with (once favorable) importance in the boy's estimation, as confirmed in Byron's next sentence: "I am not reconciled to Lord Grey, *and I never will*. He was once my *Greatest Friend*, my reasons for ceasing that Friendship are such as I cannot explain, not even to you my Dear Sister (although were they to be made known to any body, you would be the first,) but they will ever remain hidden in my own breast—They are Good ones however, for although I am *violent* I am not *capricious* in my *attachments*" (*BLJ* 1:46).

Let us pause now, halfway through this crucial letter, to reexamine the famous lines. Byron always set great store by friendship; we need to take seriously the status he here grants Grey—who, as we have seen, shares a given name with Henry Drury—although the bitterness of disillusionment may have melodramatically enhanced it. But clearly he regarded Grey as a mate bound by the sacred ties of trust, loyalty, and respect. Second, it has long been assumed that Lord Grey's unspeakable offense was an unwelcome sexual advance;²⁴ Byron's and Hobhouse's hints certainly suggest as much. Less noticed, if at all, are Byron's plurals: he has *reasons* for breaking with Grey, among which a sexual proposition may have been prominent, and perhaps the most shocking. And if not only it but his other reason(s) must also remain unspoken, they are either equally heinous or so closely related to the hypothetical primary offense as to be unintelligible independently of it. Or is Byron masking the central truth of a sexual proposition by splitting and dispersing it into several (imagined) offenses? Or does the pluralization unconsciously encrypt his positive response to an overture, or his temptation to accept it? Or did Byron value the friendship so highly, respect it so dearly, as to imagine its rupture unexplainable by one act, and so pluralizes the world in self-justification for breaking off relations without in fact having any reason but the (presumed) sexual one? This latter possibility might gain plausibility if Byron felt that he had in some way invited Grey's advance—as Frederic Raphael believes that he invited the seductions of his nurse May Gray[25]—and therefore needed other reasons for the separation; that they too remain shrouded in silence may mean that they never existed. And yet Byron's insistence upon his sound judgment, and his teasing parenthetical, begs Augusta's inquiry. Byron wanted to tell. Byron *always* wanted to tell, and usually did. If we read literally his parenthetical remark here, disclosure to Augusta might facilitate additional circulation of his secret. Why, if merely the recipient of a verbal proposition, couldn't *he* tell? What, in short, is Byron hiding? I will come back to this question.

For the moment, I want to reexamine the last sentence quoted above: "They are Good ones [reasons] however, for although I am *violent* I am not *capricious* in my *attachments.*" Emphatically reiterating the former affiliation with Grey, Byron again defends the sensible justice of his decision, indirectly citing an associational steadfastness or firmness in him that, stiffened by passion, prohibits reckless alliance and frivolous abandonments. But if we stress the personal pronouns in Byron's declaration, its meaning expands: "although *I* am [also] *violent, I* am not *capricious* in *my* attachments [as Lord Grey is in *his*]." The sentence, that is, may encode another of Byron's "reasons" for leaving Newstead abruptly, a rationale closely associated with sexual misconduct and impenetrable without knowledge of it. Read in this second way, Byron's statement charges Grey with whimsical instability in relationships, with arbitrary or self-serving motives in friendship—with, in fact, a traditional Don Juanism. And he also admits that only the *most* appalling of insults or betrayals could have shaken *him* to break a commitment in friendship. It is the cry of a boy wounded by infidelity, or flightiness, or silliness, or affectional superficiality; but its shrillness and emphasis, I suspect, also articulate an anxiety as yet but dimly (if at all) conscious over a corresponding impulse in himself to seduce, use, and abandon.[26]

Support for this reading emerges three years later in a poem, "To an Oak in the Garden of Newstead Abbey, planted by the Author in the 9th Year of his age; this tree at his last visit was in a state of decay, though perhaps not irrecoverable—15th March 1807" (Byron's losing entry in the longest romantic poem title competition!). The second stanza of this work not only accuses Grey of negligence in tending the oak; echoing the epistolary charge of the 26 March letter, Byron finds him emotionally deficient:

> I left thee, my Oak, and, since that fatal hour [for the oak? For himself, too?]
>   A stranger has dwelt in the hall of my sire;
> Till manhood shall crown me, not mine is the power,
>   But his, whose neglect may have bade thee expire.
> Oh! hardy thou wert—even now little care
>   Might revive thy young head, and thy wounds gently heal:
> But thou wert not fated affection to share—
>   For who could suppose that a Stranger would feel?

The question seethes with residual bitterness from one who *did* so suppose. The tree does not quite substitute for Byron in its suffering from Grey's potentially lethal abuse, but it carries a good deal of the young man's continuing distress over the insensitivity and caprice of a former companion, now divested of the capacity to feel.

Moore says that the discovery here related took place "some six or seven years after" the planting, and "soon after Lord Grey de Ruthen left Newstead" (1:81), although he had taken the property on a five-year lease from July 1803. Byron's recent return, in any case, to a site unvisited since he suddenly fled it for unutterable reasons brings back forcefully the circumstances requiring that flight, which then find coded expression in the verse. The "choked up" oak might very well have appeared to him to image a fate he barely escaped. Clearly, prolonged exposure to Grey had proved poisonous to boy as to oak. That by now Byron had met John Edleston, to whose charm he, the older party, was drawn, must have complicated his review of the Grey affair, which itself probably contributed to his insistence upon the purity of his passion for the Cambridge choirboy.

In the letter to Augusta, he cannot drop the subject: "My mother disapproves of my quarreling with him [Grey], but if she knew the cause (which she never will know,) She would reproach me no more. He Has forfeited all *title to my esteem,* but I hold him in too much *contempt* ever *to hate him*" (*BLJ* 1:46). Byron's suspicion of his mother's fancy for Grey and a resulting disdain laced with jealousy surely color these sentences, about which more later. For now, curiously, to the maternal audience the unspoken explanations for the estrangement appear to have shrunk to one, or are by association folded into one comprehensive "cause," which Mrs. Byron can never know. This restriction obviously privileges Augusta, and subtly invites her inquiry yet again; but it also foregrounds the (still masked) supposed sexual indiscretion as the chief offense certain to silence Mrs. Byron's complaints. Again, one wonders why an innocent Byron, with so excellent an explanation ready to hand, cannot exonerate himself for mysterious behavior by using it. Does decorum, or Byronic underestimation of female sensitivities, prevent discussion of such matters between genders, particularly within families?

The question remains, how is *Byron* implicated in the estranging event? The great irony of the succeeding epistolary line, of course, is that Byron's continuing secrecy protects Lord Grey as effectively as would the discretion of a best friend;[27] it positions Byron as guardian of the reputation of the man he professes to despise. But a bizarre logic supports that guardianship if Grey's approach found an answering, sympathetic response in Byron that terrified the boy, as well it might, given its aberrance and the current penalties for homosexual behavior, although it is difficult to believe that Byron at sixteen in a boys' public school had not yet experimented in homoeroticism, particularly since it was customary at Harrow for boys to share a bed and sleep in the buff.[28] Even were he ignorant of English law on the point, however, Byron's silence protects himself as much as Grey from shameful exposure; and the attempt to disengage himself emotionally from his former friend, and to feel only a rational "contempt" for him, collapses with the persistence of the theme in this letter. The contempt is in part self-directed, either for feeling sympathetic, or for soliciting or imagining his own solicitation of an offer, or both. Unworthy of hate, the contemptible Grey nevertheless commands much of Byron's attention just now, and siphons off a fair measure of his emotional energy. His letter goes on, after remembrances to Mrs. Byron, to promise Augusta a visit en route to Harrow, and to name three individuals, including Osborne and Murray again, whose acquaintance he values, as though still eager to populate the vacuum left by Grey, and to assure himself of his own worthiness of friendship. As for Augusta's amorous prospects, "I am sure you deserve Happiness for if *you* do not meet with it I shall begin to think it is 'a bad world we live in.'" Augusta's relational future, that is, will test a hypothesis already tempting this youth recently shocked and disappointed both by his friend and perhaps by a suspicion about himself. It is beginning to look like a very bad world indeed. Again he signs off, "Your ever affectionate Brother and Friend" (*BLJ* 1:46).

A puzzling sentence in this letter remains to be considered: "I am not reconciled to Lord Grey, *and I never will.*" The idiom is awkward, the parallel ungrammatical, unbalanced, and incomplete. "I never will be reconciled" is the presumed intention, of course, but the syntactical construction implies a missing verb, a denied action. Why the oddity of expression at precisely this point in the letter? I strongly suspect that in the heat and rush of Byron's epistolary composition, and in the anger and embarrassment of recalling the event while referring to it with censor sharply vigilant, the language of his *refusal* of Grey's proposition—or the language of an undelivered refusal—asserts itself as the language of his vow against reconciliation and any future participation in such action as Grey allegedly invited. That refusal of the sexual advance can never be said enough, if Byron did find himself intrigued by it. "I never will" is an anxiety-ridden pledge to Augusta and himself not merely that armistice with Grey is unthinkable, but that he will abstain from the behavior modeled or encouraged by his tenant back in December/January.[29]

Let me here anticipate two challenges to these arguments. First, can Lord Grey at twenty-three be fairly described as an "older man"? Indeed, may not "man" prematurely age one still more boy than adult? To middle age, twenty-three is poignantly youthful and hardly distinguishable from sixteen; to adolescence, twenty-three is practically hoary and virtually synonymous with fifty. We do not know how "boyishly" Grey may have behaved in transactions with Byron, but the scant evidence suggests to me that he usually acted his age and rank, and that Byron was flattered by the attentions of someone consciously regarded as older, more widely experienced, and a resource for worldly knowledge. Lord Grey is surely not the first or the last adult to take sexual advantage of such respect in a minor, if he did so—that Byron had already suffered May Gray's abusive manipulation probably heightened his sensitivity to adult exploitation, and possibly empowered him to invite it—but an erotic overture, itself culturally legitimate only among mature persons, from an adult to an adolescent would confirm and strengthen the subject's perception of age differential. Add the onus of transgressive sexual aberrance, imagined to be imported from an exotic world of experience, and the adolescent's perception of age difference widens in proportion to his increasing sense of threat. And as the threat would almost certainly be less from a contemporary, so would the impact of the event for the adolescent. In other words, consciousness of a capacity to attract the adult's sexual aberrance *itself* increases awareness of age differential: the wider the temporal gap, the greater the power that spans it.

Second, how can the boy disgusted by a homosexual advance become the lover of boys? The locution itself misconstrues the reality. Byron does not *become* the lover of boys; he already *is,* if perhaps immaturely, ingenuously; and his attraction to male youths is not incompatible with his alleged revulsion toward Grey. A youth suspicious of aberration in himself, particularly if the deviation is corroborated by other stigmatizing anomalies, would take alarm at any action likely to confirm that intuition of difference. If the act originates in an authority figure such as Lord Grey, it would feel all the more menacing *as authoritative,* as a substantiating gesture: it would recognize and validate the aberration as definitive of identity, offer its own anomaly in sanctioning acceptance, and judge the deviance intrinsic, possibly ineradicable. Moreover, such an intention on the part of the authority figure would be imagined to carry the trappings of a subordinating, demeaning power and would therefore trigger, in Byron at any rate, the resistance of pride, and probably also of class consciousness because the transgression of a tenant.

Now, amorous experimentation with one's school bedmate or dormitory neighbor is a very different order of engagement from the sort historically assumed to have been proposed by Grey. My hunch, however, is that Byron was less neutrally experimental or playful than sentimentally romantic in his Harrow sexual adventures: his poetry of adolescent boy-love is warm but earnest, guileless, almost painfully sincere, without a trace of the carnal nonchalance often imputed to the later Byron, whose love poetry nevertheless, as long as he composed in the genre, continued to show this tender, sentimental bent. In either case, these conjectures would appear to situate Byron at the farthest psychological remove from accommodation of Grey's invitation. And yet Byron's resistance—if he resisted—must have been grounded at least in part in a fantasy constructed from his own homoerotic experience, just as such experience would have fed any fantasy enabling his acceptance of the overture. Perceived to be constitutive of his identity, Grey's proposal, at the time or retrospectively, would give a gravity and perhaps even shocking importance to Byron's earlier erotic experience with contemporaries: it points to the propositioning Lord Grey as the adult whom the experimenting boy may become, the sooner for his acceptance of this very initiation. My point is not that the proposed sexual commerce is discontinuous with Byron's schoolboy bed-play but that, stunningly, it is not: broadly similar in a physiological sense, engagement with Grey might be seen as entirely congruous with, perhaps the inescapable consequence of, earlier dalliance.

That is one jolt of the Grey event—the revelation of continuity, even contiguity, between schoolboy sexual experimentation ("innocent lovemaking") and mature perversion. Going into December/January 1803–4, Byron could and probably did believe that his boy-love belonged to a unique, insulated, hallowed erotic structure radically distinct from the act presumably proposed by Lord Grey; and while a sense of that difference by itself might have been sufficiently menacing in prospect or in performance damaging to alienate Byron from his abuser, the evaporation of that sense of difference would only exacerbate the estrangement in a sexual identity still resistant to self-acceptance, and provoke such restless chafing about the episode as we find in Byron's epistolary reflections upon it: disappointment, guilt, perplexity, anxiety pick at it as at a loosening scab. Byron's acceptance of Grey's advance would of course have ratified even more emphatically the probability of his becoming the thing he saw, as indeed in some sense he did become it. But he might well have subsequently *used* the Grey event to justify himself in relationships with other males, by contrast representing and accepting himself in them as defensibly moral. I am persuaded that the encounter with Lord Grey, assuming its sexual content, became the foundation and rationale for Byron's later insistence on the purity of his passion for John Edleston. By that calculus in the boy's thinking, anything short of the impurity of Grey's proposed action might be admissible and defensible. Byron's rejection of Grey's overture—if he did reject it—does not, then, challenge his own homosexual predilections; rather, the passion and persistence of his protests—his homosexual panic—

interrogates them and betrays an interest thus far frightened of itself but not unprepared to be realized in more suitable partnerships.

JUST OVER FIVE YEARS LATER, Byron found himself, at twenty-one, the senior partner in a warm relationship with young Robert Rushton, handsome son of a Newstead tenant farmer. Marchand nowhere indicates how much younger than his employer this retainer was, but Robert had matured sufficiently by May of 1809 to anger the poet by accompanying the valet William Fletcher on a visit to London prostitutes in defiance of Byron's strict instructions, reported to his mother on the 19th, that the boy's "*morals* [be secured] . . . from the *temptations* of this *accursed place* [London]" (*BLJ* 1:203). A painting of Rushton and himself that Byron commissioned from the fashionable and expensive George Sanders in 1807—their postures and gestures curiously matched, their gazes similarly directed, their neck scarves similarly windswept, the boy positioned as if in adoring imitation of the man—shows Robert at about fourteen, give or take a year, to Byron's nineteen. Old enough to be Byron's sparring partner during Mrs. Byron's memorial service in April of 1811, Robert had also attended the poet as page part way on this first continental tour (and would again in 1816), although not old enough, in Byron's proprietary view, to travel safely in Turkey, even in his lordship's entourage. This custodial concern quickens into possessiveness and even jealousy in Byron's outrage over Fletcher's contribution to Rushton's delinquency among the whores, but in varying degrees it informed all of his dealings with Robert, whose bedroom at Newstead adjoined his master's on the top floor (Marchand 1:175), and whose feminine features inspired rumors that Byron's live-in mistress cross-dressed. It appears again in Byron's facilitation of Robert's immunization against smallpox, a crude process involving infection with cowpox (*BLJ* 1:187–88).

I introduce Rushton in this context because of a coincidence of subjects in Byron's 15 August 1809 letter from Gibraltar to his mother, reporting Robert's return to England, on Byron's order, in the company of Joe Murray, longtime servant at the estate: "Pray show the lad any kindness as he is my great favourite, I would have taken him on ‹but you *know boys* are not *safe* amongst the Turks—› Say this to his father, who may otherwise think he has behaved ill" (*BLJ* 1:221–22). Then follows, after a conventional closure, this postscript: "So Ld. Grey is married to a rustic, well done!" (*BLJ* 1:222), in response to Mrs. Byron's: "Lord Grey de Ruthyn has married a Farmer's Daughter" (Marchand 1:180n). Byron's addendum may, of course, merely notice his mother's announcement in equivalent marginalization. But his relegation of Lord Grey to the regions of afterthought might be calculated, as assuredly is his next sentence: "If I wed I will bring you home a sultana with half a score of cities for a dowry, and reconcile you to an Ottoman daughter in law with a bushel of pearls not larger than ostrich eggs or smaller than Walnuts" (*BLJ* 1:222). Five years after the estranging event, Byron remains eager to differentiate himself from Lord Grey, now twenty-nine, and to widen the distance between them: if he, unlike Grey, marries at all, he, unlike Grey, will marry wealth and position. But only two sentences back, Byron has affirmed his proprietary claims on another "rustic" in age differential to him approximately as he was to Grey—a boy whom he has just committed to English safekeeping against a foreign menace presumably of the sort posed by Grey against himself in December/January 1803–4.

Writing of the Turkish threat, Byron could scarcely not have recalled his experience with its British variant, if that was Grey's offense, in which case Byron would be particularly sensitive to Robert's endangerment. But not only from Turkish men. By now Byron has known the "pure" John Edleston and the impure Charles Skinner Matthews and other Cantabrigians of Matthews' aberrant sexual persuasion, and is prepared to take advantage of homoerotic hospitality among the Ottomans.[30] Marchand, citing Hobhouse's conversation with Benjamin Robert Haydon while sitting for his portrait in 1838, declares that "Byron's initiation in the vices came probably earlier even than Hobhouse supposed, certainly as early as his sojourn in London in the early months of 1806" (1:118n; see also 1:90n). The dispatching of Robert Rushton spares the boy exposure not merely to randy Turks but to knowledge of Byron's liberated congress with them, "saves" him for resumption of a relationship with the returned Byron presumably very different from the indulgences of the Turkish tour. Whether Byron would have seen in his association with Robert the inverse of his with Grey, we can only conjecture; but that the writing about Rushton calls to mind a(nother) sexual episode in the life of Lord Grey deserving and now permitting derision seems probable. Byron's ambivalence about disclosing his reason for sending Robert home—the blotted but decipherable line—matches exactly his hesitating willingness to be drawn by Augusta on the estrangement from Grey, as we shall see: the crossed lines practically invite Mrs. Byron—supposing she *did* know what he spoke of—to wonder how safe boys might be in the company of her son.

Lord Grey appears once more in Byron's correspondence with relevance to our concerns in these pages. In August of 1808 he preferred "a general charge of misconduct" against Owen Mealey, Byron's gardener at Newstead, but without particulars, which Byron then requested before acting, even while pointedly wondering, twice, whether Grey had not been misinformed of Mealey's "delinquencies" by an unreliable servant grapevine. Here, of course, are Byron's silences on Grey reheard in Grey's on Mealey; or more exactly in his reporting only general suspicions of unverified transgressions, Byron promises "reparation" if "grounds of [the] complaint" are forthcoming, but casts such doubt over the likelihood of Mealey's guilt as to discourage further inquiry. The remainder of the letter, however, without apparent motivation or comment, other than the overhanging suspicion of misconduct at Newstead, revisits the separative event of 1803–4. As with Augusta, Byron does and does not want to talk of it: "I cannot conclude without adverting to circumstances, which though now long past, and indeed difficult for me to touch on, have not yet ceased to be interesting" (*BLJ* 1:168). Really, one wants to ask? To whom? And why? What has vitalized interest in those painful circumstances "now long [not quite five years] past"? Then: "Your Lordship must be perfectly aware of the very peculiar reasons [mark the plural] that induced me to adopt a line of conduct, which however painful to me it certainly was, became unavoidable" (*BLJ* 1:168). The curious phrasing suggests that Byron's adopted line of conduct—presumably his dissociation from Grey—was *not* abrupt in spontaneous response to a catalytic event but rather developed over time, from accumulated reasons: what I did *became* inevitable, he appears to say, through the repetition or duration of its causes (unless "became" merely avoids a stylistically awkward repetition of "was"; but such niceties do not normally distinguish Byron's epistolary prose).

Having recommended memory, Byron declines to jog it: "On these [reasons] I cannot enter at large, nor would the discussion be a pleasing one, while any farther explanation is unnecessary" (*BLJ* 1:168). But what *prior* "explanation" has been offered, and by whom? Does this sentence mean that Byron will not be any more particular in explaining his grievance against Grey than Grey has been in his against Mealey, since explanation is in any event superfluous? Besides, he closes the door on it: "—at the same time, though from these and other causes, much intercourse between us must entirely cease." Are there really, as the subordinate clause indicates, yet additional unspoken reasons for continuing their estrangement? Or is Byron padding, rationalizing, and in what follows, deflecting?

> I have still so grateful a recollection of many favours you have conferred upon me as a boy, that I shall always be happy, when we do meet, to meet as friends, and endeavor to forget we have been otherwise. If ever you sojourn again in Notts, I hope you will pay Newstead a visit, I shall be there from September till January, for the present month I reside in Brighton. (*BLJ* 1:168)

This is conciliatory but cool, and it instantly compromises the willingness to meet as friends with the "endeavor," without guarantee of success, to forget enmity. It foregrounds the favored boy as rationale and basis for any future encounter, and thus both remembers the disfavored one and subordinates the courteously diplomatic young lord who in any case elides himself from the explicit invitation to visit Newstead Abbey, not its owner, who is presently absent anyway. The letter satisfies the requirements of decorous hospitality, but with gritted, almost bared teeth.

Lord Grey, however, by his own testimony, is imperfectly if at all aware of the reasons inducing the painful line of conduct that Byron here recalls. His response to this letter very differently remembers the separation: "We parted in 1804 the best of friends, your letters afterwards were most affectionate. . . . You say the break was painful to yourself, I need not say to you who know I have not the power to command my feelings when [deeply?] wounded what my sensations were."[31] It is difficult to believe that Byron could have written affectionately to Grey while so relentlessly impugning his conduct in letter after letter to Augusta and Mrs. Byron. In the absence of corroborative evidence pointing to an amicable separation—which in any case Grey could not have dared to produce in self-defense—one is tempted to read the tenant's version as a self-protective lie. And yet his profession of wounded sensations sounds truthful enough if the boy had repulsed an erotic proposition, or accepted one (or more) for that matter, and decamped as a consequence. Marchand speculates that Byron "may have cut the acquaintance without revealing to Grey the extent of his shock at the time" (*BLJ* 1:168n), in which case Grey's "sensations" would have been "wounded" by Byron's prolonged absence, after January 1804, not by a dramatic rupture with accusations and explanations flung back and forth. Grosskurth posits Byron's jealousy of his mother's attractions for Grey as motivation for his fabrication of the dramatic parting, itself a cover for dalliance with Grey (41). Still assuming a sexual overture, one can imagine—if uncomfortably, with disappointment—a frightened, guilty Byron skulking off into the night toward Harrow without confronting Grey—more easily, in fact, than imagining his massive duplicity in continuing "affectionate" correspondence with the tenant. On the other hand, the returned schoolboy, anxious about interpretations of his flight from Newstead, might have observed the proprieties by penning a formal acknowledgment of his host's hospitality, which Grey then remembered or misinterpreted as "affectionate." It is in any case possible, and in my view likely, that Byron departed Newstead, perhaps without vocal recrimination or explanation but in circumstances—whether long prevailing or recently developed—that left no reasonable doubt about his reasons for doing so, even if only he and Grey were privy to them. Thus Byron's certainty of Grey's awareness, and thus the space for dissimulation in Grey's response.[32] Nevertheless, Grey prevaricates. And yet what choice has he? He cannot commit to writing any word construable as an admission of improper behavior toward the boy, but neither can he afford, despite the warning, to leave Byron's mysterious remarks unchallenged. So he pretends ignorance of rationale, imagines affectionate letters, and melodramatizes his pain with the impression that it was the worse for the incomprehensibility of its cause.[33]

2 : Virgilian King : 5 July 1804

ALTHOUGH BORED AT BURGAGE MANOR in the company of "old parsons and old Maids" (*BLJ* 1:47), Byron writes to Augusta on 2 April 1804 in a lighthearted vein; but the Grey specter lurks just below his consciousness, and subtly shapes part of his discourse:

> I shoot a Good deal, but thank God I have not so far lost my reason as to make shooting my only amusement. [Shooting *was* Grey's favorite pastime.] There are indeed some of my neighbors whose only pleasures consist in field sports, but in other respects they are only one degree removed from the brute creation. These however I endeavor not to imitate, but I sincerely wish for the company of a few friends *about my own age* [my italics] to soften the austerity of the place.

And he elaborates wittily on how the "Gravity" of Burgage Manor trains him for "an Archbishopric" (*BLJ* 1:47). Behind the aristocratic snobbery registered here is recollection of sporting days and nights with Grey at Newstead; and although Fieldingesque squires most immediately constitute that "brute creation" from which Byron differentiates himself, the phrase may also faintly inscribe a sexual anxiety—an erotic as well as social distinction. The stipulation for young friends rejects not merely the "parsons and . . . Maids" of present company but also the older Grey, who may now, in disillusioned aftermath, seem hopelessly corrupted by age and experience. Observing that Augusta's and a Harrow friend's letters are his only "resources for driving away *dull* care," and then insisting that hers alone are his "only pleasure," Byron signs off, this time reversing the order of his relatedness to "Friend and Brother," as though both offering and needing the first, in active expression, more urgently.

Another week sees a striking shift in Byron's attitude toward the sporting life:

> . . . by the bye, I do not dislike Harrow I find *ways* and *means* to amuse *myself very pleasantly* there, the friend whose correspondence I find so

amusing is an old sporting companion of mine, whose recitals of Shooting and Hunting expeditions are amusing to me as having often been his companion in them, and I hope to be so still oftener. (*BLJ* 1:48)

The boldness of the contradiction disappears if we assume that the earlier letter alludes principally to Grey, and the second altogether forgets him, or "endeavours" to erase epistolary evidence related to him. What in the second renders such shooting escapades acceptable is that the companion in them is not Grey; that the companion is of similar age and experience; and that the companion makes tales of their outings—turns experience into an entertaining, performative speech act co-starring themselves. (The event with Grey, then, has not spoiled pleasant memories of other shooting parties.) I stress this last reason because "reciting" is much on Byron's mind as he writes. The passage I quote continues a sentence beginning this way: "If I speak in public school it will not be till the latter end of June or the beginning of July, you are right in your conjecture for I feel not a little nervous in the anticipation of *my Debut* as *an orator*" (*BLJ* 1:48).

This is the first mention in Byron's surviving correspondence of his Harrow Speech Day engagement,[1] although he must have written of it to Augusta in a letter now lost, for the quoted passage appears to resume a conversation on the subject; and the context of the reference is important. As a shy, lame, unpopular, and except for title undistinguished boy, Byron is understandably anxious about a major public trial—an opportunity to match and measure himself against other boys, a chance to move up toward recognition as a respectable voice and identity in the school. The stakes are high, and his conditional "If" acknowledges the possibility of withdrawal at the same time that the reflections on happiness at Harrow (albeit expressed in the double negative: "I do not dislike Harrow") look ahead to increased pleasure after a successful Speech Day performance. That wish colors his contradiction of Augusta's assumption of discontent, which almost certainly rests upon his prior claim of it. There is also a swagger, a flash of bravado, in the phrase, "*my Debut* as *an orator,*" although it is not without a trace of self-irony as well. Having muted himself for months about an event presumably needing articulation for relief of pressure, his speech the victim of his own self-suppression, Byron is about to be *featured* as a speaker, not principally *as* himself, of course (although this will change with his second and third performances) but with his speaking skills the focus of everybody's attention in his premiere as "orator." The opportunity is potentially liberating, and on his performance rides the question of his future plausibility as acceptable schoolmate; indeed, his *career* as Lord Byron is already implicated, for the quoted phrase reverberates with the timbre of the upper House.

Three weeks to a month later, in a letter to his mother (1–10 May 1804? *BLJ* 1:49–50), Byron reports comfort with Harrow peers but confesses to "scrapes with Drury and the other Masters," and curiously recycles parts of the complaint he had voiced to the same audience almost exactly a year earlier, although the culprits have changed and multiplied, and Byron's discourse itself has compulsively expanded:

> I have gotten into two or three scrapes [an underestimation?] with [Dr.] Drury and the other Masters, which are not very convenient, the other day as he was reprimanding me, (perhaps very properly) for my misdeeds he uttered the following words, "it is not probable that from your age and situation in the School your Friends will permit you to remain longer than Summer [term], but because you are about to leave Harrow, it is no reason you are to make the house a scene of riot and Confusion." this and much more said the Doctor. (*BLJ* 1:49)

If the headmaster truly said something like this representation, what did he mean, and how did the boy interpret him? Is the reprimand (and threat of expulsion) an assessment of Byron's scholastic record, a comment on his untimely progress for a boy of his age? Is it the wish of an exasperated headmaster to be rid of a fractious boy? And to what "Friends" does Drury allude? To any at the school, including himself, who have Byron's best interests at heart? To those who control the government's purse and pay his tuition bills? This last possibility may be supported by subsequent evidence in the letter, but if the headmaster refers to local "Friends," the conception of friendship is at best odd, for friends are thus made the agents of rejection and abandonment—of abuse, as Byron had already experienced it and them.

Moreover, Drury's attribution of the expulsive act to nameless others repeats the indirect, mediated message on Henry's part that so angered the boy. What follows is the solidification of probability into fait accompli: "because you are about to leave" assumes the pupil's accession to an administrative decision to that effect, and on its face provides reason enough for a hot-tempered lad to create the "Confusion" it decries. The language foresees the end of Byron's Harrow career while appearing merely to threaten it as discipline. But there is more, and another kind of threat, by now familiar: "I am informed From creditable authority that Dr. Drury, Mr. Evans and Mark Drury [the headmaster's brother and a Harrow tutor] said I was a *Blackguard,* that Mark Drury said so I *know,* but I am inclined to doubt the authenticity of the report as to the rest." (*BLJ* 1:49). Perhaps then the "creditable authority" is not so creditable after all, if it reports so hurtfully on the two respected teachers. Byron is caught between his wish to clear his favorites and his fear that the entire pedagogical establishment may be corrupt and leagued against him. Notice the first-person plurals in this continuation: "perhaps it is true perhaps not, but thank God they may call me a Blackguard, but they can never make me one"—which is to deny the power of language to transform character but not to wound it.

Plainly, however, the suspicion of conspiracy prevails over more charitable instincts, and inspires defiance: "If Dr. Drury can bring one boy or any one else [as though by coercion?] to say that I have committed a dishonorable action, and to prove it, I am content, but otherwise I am stigmatized without a cause, and I disdain and despise the malicious efforts of him and his Brother." (*BLJ* 1:49). Embedded in this (undelivered) challenge may be one explanation for Byron's silence on Lord Grey. It is not enough for Dr. Drury's hypothetical tattle to charge "dishonorable action"; proof is requisite. Moreover, for Byron to bring the charge against Grey without incontestable proof would implicate him if Grey were not "proved" guilty, possibly if he were, and in any event involve him in discussions embarrassing and threatening to a boy probably already baffled by homoerotic interests. Furthermore, as we have seen, Byron may not have resisted Grey's overtures; if he succumbed to them, he could hardly bring the charge publicly without risking disclosure of the truth. One can imagine, in such a circumstance, Byron hearing brought against himself the very challenge he has just laid on Dr. Drury's desk: and Byron was savvy enough to imagine it, too.

That "Blackguard" includes sociological as well as delinquent implications in Mark Drury's use of it is clear as Byron continues:

> His Brother Mark not Henry Drury (whom I will do the Justice to say has never since last year, interfered with me [the verb and the syntax both privilege the writer and his agenda over the schoolmaster and his, so that the attribution of "Justice" manages to subordinate the tutor] is continually reproaching me with the narrowness of my fortune, to what end I

Meanwhile, however, as high as he has soared, so low does he now sink, in what reads like a startling anticipation of the abrupt discontinuities, incongruities, and tonal shifts of *Don Juan* (composed, like this letter, in stages):

> But why this upstart Son of a Button maker is to reproach me about an estate which however, is far superior to his own, I know not, but that he should call me a Blackguard, is far worse, on account of the former I can blame only Hanson (and that officious Friend [Fiend?] Lord Grey de Ruthyn, whom I shall ever consider my most inveterate enemy), it is a mere trifle, but the latter I cannot bear, I have not deserved it, and I will not be insulted with impunity. (*BLJ* 1:49)

The earlier restraint gives way to vitriol, in the first instance of a nastily snobbish cast, by which the slur upon Mark's blood and class repays Mark's upon limited aristocratic fortune, perhaps because, we now learn, disclosures about Byron's estate may be traced back to the attorney Hanson and Lord Grey—presumably Hanson's "officious Friend" but no longer Byron's. How information about Byron's fortune could pass from Hanson to Grey and thence to Mark Drury is unclear: although Hanson had it, would he carelessly communicate it, especially to the Newstead tenant? And if Harrow needed it, why go to Mark and not to his brother the headmaster? Or perhaps the information came from Dr. Drury to Mark? And what possible interest could have linked Grey and Joseph or Mark Drury? An easier and likelier explanation might suggest that, given Byron's pensioner status at the school, the size of his fortune cannot ever have been much of a secret.

But the boy needs a villain, a scapegoat; he seizes upon Hanson who *does* know the family's finances, and, still lacking a reason to account to his mother for the estrangement from Grey, conveniently associates the two men in indiscreet revelation without implicating himself. By comparison with the charge of blackguardism, perhaps the financial insult is a "mere trifle," but if so it occasions a disproportionately substantial response. Byron, I suspect, wishes to tar Mark Drury with the blackest brush he can find, and so links him, too, to the "inveterate enemy" Grey. Curiously, with Hanson and Grey in Byron's hand, Mark is exonerated of one crime: "I can *only* blame" Hanson and Grey, he writes. But the partial exoneration only clears the way for incrimination on unpardonable grounds:

appearing merely to threaten it as discipline. But there is more, and another kind of threat, by now familiar: "I am informed From creditable authority that Dr. Drury, Mr. Evans and Mark Drury [the headmaster's brother and a Harrow tutor] said I was a *Blackguard,* that Mark Drury said so I *know,* but I am inclined to doubt the authenticity of the report as to the rest." (*BLJ* 1:49). Perhaps then the "creditable authority" is not so creditable after all, if it reports so hurtfully on the two respected teachers. Byron is caught between his wish to clear his favorites and his fear that the entire pedagogical establishment may be corrupt and leagued against him. Notice the first-person plurals in this continuation: "perhaps it is true perhaps not, but thank God they may call me a Blackguard, but they can never make me one"—which is to deny the power of language to transform character but not to wound it.

Plainly, however, the suspicion of conspiracy prevails over more charitable instincts, and inspires defiance: "If Dr. Drury can bring one boy or any one else [as though by coercion?] to say that I have committed a dishonorable action, and to prove it, I am content, but otherwise I am stigmatized without a cause, and I disdain and despise the malicious efforts of him and his Brother." (*BLJ* 1:49). Embedded in this (undelivered) challenge may be one explanation for Byron's silence on Lord Grey. It is not enough for Dr. Drury's hypothetical tattle to charge "dishonorable action"; proof is requisite. Moreover, for Byron to bring the charge against Grey without incontestable proof would implicate him if Grey were not "proved" guilty, possibly if he were, and in any event involve him in discussions embarrassing and threatening to a boy probably already baffled by homoerotic interests. Furthermore, as we have seen, Byron may not have resisted Grey's overtures; if he succumbed to them, he could hardly bring the charge publicly without risking disclosure of the truth. One can imagine, in such a circumstance, Byron hearing brought against himself the very challenge he has just laid on Dr. Drury's desk: and Byron was savvy enough to imagine it, too.

That "Blackguard" includes sociological as well as delinquent implications in Mark Drury's use of it is clear as Byron continues:

> His Brother Mark not Henry Drury (whom I will do the Justice to say has never since last year, interfered with me [the verb and the syntax both privilege the writer and his agenda over the schoolmaster and his, so that the attribution of "Justice" manages to subordinate the tutor] is continually reproaching me with the narrowness of my fortune, to what end I

know not[;] his intentions may be Good, but his manner is disagreeable, I see no reason why I am to be reproached with it. (*BLJ* 1:49)

Worth noting is the relative mellowness of this passage, a moderation compatible with that of the two previous quotations where only "disdain," "despise," and "malicious" capture the ire of Byron's earlier complaint. But why the temperate tone? What "Good intentions" does Byron suppose might author Mark Drury's taunts about his fortune? What does Byron read behind Mark's "disagreeable manner" that somehow redeems or mollifies it? Or for what reason does he uncharacteristically seek charity where little may abide?

The temperance is smart rhetorical strategy. Byron here lays the reasonable foundation upon which he will momentarily mount his assault against Mark Drury: it is the contrasting but solid base, showcasing rationality and fair-mindedness, that helps to validate what might otherwise seem excessive, even hysterical in the forthcoming fulmination. Second, Mark is right about the fortune, Byron knows that he is right, and knows that his mother knows it; and Byron's acknowledgment of that lamentable and embarrassing truth for the moment restrains his wrath over being "reproached" about it. Besides, Mrs. Byron would certainly approve of any "Good intentions" that included the counsel of frugality—a motive she might reasonably assign to Mark Drury from this account of him. Her son finesses the question of motive to pursue the issue of manner(s), which is a kind of metonymy for what Byron regards not merely as the discourteous, unseemly publicity of one's financial condition but, more egregiously, the disrespectful, unacceptably invasive and dishonoring conduct of a commoner toward a lord. Mark Drury's reproaches for reduced fortune trample decorum and therefore cannot be countenanced by an aristocrat, or by an aristocrat's mother. That is the seed buried here, to flourish later in the letter (and in time).

His indignation thus contained, Byron can continue to his mother as he might have continued to Dr. Drury, not so much denying the charge or rationalizing his own conduct and appearance as making the best of an unhappy circumstance, which of course confirms Mark Drury's assessment. But he concludes with a claim to at least superficial equality with most peers that strikes an unintentionally ironic note: "I have as much [spending?] money, as many Clothes, and in every respect of appearance am equal if not superior to most of my schoolfellows, and if my fortune is narrow, it is my misfortune not my fault" (*BLJ* 1:49). While Mrs. Byron might be gratified by three-quarters of this statement, it seems principally designed for self-assurance. And the deep wish for *physical* conformity fathers the poignant claim for it (suppressed consciousness of his lameness emerges later in this letter, too). The final quoted clause may even disguise a defense of lameness, since he has already, if falsely, asserted equality of fortune: good "appearance" is his metonymy for normality of physique. "Do not blame me," Byron appears to advise his mother (and Dr. Drury and Mark), "for an aberration beyond my control," with just the whisper of an implication that it was within hers,[2] as was preservation of the Gordon fortune against paternal Byronic plunder.

That encoded wish, in any event, inspires the marvelous rhetorical leap of Byron's succeeding lines, although they are driven as well by anger over Mark's sneering belittlement:

> But however the way to *riches* to *Greatness* lies before me, I can, I will cut myself a path through the world or perish in the attempt. others have begun life with nothing and ended Greatly. And shall I who have a competent if not a large fortune, remain idle, No, I will carve myself the passage to Grandeur, but never with Dishonor. These Madam are my intentions. (*BLJ* 1:49)

This is eloquent speech, noticeably distinct from its context in rhythm, syntax, pitch, passion: it approximates the language of classical oratory and theatrical declamation; it attempts—and almost achieves—the style of classical heroes (chiefly of Homer and Virgil) whose exploits the boys have been studying, translating, imitating, with nothing yet of the Horatian influence so distinct in later writings. Although something slightly absurd attaches to such high-minded rhetorical posturing in a sixteen-year-old, there is basis for admiration here, too, for the ambition is full of energy and resolve: one feels the pulse of desire to overcome whatever the handicap laid on him by (mis)fortune, and to invest her benefits for premium return. The lines carry conviction no matter how formulaically framed: youthful declaration of mission, after all, is the first stage of its completion. More important for the purposes of this paper, the passage probably reflects Byron's preparations since early spring (Marchand 1:82–83) for his first Speech Day. The lines do not echo the speech he will deliver, but they catch something of the spirit, pace, style, and dignity of his Virgilian declamation.

Meanwhile, however, as high as he has soared, so low does he now sink, in what reads like a startling anticipation of the abrupt discontinuities, incongruities, and tonal shifts of *Don Juan* (composed, like this letter, in stages):

> But why this upstart Son of a Button maker is to reproach me about an estate which however, is far superior to his own, I know not, but that he should call me a Blackguard, is far worse, on account of the former I can blame only Hanson (and that officious Friend [Fiend?] Lord Grey de Ruthyn, whom I shall ever consider my most inveterate enemy), it is a mere trifle, but the latter I cannot bear, I have not deserved it, and I will not be insulted with impunity. (*BLJ* 1:49)

The earlier restraint gives way to vitriol, in the first instance of a nastily snobbish cast, by which the slur upon Mark's blood and class repays Mark's upon limited aristocratic fortune, perhaps because, we now learn, disclosures about Byron's estate may be traced back to the attorney Hanson and Lord Grey—presumably Hanson's "officious Friend" but no longer Byron's. How information about Byron's fortune could pass from Hanson to Grey and thence to Mark Drury is unclear: although Hanson had it, would he carelessly communicate it, especially to the Newstead tenant? And if Harrow needed it, why go to Mark and not to his brother the headmaster? Or perhaps the information came from Dr. Drury to Mark? And what possible interest could have linked Grey and Joseph or Mark Drury? An easier and likelier explanation might suggest that, given Byron's pensioner status at the school, the size of his fortune cannot ever have been much of a secret.

But the boy needs a villain, a scapegoat; he seizes upon Hanson who *does* know the family's finances, and, still lacking a reason to account to his mother for the estrangement from Grey, conveniently associates the two men in indiscreet revelation without implicating himself. By comparison with the charge of blackguardism, perhaps the financial insult is a "mere trifle," but if so it occasions a disproportionately substantial response. Byron, I suspect, wishes to tar Mark Drury with the blackest brush he can find, and so links him, too, to the "inveterate enemy" Grey. Curiously, with Hanson and Grey in Byron's hand, Mark is exonerated of one crime: "I can *only* blame" Hanson and Grey, he writes. But the partial exoneration only clears the way for incrimination on unpardonable grounds:

Mr. Mark Drury rides out with his Son,³ sees me at a distance on a poney which I hired to go to the bathing place which is too far for me to walk, he calls out, tells his son I am a Blackguard, This son, who is no friend of mine comes home relates the story to his companions, possibly with a few exaggerations, but however the Greatest part was true, and I am to be considered as such a person by my comrades, it shall not be, I will say no more, I only hope you will take this into your consideration and remove me at Summer from a place where I am goaded with insults by those from whom I little deserved it. (*BLJ* 1:50)

Several items in these lines require comment. First, the apparently irrelevant explanation of the pony warrants inclusion in this letter on at least two grounds: (1) the expenditure must be justified to Mrs. Byron, else it will appear an extravagance—and yet even so validates the master's earlier charge of straitened circumstances. Apart from Byron's keenness to picture himself on horseback, however, why mention the situation at all *only* to explain it? (2) Byron suspects that the lameness requiring use of the pony for the two-mile trip to the bathing pool provides Mark Drury with a reason for disliking and taunting him.⁴ As Byron understands the charge, his blackguardism *includes* the physical handicap or is a figure for it, and at all events helps to account for Drury's bias against him. Projecting his own embarrassment and chagrin onto Mark, Byron imagines the master appreciating his need of the animal, attaches it to Drury's other "reasons" for naming him "Blackguard," and so mentions the detail in his narrative to Mrs. Byron.

Second, Mark Drury and Byron ride at some "distance" from each other, so that the master must "call out." The phrase bristles with dueling resonances, to which Byronic history would have peculiarly sensitized the boy, and sharpens the edge of the narrative's already contentious cast. But beyond that, one wonders *what* Drury "calls out": a greeting? Or does he shout, expressly so that Byron may hear the offending epithet pronounced to his son, presumably on horseback at his father's side? "There is Lord Byron the Blackguard," Mark supposedly trumpets, with a wicked laugh! Byron evidently wishes to conjure such an image in his mother's imagination; for the "calls out" is superfluous—possibly one of the embellishments of which the Drury brother is suspected—unless Mark truly did "call out" for Byron's benefit, or, in the victim's view, Mrs. Byron's belief that he had would advance the boy's cause with her. Such action, if accurately reported, seems extraordinarily ill-spirited in a master, particularly in the presence of a son through whom circulation of the incident among other schoolmates is guaranteed. Small wonder that Byron felt it as a deliberate attempt to humiliate him before his fellows.

Third, the conclusion to Byron's letter suggests that the whole of it may be shaped by an agenda: he wishes to leave Harrow and would persuade his mother to sanction withdrawal. The desire does not necessarily interrogate earlier portions of the letter, but it may invite skepticism, particularly in light of Byron's suspicions of the Drury boy's "exaggerations." Until shown otherwise, we must believe "the Greater part was true" of Byron's account as well.

Fourth, his final clause in the letter is curiously ambiguous: "I am goaded with insults by those from whom I little deserved it." If an idiomatic expression of modesty, the line nevertheless asks whether he just a little *did* deserve the goading, too. And for what? Or did he deserve it from others better entitled than Mark to goad him from superior positions of wealth, status, intellect, physical aptitude? And does he deserve from some *much* goading? The intent is reasonably clear—he has been undeservedly goaded at Harrow—but Byron is also conscious that in some respects he is a fair target. And that, too, perhaps more than literal victimization, encourages his departure. (But this is a late development in the letter. No less than six times within it Byron questions the justice of what has happened to him, whether always as rhetorical ploy is not certainly determinable.)

As an additional gloss on Byron's relations with the Harrow faculty, here are lines from his poem "To the Duke of D[orset]," another "farewell" lyric composed, writes Byron, in the summer of 1805, just before he left the school:

> . . . let not this [your status, wealth, illustrious name] seduce thy soul,
> To shun fair science, or evade controul;
> Tho' passive tutors, fearful to dispraise
> The titled child, whose future breath may raise,
> View ducal errors with indulgent eyes,
> And wink at faults they tremble to chastise. (ll. 11–16)

Byron's note to line 13: "Allow me to disclaim any personal allusion, even the most distant. I merely mention generally, what is too often the weakness of Preceptors" (*CPW* 1:369). Other data examined in this paper, albeit largely Byron's own testimony, attest the truth of this disclaimer and together with it point to discrimination and inequity in preceptorial treatment of at least one blue-blooded boy at Harrow—specifically, manifestations in discipline of the verbal bias Byron believed provoked among the masters by his lameness and economic status. That envy of Dorset's immunity emerges in these verses does not preclude the probability of Byron's conduct having elicited fewer winks, and his rank fewer indulgences, than he thought himself entitled to.

His only additional surviving correspondence before Byron's departure for the summer holiday requests of Hanson a reservation on the Edinburgh coach for 25 July, but two very important, even formative events marked the end of Byron's school year. The first was the boys' recitation, for critiquing by the headmaster, of their compositions prior to delivery before the school in what was covertly, I suspect, an audition or screening of candidates for participation in Speech Day; the second was Byron's performance on the Speech Day program.

Preparing his biography of the poet, Thomas Moore asked Dr. Drury to verify reports of Byron's precocity in the elocutionary arts. Here is the headmaster's reply:

> The upper part of the school composed declamations, which, after a revisal by the tutor, were submitted to the master: to him the authors repeated them, that they might be improved in manner and action, before their public delivery. I certainly was much pleased with Lord Byron's attitude, gesture, and delivery, as well as with his composition. All who spoke on that day adhered, as usual, to the letter of their composition, as, in the earlier part of his delivery, did Lord Byron. But to my surprise he suddenly diverged from the written composition, with a boldness and rapidity sufficient to alarm me, lest he should fail in memory as to the conclusion. There was no failure; he came round to the close of his composition without discovering any impediment and irregularity on the whole. (Moore 1:36)

Astonishingly, Byron claimed at the time to have no recollection of his extemporaneous additions, protesting to Dr. Drury that he had faithfully delivered his prepared text. Drury concluded that the boy, "fully impressed with the sense and substance of the subject . . . hurried on to expression and colourings more striking than what his pen had expressed."

Here, of course, is the incipient *improvisatore,* the performer inspired by his own performance to extemporize from it, the imaginative, agile mind that will spin the threads of countless *Don Juan* stanzas themselves of "striking colour" and endless variety. But Dr. Drury—and with his prompting, Byron—had also heard the budding orator. Both were impressed, Drury with Byron's natural gift, Byron with Drury's opinion of it. In *Detached Thoughts,* the poet remembered:

> My qualities were much more oratorical and martial—than poetical—and Dr. D[rury] my grand patron—(our headmaster)—had the great notion that I should turn out an Orator from my fluency—my turbulence—my voice—my copiousness of declamation—and my action—I remember that my first declamation—[that is, the composition recited before Dr. Drury] astonished him into some unwonted (for he was economical of such) and sudden compliments—before the declaimers at our first rehearsal. (*BLJ* 9:42–43)

Well might Byron take pride in such kudos, for the Reverend Doctor Drury brought sterling credentials to his assessment of oratory and of theatrical affairs generally. His uncle, the older brother of his father Thomas, was an (albeit undistinguished) playwright; behind him, to one expired branch of the family may be nominally traced London's Drury Lane and the theater it boasts. Fifty years after the event, the bishop of Oxford, Dr. William Jackson, recalled and performed "a severe poetical phillipic" composed and recited against himself by young Joseph Drury when the two were Westminster schoolmates.[5] Along with his Harrow mentor Dr. Robert Summer, Dr. Drury was celebrated at the school for his "high and noble tone of feeling, a most ready and persuasive eloquence, a richness of language and copiousness of illustration, aided by a particularly fine delivery" (Drury Memoir 8). His occasional sermons from the pulpit of the parish church "always produced a considerable impression; and, though youth is not commonly very tolerant of sermons, yet the uniform attention with which his addresses . . . were received by that class of his auditors would have surprised every one accustomed to see the usual impatience and restlessness of boyhood" (Drury Memoir 24). He was among the earliest to recognize the genius of Edmund Kean (at Exeter in 1810–11) and to patronize his ascendancy to stardom. The impact of such gifts, arts, discernment, and interest during Dr. Drury's headmastership redrew the extracurricular profile of the school and substantially contributed to the enhancement that brought Harrow, under Drury, to heavy subscription and fame among Britain's elite. To the role of elocution in differentiating the institution, Charles Drury bears witness:

> During the mastership of Dr. Drury considerable emulation was excited, among the elder youths, to excel in elocution; and continued, with increasing force, during the whole twenty years that he held it. Public speaking at school has, in general, been a very heavy business: the awkward and constrained manner of the young orators often renders it rather painful than otherwise to witness their efforts. But the number of those who, during that period, acquired certain degrees of ease, grace, and force of delivery, was so large in proportion to others, whom no practice or instruction could improve in the accomplishment, that the Harrow speeches acquired a celebrity, and drew together a confluence of auditors, altogether unprecedented in any other place of education. This attention to school speaking, under a preceptor in the art, who was himself much distinguished for his oratorical powers, was not without its good effect. It could not supply ideas, or enrich language to any great extent (although something would necessarily adhere to the mind out of that which was recited with strong feelings of interest), but it undoubtedly gave much ease and confidence; and Harrow had long to boast of a very great proportion of the best speakers in the two Houses of Parliament. From Mr. Perceval and Lord Harrowby, some of the earliest who practiced it at this school, down to Sir Robert Peel, one of the latest who studied it under Dr. Drury, there was ample cause to justify and applaud the attention paid to the study. Nor have there been wanting, either in the pulpit or at the bar, gentlemen, who have had reason to look back with much satisfaction to their early efforts of elocution at Harrow speeches. (Drury Memoir 23)

Looking back at his own earliest, public effort, the 1804 *"debut,"* Byron generously assigns exclusive credit:

> When Probus' [Dr. Drury's] praise repaid my lyric song,
> Or plac'd me higher in the studious throng;
> Or when my first harangue receiv'd applause,
> His sage instruction the primaeval cause,
> What gratitude, to him, my soul possest,
> While hope of dawning honours fill'd my breast.
> For all my humble fame, to him alone,
> The praise is due, who made that fame my own.
> ("Childish Recollections," ll. 349–56; 1806–7)

How sweet Dr. Drury's unexpected praise must have sounded to ears so often bruised by taunts, insults, threats, and reprimands, from peers and instructors alike, not to mention the reproaches of a parent and the (presumed) indecencies of a tenant—and how psychologically gratifying that it conferred honor in the company of Byron's competing rhetors: it acquaints the boy with the taste of stardom. Perhaps for the first time at Harrow, Byron distinguishes himself, satisfies the faculty by whom he has felt besieged, and is publicly complimented: one hears the pride, many years after the fact, in the announcement of his achievement against rivals for praise. Just as important, the event charted a course for further distinction, for claiming a place of recognition and respect among peers: for marginalizing if not erasing the stigmas by which he had thus far been defined. Orators were not handicapped by bad feet; in any case, Dr. Drury had complimented his action. And skilled oratory, unlike the martial arts, did not evolve from or in any way implicate his physical disability, or call attention to it (he then thought; but this plus is instantly sabotaged). Furthermore, Dr. Drury the gentleman had praised a capacity requisite in the distinguished nobleman, and thus in some degree ratified the title of which Byron was so proud. Drury had in effect authorized a parliamentary career for the young lord. It was, unmistakably, a pivotal occasion.

By 1807, Byron's thinking, aided by his Speech Day triumphs, poetic achievements, and attorney's fretfulness, had complicated itself into a dilemma. *Fugitive Pieces* and *Poems on Various Occasions* had garnered "many very flattering literary Critiques, from men of high Reputation in the Sciences, particularly Lord Woodhousie [*sic*], & Henry Mackensie; both *Scots,* & of great Eminence as *Authors* themselves, I have received also some most favourable Testimonies from *Cambridge* . . . encouraged by these & several other Encomiums, I am about to publish a volume at large [*Hours of Idleness*; the others had been privately printed]" (*BLJ* 1:113). Thus Hanson's concern; thus Byron's conflict and defense: "I coincide with you in opinion that the *poet* yields to the *Orator* [does capitalization privilege the latter?], but as nothing can be done in the latter Capacity till the expiration of my *minority,* the former occupies my present Attention"—that is, as stopgap measure, time-filler, I am a poet, with my real career on hold. But no, on second thought, as the revisionary imagination kicks in, not quite right; poetry deserves better than that. So: "& both *ancients* & *moderns,* have declared, that the two pursuits are so nearly similar, as to require in a great measure the same Talents, & he who excels in the one, would on application succeed in the other." Pursuit of the one is pursuit of the other, and the dilemma is deferred. After all, "Lyttleton, Glover, & Young (who was a celebrated *Preacher* & a *Bard*) are instances of the Kind, *Sheridan* and *Fox* also, *these* are *great* names, I may imitate, I can never equal them" (*BLJ* 1:113). And for the time being the professional dilemma is solved: I can be both poet and orator on the model of prominent practitioners, if more modestly than they. For the 1807 Byron, then, both professions appear to profit by proximity to and overlap with the other. A discourse beginning as an elaborate apology for practicing poetry on an interim basis winds its way around to claiming the equality of poetry and oratory as lordly employments. Both appear viable career choices for this nineteen-year-old.[6]

IF MARCHAND IS RIGHT that Byron had long since chosen a text for performance on Speech Day, 5 July 1804, and had been preparing for it through the spring, then he would also have chosen *his* role of the three available in the *Aeneid* 11 colloquy, and probably by now have memorized it. But at some point before the Speech Day bills were printed, he changed his mind and traded roles with classmate Thomas Leeke, surrendering the part of Drances to him and assuming the role of King Latinus.[7] Grimly he saw that even oratory provided no refuge from reminders of his lameness, for Turnus (played by Robert Peel, future prime minister)[8] refers to Drances's "flying feet" (or "timorous feet," in the translation Marchand uses: "Will thy bravery ever be in that windy tongue and those timorous feet of thine?" [1:84]), an image likely to arouse hoots and titters among an audience of boys, especially if directed at a hobbled lad. To be Drances would put Byron at risk of hearing more of the ridicule already plaguing his Harrow days, only this time while spotlighted in the center of things. Further, as Tyerman points out (17), Latinus *sits* throughout the scene. And his seat is a throne.[9]

Reciting in Latin, the three boys presumably performed a portion of the counsel chamber scene from lines 302–445 of book 11, with expository sections omitted. Latinus and Drances have about the same number of lines; if Peel recited Turnus's entire speech—as might be expected, given his reputation for oratory at the time—his portion was twice as long; but it may have been cut to balance his mates'.[10]

Before examining other factors favoring Byron's switching of parts, I should notice the assumption behind our assumption that the reference to "flying feet" turned Byron away from the Drances part: namely, that the schoolboys in some degree identified the actor with the role he performed, and, more important, that the actor himself did so.[11] The sensitivity that prompted Byron to reject the Drances role once having mastered it would if anything be heightened as a consequence of the miscasting, and would doubtless encourage his scrutiny of other roles for potential backlash against himself before electing them. News of his tradeoff, however, and the (named or hypothesized) reasons for it, would almost certainly have circulated around the school, and so renewed attention to the disability. Caught, then, as Drances or as the former Drances, Byron must have painfully anticipated embarrassment on 5 July. In short, *acting a part* provided both opportunity and risk: identified with a role, one might use it to make a statement that became one's own, with pertinence to one's present circumstances, since one's personal circumstances were already implicated for the audience in the performance. That is, one might in the recitation become a subtle allegorist. Or one might be victimized by an unwise selection of roles. Something like this way of thinking informed Byron's choices of texts for all three of the Speech Days in which he participated.

But inducements other than his lameness also urged Byron's surrender of the Drances role. For one, Virgil's characterizing introduction to Drances's speech identifies him as "spiteful . . . spurred by stings of his insidious envy / Of Turnus's glory."[12] Envy of others' successes with the masters and in other aspects of Harrow life may have helped excite Byron's oratorical ambitions, but he would have found indecorous at best and probably indecent the public intimation of such a motive in an aristocrat at a boys' school. While Byron was like Drances a "man of faction" and about to become more distinctly so in the corporate protest against a new headmaster, to showcase one's factionalism and partisanship could alienate potential allies in the unstable world of adolescent associations. Moreover, Drances is "on his mother's side / of noble birth, but low-born on his father's." Byron, of course, can point to biological aristocracy in both bloodlines, but the myths associated with his paternal ancestry suggested "low" behavior well enough, and the size of his estate had already, and painfully, been locally impugned as insufficiently patrician. Drances, on the other hand, is "lavish with wealth" (a phrase used to his discredit, says R. D. Williams, 405), a particularly regrettable attribute to have linked to his impersonator, with Mark Drury and perhaps others insinuating Byron's relative impoverishment. Mrs. Byron had more than once embarrassed the son among his schoolmates, having behaved while visiting him at the Dulwich school, before his transfer to Harrow, in a manner unworthy of gentility, inspiring one lad to remark to the mortified boy, "Byron, your mother is a fool"; his resigned reply, "I know it" (Marchand 1:62). My point is that even indirect reminders of Byron's parental heritage and depressed estate would hardly have advanced his reputation among the boys, and might have reinforced its disreputable cast or additionally damaged it. The less said or implied about those matters, the better. Drances's speech itself conveys none of this characterizing information, but it need not have done so for spectators' comprehension: the *Aeneid* was standard curriculum fare at Harrow, especially in the fifth and sixth forms. Most of Byron's audience would know from classroom drills the character he portrayed, and be well positioned to make connections unflattering to him.

Drances speaks second in the colloquy, after King Latinus, who proposes making peace with Aeneas and settling Teucrians on Latin land. Of similar mind, Drances is less driven by a desire for peace, however, than for Turnus's undoing. Accusing the king of seeking advice where none is necessary, since the course of action is obvious to royalty and subject alike even if fear checks speech about it, Drances charges Turnus with a reckless warmongering responsible for many warriors' deaths and the city's mourning. And he counsels Latinus against forswearing his pledge to give daughter Lavinia to Aeneas, as a seal of peace, even though Turnus threatens violence in order to have her himself. Here is a triangle conceivably interesting to Byron for personal reasons, a proposed marriage designed to end an old feud, jeopardized by the claims of a rival suitor. It varies somewhat Byron's situation with Mary Ann Chaworth, but as Drances he would oppose liberation of the maiden for the rival's possession. He would argue, in short, against the grain of his own attachment to the Mary Ann unavailable to him, because pledged to another man, more established and revered than he, in a paternally sanctioned betrothal. The Drancenian argument in Byron's mouth would cross his own peacemaking stakes in repairing the Chaworth-Byron breach wrought by his great uncle's— the fifth lord's—lethal duel with William Chaworth, Mary Ann's grandfather and his own distant kinsman. But Drances's sly insinuation that Turnus is by rank and worth undeserving of Lavinia might have unsettled the young lord who, though titled, knew himself dimmed, in Mary

Ann's eyes, against the dash, color, and elegance of John Musters, her fiancé, and less prepared than he to support a household. That Byron could have remained oblivious to these loose parallels seems to me unlikely in one of his already finely tuned self-consciousness; but even so he may have instinctively resisted a role requiring passion in a cause antithetical to the desire binding him to Mary Ann.

Further, Drances, if aspiring to heroic leadership, nevertheless situates himself as suppliant to Turnus, "beseeching" him to subordinate personal achievement and satisfaction to civic responsibility and the social good—all of this in prolix speech bearing out the narrator's charge of "lavish words" and ironizing Drances's own sense of the superfluity of additional counsel, a windy excess unappealing both as character trait and as performance to restive schoolboys. Blaming Turnus for "all these trials of Latinus," Drances implores him, although perceived as antagonist in the debate, to "pity us, / your fellow citizens; put off your pride, / and beaten, leave the field." Imagine the potential damage to one's schoolyard image if identified with the character delivering these lines—especially if one had worked diligently, combatively, as Byron had done, to overcome an assumed frailty and earn a playing-field reputation as an intrepid, scrappy presence, the usual victor (by his own testimony, anyway) in skirmishes there. Drances's speech can be heard as defeatist, and indeed is taken as cowardly in Turnus's refutation, which includes the reference to Drances's "flying feet." That phrase is a scurrile metonymy for cowardice, and in context—"Will Mars be always in your windy tongue / and in your flying feet?"—accuses Drances of hypocrisy, of big, brave words unproved by deeds, and recognizes as a continuing policy of craven appeasement what might on another tongue have been interpretable as the civic compassion of the discourse.

Moreover, when Drances wonders whether the "downy palace" of Turnus's desiring is worth the sacrifice of more "sad souls" of his countrymen, he insults any heart—especially one of only sixteen years—prepared to give the world for love. Finally, Drances's promotion of the contest between Turnus and Aeneas as the swiftest and most economical means of settling the conflict may, in light of his other recommendations and of Turnus's rejoinder, look like apprehensive transference or abandonment of martial obligation, a shirking of civic duty masking itself as humanitarian sympathy. The self-serving, divisive, deliberately provocative, and slickly insolent properties of Drances's speech well define a contemptible character in no respect an enviable part for a lovesick boy eager to be regarded as bold, tough, and decent by his mates. It is hard to imagine Byron, even "in character," enduring with patience, and without answering, the blistering censure about to be laid upon Drances by an enraged Turnus—and in the voice of the virtuoso Robert Peel. For Drances is quintessentially a blackguard. To be so denounced before the school, while rumors of his own alleged knavery circulated, would for Byron have been insupportable.

But why Latinus instead? The king's role might *not* have been Byron's first alternative choice. If the Turnus selection was of comparable length, it is possible that he first asked Peel, not Leeke, to trade roles with him, for Turnus's is manifestly the more fiery and theatrical of the three speeches, and therefore more consistent with Byron's two subsequent selections and with the kind of declamation that Dr. Drury said the boy preferred—speeches full of passionate vehemence. If on the other hand Peel had elected to recite all of the approximately one hundred lines of Turnus's speech, Byron might well have opted for Latinus's as the more easily mastered in the relatively short time remaining for a second memorization. Or Peel, with an already infallible instinct for grand oratory, might reasonably have refused to relinquish Turnus's part. I am in any event assuming that Byron chose Latinus's role partially by default, more because he dared not "be" Drances than in order to express himself through the royal persona.

Still, Latinus did speak first, from a throne, as king. The part had snob appeal. A nobleman should have it, and neither Peel nor Leeke could claim high birth. Further, Latinus proposes a solution to the crisis without sounding defeatist; his is the positive, active version of Drances's negative, passive plan for peace: the difference is moral, tonal, attitudinal. And yet some portions of Latinus's speech sound the world-weariness affected by Byron's early lyrics: "each must be his own hope, but now you know how poor a thing that is." Transferred to a Romantic context, these lines would appeal to the melancholic Byron, part-time resident of the Peachy Stone in the Harrow churchyard, where, like Juan ruminating in the woods, he is supposed to have brooded away hours of isolated meditation, a perfect paradigm of the poses populating "graveyard" verse. Otherwise, apart from Latinus's generous dispensation of gifts to the Trojans—in the circumstances, bribes—little in the speech would appear to draw Byron to it. The end of it seems at first particularly antipathetic, for Latinus effectively divests himself of "the emblems of my sovereignty" (a situation curiously similar to that of the

Lear whom Byron will later impersonate) and dispatches them by ambassador to the Trojans. But there is Latinus himself, not merely king but father; and as father he may attract and answer that persistent desire in the young Byron to be recognized by, and eventually as, himself the Father, as we have just seen in his relations with the elder Drury. Peter Manning has persuasively argued for the ambivalent appeal of that paternal presence, and Byron's attraction to the role of Latinus may be another expression of it.[13]

Moreover, Byron has shifted into a valedictory mode. He plans to leave Harrow, to lose the "territory" now in some measure made his own. Like Latinus, he is himself of "uncertain mind" and beset by foes; rumor has stripped him of the material status supposed synonymous with lordship, and smeared him with charges of criminality and vagabondage. His is decidedly "a troubled state" at Harrow, where "good counsel," including that of solicitor Hanson, would be no less welcome than in Latinus's chamber. The role is a compatible one.

How he would have acted it, we can only surmise. Eye-witness testimony from a later time reports that Harrow speakers "waved their white gloves in the genuine old 'Pump action' which immemorial custom has determined to be the most impressive gesticulation for such occasions, and looked over their stiff collars with eyes flashing with the fire of Shakespeare or Macaulay, or sparkling with the milder flame of Sheridan or Moore."[14] Conjectures about Byron's manner may be informed by recollections that Dr. Drury was sensitive and attentive to oratorical technique, and required rehearsals (of an uncertain number) before Speech Day performances.[15] And Byron's alleged and demonstrated preference for passionate declamation can perhaps be read back into his impersonation of King Latinus. No record of Dr. Drury's rhetorical instruction has come to my attention, but we know that Dr. Keate, Eton headmaster from 1809 to 1834, practiced oratory, taught the boys elocution, gesture, and delivery, and may through his students deserve whatever credit is not claimed by Harrow for the improved quality of parliamentary debate during their tenure in the Houses.[16]

Similarly at Shrewsbury, the headmaster "evidently took an immense amount of pains in coaching the boys,"[17] "training the selected [speakers] for some time before the appointed day."[18] In witness to the gravity attending Speech Day and to the seriousness with which boys were expected to address speaking opportunities: "Dr. Samuel Parr was present on more than one [Shrewsbury] Speech Day, sitting in the place of honour next to the Head Master, with his pipe in his mouth and his spittoon before him, and occasionally signifying his approval by quietly tapping two fingers of one hand on the palm of the other, an amount of applause which Dr. Butler took care to assure the boys meant a great deal from so great a man" (Fisher, 317). The school retains texts of speeches, in boys' scripts, with marginal directions for emotional representation and accent marks over syllables to be stressed, in the hand of Dr. Drury's approximate contemporary Dr. Samuel Butler, Shrewsbury headmaster from 1798 to 1836. The record of the 11 June 1821 Shrewsbury event shows expressive markings for Drances, impersonated by one Master Gretton, in the *Aeneid* 11 passage from which Byron recited, but no transcriptions of Latinus's or Turnus's speeches. Still, from Dr. Butler's directions to young Gretton, we may perhaps extrapolate a sense of the dramatic registers expected or sought of boys performing roles as well as speeches on the Shrewsbury stage; and it is perhaps safe to assume that their fellow declaimers in other venues, at least under oratorically astute masters, would also have stretched to capture the emotions of the characters they played. Here, at any rate, are Dr. Butler's directions as they appear down a column to the left of Gretton's thirty-three-line transcription of Drances's speech: "Taunt, Insult, Defiance, Regret, Insult, Counsel, Intimidation, Taunt, Authoritative interrogation, Reproach, Remonstrance, Contempt, Exhortation, Regret, Taunt, Passion, Admonition with insult."[19] A challenge to a mature actor, surely, but to a schoolboy! From such dramatic coaching, assuming its cultural and theatrically performative typicality, we can nevertheless derive a fuller sense of how much Byron's sacrifice of the Drances part cost him, for it anticipates the villainy of Zanga and the emotional extremity of Lear that helped draw him to those roles. The appeal of melodramatic representation, however, cannot yet overcome the anxiety for reputation, or more especially the embarrassment of physical difference, and like many another actor Byron hides an identity ashamed of itself in a persona extravagantly exposed.[20]

First Interval

LESS THAN THREE WEEKS after her son's oratorical debut, Mrs. Byron wrote to Hanson, "I was informed by a Gentleman yesterday that he had been at Harrow and heard him [Byron] speaking, and that he acquitted himself uncommonly well" (Prothero 1:27). This judgment may have been merely a polite response to an inquiring parent anxious for a favorable report, but there is no reason to doubt it either, and in light of Byron's eagerness to perform again and to have Augusta hear him, it gains credibility. There is, moreover, Byron's own testimony. In what Moore calls his "evident satisfaction" (1:65), Byron brags to his journal: "When I was a youth, I was reckoned a good actor. Besides Harrow speeches (in which I shone) I enacted Penruddock in the Wheel of Fortune, and Tristram Fickle in Allingham's farce of the Weathercock, for three nights (the duration of our compact) in some private theatricals at Southwell, in 1806, with great applause. . . . [T]he whole went off with great effect upon our good-natured audience" (1:65).[1] This last gesture of modesty toward an indulgent audience does not much temper Byron's thespian pride. More important is the firm linkage in his mind between speechmaking and acting: his discourse imagines oratory as a species of performance, as itself theater. The platform of declamation at Harrow was literally for him a site of drama, a scene designed for "enactment," a public venue for self-construction. The connection then requires an accommodating interpretation of the boy's conceptualization of Speech Day "performance."

But his summer was an uneasy holiday. Mrs. Byron canceled her son's plans to travel with classmates and made him remain with her at Burgage Manor in Southwell, where her temper appears to have fueled his. The two quarreled throughout the vacation, although their squabbles, now and ever, appear to have had about them a beguiling, almost recreational air: indisputably hostile, even mean on both sides, yet media for engagement, more valued than dreaded, tense rapprochement, source and channel of energy. For one thing, Mrs. Byron continued the flirtations with Lord Grey that so scandalized and outraged her son, already sensitive to proprieties if often willing to flout them. But Byron's disturbance over this relationship may have reflected a two-pronged jealousy. Himself the prior object of Grey's (however unwelcome) attentions, he now sees or imagines them transferred to a mother who, despite her frequent severity toward him, remained his own possession, to play and exploit to advantage, for he was as irresistible to her as to many; and her gullibility and malleability conditioned—spoiled—him to expect and maneuver for similar indulgence from others. To watch this woman—only with difficulty imagined by the son as a sexual creature—encourage the very sexual advances that he had rejected (or accepted) from the same man must have been deeply shocking to Byron, and not only on account of his parent. For Lord Grey, responding in any degree erotically or even politely to Mrs. Byron, or in ways that she could interpret as encouraging, would have affirmed exactly that capriciousness in relationships of which Byron had already suspected him, and raised questions, too, in the boy's mind about the sexual dynamics of their earlier association, even uncertainty about his interpretation of the estranging incident.

Mrs. Byron's flirtation with Grey emblematically turns the Newstead tenant into a father substitute for the boy, and the episode between them—symbolically invigorated now by Mrs. Byron's efforts to reconcile her son and her presumptive suitor—effectively into an incestuous affair, in intent if not in deed, and so intensifies its repulsive (or fearfully intriguing) aspects. It may not be implausible to conjecture that Byron's first acquaintance with incestuous passion came not with Augusta but with the surrogate mother May Gray, belatedly dispatched after the molestative damage had been done, and with the symbolic potential stepfather uncannily carrying the same surname as the maid. In any event, Byron's probable sense during the 1804 summer that his mother and Lord Grey had individually turned away from him toward each other must have felt alienating as well as disgraceful; but the match may also have looked to the boy like a joint conspiracy of one despised, one unreliable, and two untrustworthy adults against him—and to us like a version of the Humbert-Humbert syndrome, Grey's (like, in another sense, Gray's) use of the mother to get at the child.

Mary Ann Chaworth, attractive to the young lord partly because descended from the victim of his ancestor's sword and partly because inaccessible as an engaged woman,[2] had already turned against him the previous summer, in a thoughtless but scorching repudiation that he overheard, or heard cruelly reported: "Do you suppose I could care anything for that lame boy?" she is supposed to have (rhetorically?) asked her maid (Marchand 1:78). This doubly and bitterly stinging rejection targets both the deformity and the youth; worse, it exposes Mary's hypocrisy and admits the insincerity, the pretense, the capriciousness of her prior attentions to him; in effect and retrospect, it classifies her, in affective insincerity, with Lord Grey. The remark was critically wounding, and could only have reinforced Byron's growing suspicions of stability and integrity in relationships.

But despite the rejections, Byron found himself drawn back to Annesley during the 1804 summer. No record of his visits survives, save a revealing snippet of conversation with Mary Ann: "The next time I see you," Byron reportedly said, "I suppose you will be Mrs. Musters," hardly daring to hope for a denial but inviting it. Her excited but insensitive reply, "I hope so" (Marchand 1:88), cut sharply, not only because giving no encouragement to the lilting hypothetical of his statement, but effectively excluding him from future relation with her as a married woman, and even tainting the present moment with expectations of connubial bliss. Apart from several lyrics—"To Emma" of 1805 the finest among them—it was some years before Byron could write extensively of this relationship and estrangement in "The Dream," when his separation from Lady Byron was raw, but its impact was perhaps as devastating to the sixteen-year-old as the rupture that recalled it to the maturer mind in 1816.[3] For it confirmed the inaccessibility of the ideal woman, and became, with reinforcement by his earlier disappointment in Mary Duff, paradigmatic of separations later endured and engineered, if it did not in fact spawn and find itself rewritten in them.

For the son's opposition to her interest in Grey, the mother retaliated. With an unfailing timing and an eerily acute sense of how to hurt him, she reported, probably during the summer 1804 holiday (Marchard 1:88 and n), "Your old sweetheart Mary Duff is married." Byron had first met his distant cousin (on the Gordon side) in 1796, when they both were eight, and he never forgot the emotion she excited in him, at least partly because, as his "first love" unstained in imagination, she gathered luster as years passed and experiences accumulated. Mrs. Byron claimed that leaving her was Byron's single regret in departing Scotland for Newstead Abbey. Long after the marriage here announced, Byron in his journal puzzled over the intensity and persistence of his feelings for Mary Duff.

> How very odd that I should have been so utterly, devotedly fond of that girl, at an age when I could neither feel passion, nor know the meaning of the word. . . . [W]e were both the merest children. . . . I recollect all we said to each other, all our caresses, her features, my restlessness, sleeplessness . . . my tormenting my mother's maid to write for me to her, which she at last did, to quiet me. . . . I remember, too, our walks, and the happiness of sitting by Mary . . . and . . . gravely making love, in our way. How the deuce did all this occur so early? Where could it originate? I certainly had no sexual ideas for years afterwards; and yet my misery, my love for the girl were so violent, that I sometimes doubt if I have ever been really attached since. (*BLJ* 3:221–22)

But this extended (and there is more) lyrical meditation on making love "in our way" with Mary Duff that yet wonders at the very possibility of it in prepubescent children, as though all strong attraction must be sexually grounded, is set in motion by the stunning intelligence of her marriage, which fell "like a thunder-stroke—it nearly choked me—to the horror of my mother and the astonishment and almost incredulity of every body. [And earlier in the same journal entry:] I really cannot explain or account for my feelings at that moment; but they nearly threw me into convulsions" (*BLJ* 3:222). Although data is limited, the boy's physiological experience was probably psychogenic, something close to neurocirculatory asthenia, a paroxysm induced by severe emotional stress.[4] But whatever it was, its cause cannot be mistaken: the remembered Mary had been happily free from carnal pollution until Mrs. Byron's comment placed her on the nuptial couch. And yet, despite the overprotesting protest, Byron cannot leave her there, by spouse possessed:

> Lately, I know not why, the *recollection* (*not* the attachment) has recurred as forcibly as ever. I wonder if she can have the least remembrance of it or of me? . . . How very pretty is the perfect image of her in my memory—her brown, dark hair, and hazel eyes; her very dress! I should be quite grieved to see *her now*; the reality, however beautiful, would destroy, or at least confuse, the features of the lovely Peri which then existed in her, and still lives in my imagination, at a distance of more than sixteen years. (*BLJ* 3:222)

The journalistic meditation is at once a psychologically successful and an intellectually baffled attempt to restore maidenhood and to reinstate the paradise of Mary and George's play. The announcement of her union assaults the veritable paradigm of attachment—matching Mary Chaworth's of separation—that Byron's association with her had configured. But the journal account still finds him rejecting a meeting and grasping at scraps to reassemble that prototype, still a "Peri" imaginatively his mate. And the compliment may bite, or anyhow gently nip: originally, from the Persian, a beautiful, graceful, but demonic or malevolent female elf commissioned to plague humankind, the peri also had to perform long penitence, which ultimately earned divine favor but not exoneration. Although the malign edge appears to have dulled or even vanished in the English lexicon by the late eighteenth century, the word may have subtextually retained just enough of it to register Byron's resentment, his sense of ill-treatment later reiterated. It is possible that Byron knew the word in 1796, for the *OED* tracks its earliest English appearance to Richardson's *Persian Dictionary* of 1777. A likelier source for Byron is Beckford's *Vathek* (1786); and he may have heard it on his first foreign tour before using it in *The Bride of Abydos* (1:5; 1813). Moore picks it up for *Lalla Rookh* in 1817. But even if not a later acquisition, Byron's use of "Peri" attempts to reframe as exotic myth his youthful experience with Mary Duff, to seal it off against current actuality, to shield it against any encounter with the actual "*now.*"

Acknowledging the (unlikely) possibility that Byron reciprocates his mother's announcement with an overreaction calculated to frighten her for sadistic disclosure, we can nevertheless accept his shock at another loss of idealized femininity (a metonymy for innocent, utterly pure union), with the mother as secondary rupturing instrument. Also forming in the boy's mind may be the specter that marriage is itself a separative agent: in uniting, it inescapably takes away, fractures multiple attachments by removing two persons from circulation, or by so redefining other ties as irreparably to weaken them. Byron's confessed inability to explain or account for his "feelings" is at least in part an unwillingness to measure the magnitude of his investment in Mary Duff, and to investigate the impact upon his imaginative faculty of her loss—which he then bravely does in nostalgic prose that reconstructs a still attached "Mary Duff." He struggles, alternatively, under premonition of "convulsions," to mute his mother on the subject in his presence;

but if in any degree tactical, the strategy backfires: containment of the marital news in one quarter forces its dispersal in others, the result of which is publication of Byron's failure as lover. The mother, in short, impairs the son's potential as a successful mate, and further alienates herself from him.

Nor is it likely that Mrs. Byron could have refrained from retailing particulars of Byron's psychological reaction to her announcement, the dissemination of which would have embarrassed him and additionally problematized a manhood already sometimes under (at least self-) interrogation. Indeed, so rankling did Byron find his mother's mismanagement of the news—a vexation in part displaced from Mary and permitting her rehabilitation—that he returns to it toward the end of his entry: "I think my mother told the circumstances (on my hearing of her [Mary Duff's] marriage) to the Parkynses, and certainly to the Pigot family, and probably mentioned it in her answer to Miss A[bercromby], who was well acquainted with my childish *penchant,* and had sent the news on purpose to *me*—and thanks to her!" (*BLJ* 3:223). Miss Abercromby and Mrs. Byron, that is, conspire with Mary Duff in a betrayal that isolates, discredits, and humiliates its object. And all of this is part of the matched set of heavy psychic baggage that Byron dragged along to Harrow.

One bright interlude illuminated Byron's otherwise gloomy summer holiday, but even it closed darkly. His relationship with Elizabeth Pigot proved satisfactory, even rewarding while it lasted, for in the Pigot household he found comfort among a welcoming surrogate family that "required no pretense and imposed no emotional strain" (Marchand 1:87)—thus his distress over being exposed as emotionally overwrought by the news of Mary Duff's wedding. He and Elizabeth spoke of love with an abstraction unthreatening to Byron (1:87), but he wrote more concretely and intimately of his feelings, without avail. A somewhat stilted letter of 29 August 1804 compliments with gratitude Elizabeth's drawing of the Byron Arms, finds in the gift reassurance "that *you* have not entirely *forgot* me" (though reminding her of another promised gift), regrets her continuing absence, and anticipates hearing her sing to him, her "affectionate Friend" (*BLJ* 1:51). On a more famous occasion she tore out a sheet of his inscribed verses from a book he returned to her, and shortly left the Southwell household for a prolonged period. No causal logic appears to link her departure with his poetic disclosure of affection; but no pining adolescent of Byron's bruised and conditioned sensibility could have resisted imagining one. Miss Pigot can be slotted into the already painfully familiar calculus of abandonment following declaration of affection.

Augusta, mercifully, is the exception. Byron's half sister has by now emerged as a virtual substitute for the abandoning Marys, the abandoning mother, and the abandoned Grey. We have already heard Byron name himself Augusta's "warmest and most affectionate Friend" and herself the "*nearest relation* I have in the world by ties of *Blood* and *affection.*" This cry *for* a near relation and friend arises out of familial loneliness following the estrangement from Lord Grey (effecting increased distance from his mother) on the family estate, that locale itself perhaps contaminated in the boy's eyes by the misconduct of its tenant (or, considering Byron's later use of it, initiated, readied, and equipped for him). The disaffiliations of four important women over the 1804 summer can only have aggravated that sense of estrangement. He reaches out for an Other, who is not entirely Other, and who as blood relation may be—and have reason to be—the more steadfast friend, a bond all the stronger for its doubling.

And yet the affiliation with Augusta is already problematic. Brother and sister have never shared a residence. More important is Augusta's unstable status as kin. She is and she is not his sister; as half sister she inhabits a middle ground, an indeterminate precinct wherein her kinship equilibrates with her lack of it, her blood tie with its dilution. Augusta was in fact as devoted to Byron as any associate, ever, at least until set upon by Lady Byron and her coterie, but her technical blood relationship situates her in a neither/nor modality, where she is as likely to meet the expectations of filiality or full sisterhood as to withdraw entirely from such responsibilities—as likely, in blood, to retreat as to advance. The equivocating designation *half sister,* in other words, identifies a relationship expressly compromised by its lukewarm nomenclature. Augusta's filial status even at the time asks for investigation and definition. I suspect that its very nominal indeterminateness constitutes an attraction for the adult as well as the teenaged Byron. In 1804 he could think of Augusta as a replacement friend for the lost friends, and as a steadier, more trustworthy familiar mainstay than the mother had ever been and had lately proven herself to be. Whether the reduced blood ties later enabled her brother's violation of taboo with Augusta would be difficult to prove, but one might argue that the incestuous act psychologically rebelled against precisely this enigmatic state in an effort to stabilize Augusta in an unequivocal association (or, alternatively, that the very fluidity of half sisterhood matched Byron's resistance to relational rigidities).

Apart from the letters to Elizabeth Pigot mentioned above, and his acceptance of John Hanson's invitation to visit for a hunting expedition (Byron's enthusiastic reception throws into illuminating relief his earlier disparaging discourse on shooting—each message neatly tailored to its audience), none of Byron's holiday correspondence (if any) survives. Back at Harrow, however, he writes promptly to a lovesick Augusta, posing as a rake whose cynicism does not mask the summer wounds that inspire it, and with an attitude that replicates and perhaps avenges against the gender the mockery he has felt from Mary Ann Chaworth: "I feel a little inclined to laugh at you, for love in my humble opinion, is utter nonsense, a mere jargon of compliments, romance and deceit; now for my part had I fifty mistresses, I should in the course of a fortnight forget them all, and if by chance I ever recollected one, should laugh at it as a dream, and bless my stars, for delivering me from the hands of the little mischievous Blind God" (*BLJ* 1:52). The occasion of Augusta's unhappiness is General Charles Leigh's continuing objection to his son's proposed match with her. And the principal ground of his objection is her relatively small income, precisely the snobbish rebuke Byron felt at Harrow even before hearing it pinned on Mark Drury. That Augusta is similarly victimized reinforces the rapidly ripening filial bond, as does her troubled love life, which allows her brother's attempted assumption of the role of the experienced, jaded profligate. His effort only partially succeeds, for what we hear is a (young Manfred's) wish to forget, and a milder version of the defensive, compensatory cynicism of *Don Juan*'s narrator, who also cannot forget. Nevertheless, the remainder of this letter, like the quoted excerpt, is so high-spirited and cheerful that Byron apologizes, at the end of it, for his "levity."

His postscript explains why, by contrasting his autumn with his summer circumstances. It begins with a second confession of tension between himself and Mrs. Byron, this one anchored in maternal upset with Augusta which implicitly establishes the solidarity of offspring against the parent (compare the matrix of conflict in *King Lear*, the text from which Byron excerpts his recitation for 4 July). It is as though Augusta's offending epistolary silence authorizes not only the son's discord with his mother but his separation from her, even if only to return to school: "I left my mother in Southwell, sometime since, in a monstrous pet with you for not writing, I am sorry to say the old lady and myself, don't agree like lambs in a meadow" (*BLJ* 1:53). But for this strife Byron uncharacteristically appears to blame his own fidgeting, "which my precise mama objects to, we differ, then argue, and to my shame be it spoken fall out a *little,* however after a storm comes a calm" (the cliché, I suspect, also reflecting the *Lear* passage in rehearsal). The relational rhythms tracked here accord with other records, but Byron's simile subverts his acceptance of responsibility, for it *defends* his "fidgeting" as natural and his mother's "precision" as aberrant; and he minimizes the seriousness of their disputes both by reducing their scale and assuring Augusta of ever-returning calm. The effect—perhaps the intention—is to render himself a bluff, sprightly, good-natured fellow whose domestic squabbles are inconsequential. Thus, too, the offhanded inquiry into the well-being of his Aunt Sophia (Maria Byron) in a nonsequitur that almost, facetiously, wishes her dead: this is the mandatory query of the absent son about relatives' health, and marks a familial concern despite the quarrels at home.

More important are his remaining reflections, bracketed by "Adieus" but postponing ending, on Harrow life and friends:

> Adieu. I am happy enough and comfortable here, my friends are not numerous but select, among them I rank as the principal Lord Delawarr who is very amiable and my particular friend, do you know the family at all? Lady Delawarr is frequently in town, perhaps you may have seen her; if she resembles her son she is the most amiable woman in Europe. I have plenty of acquaintances, but I reckon them as mere Blanks, Adieu, my dear Augusta,—(*BLJ* 1:53)

The affected insouciance does not entirely conceal a social uneasiness: "happy enough" wishes its qualifier erased, as "not numerous" wants company and "select" rationalizes. And by the end of the postscript Byron's privileged group shines ever more brightly and importantly against the dull "Blanks" of mere acquaintance. Delawarr's amiability and *his* friendship for Byron, along with his title and possibly his family, earn him "selectivity" and priority, and the implicit contrast of Lady Delawarr with Mrs. Byron in the epistolary context registers admiration if not regret and envy. Moreover, the amiability hypothesized between mother and son contrasts with the wrangling of the Byronic pair just described, and maybe even offers the woman's company as cheering antidote to Augusta's gloom. Byron is well known to have singled out favorites among Harrow boys, but this foregrounding of a "special" relationship in a letter full of cynical swagger about the "utter nonsense" of strong and lasting attachment, in the process of bidding a beloved adieu, is noteworthy enough to follow up.

Delawarr is himself the addressee and subject of several of Byron's subsequent farewells: as the "Euryalus" of "Childish Recollections" (1806),[5] "fair" Delawarr is distinguished for his noble ancestry, honesty, integrity, "form unmatch'd" (309), and "heart untainted" (310), but specifically *not* for an orator's tongue: "Yet, not the Senator's thunder thou shalt wield" (311), even though professional respect may await him in "polish'd courts" (of law?) (315). "Childish Recollections" and two lyrics lament a "dissention," grounded in envy, that severed the bond between Delawarr and Byron ("To [George, Earl Delawarr]" and "L'Amitie Est L'Amour Sans Ailes"; *CPW* 1.119–121 22–25); and Byron's letter to the Earl of Clare in 1807, two years after the alienating event, apologizes for his "*en cavalier*" treatment of Delawarr, to whom he has also apologized "with very faint hopes of success," although he blames the misinformation of associates for his conduct toward the favored schoolmate (*BLJ* 1:134; 20 August 1807). I pause over this relationship not merely to emphasize the absence of oratorical competition between the two schoolmates but also to highlight early signs of the tenuousness of Byronic association felt intensely and remembered devotedly, as Byron's lyrical reflections make manifest.[6]

But let us look more closely into this adolescent relationship in light of Byron's letter to his sister a week later, responding to her prompt reply:

> You tell me you don't know my friend Ld. Delawarr he is considerably younger than me, but the most good tempered, amiable, clever fellow in the universe. To all which he adds the quality (a good one in the eyes of women) of being remarkably handsome, almost too much so for a boy. He is at present very low in the school, not owing to his want of ability, but to his years, I am nearly at the top of it, by the rules of our Seminary he is under my power but he is too good-natured ever to offend me, and I like him too well ever to exert my authority over him. If you should ever meet, and chance to know him, take notice of him on my account. (*BLJ* 1:54)

That Byron writes to a woman will not wholly account for his stress upon Delawarr's handsomeness, for that "quality" reappears in the poetry about George; and the reflection upon the near excess of beauty in him almost apologizes for sensitivity to it. Amiability continues to define Delawarr, distinguishing this alliance most notably from Byron's domestic conflicts, and perhaps suiting Delawarr for the "domestic happiness" which "Childish Recollections" predicts for him (321). But Byron's hierarchical consciousness is pronounced, his seniority and empowerment by the system, even under restraint, being a valued circumstance. "To [George, Earl Delawarr]" speaks of "This love which you feel, was the love of a brother, / Nor less the affection I cherish'd for you," but almost certainly the remark enjoys the adulation of the younger for the elder "sibling." It may also fantasize a familiar association, or try to rationalize a homoerotic one, for within a few lines of confiding to Augusta his difficulty in suppressing dislike of the "eccentric" Mrs. Byron, Byron is back on Lord Grey, "that agent of my cordial, deliberate detestation" (*BLJ* 1:54):

> She [Mrs. Byron] wishes me to explain my reasons for disliking him [Lord Grey], which I will never do, would I do it to any one, be assured you my dear Augusta would be the first who would know them. She also insists on my being reconciled to him, and once she let drop such an odd expression that I was half inclined to believe the dowager was in love with him. But I hope not for he is the most disagreeable person (in my opinion) that exists. He called once during my last vacation, she threatened, stormed, begged, [*sic*] me to make it up, he himself loved me, and wished it, but my reason [note the singular, perhaps dictated by the contextually threatening language of affection] was so excellent that neither [Mrs. Byron nor Lord Grey] had effect, nor would I speak or stay in the same room, till he took his departure. No doubt this appears odd but was my reason known, which it never will be if I can help it, I should be justified in my conduct. Now if I am to be tormented with her and him in this style I cannot submit to it. You Augusta are the only relation I have who treats me as a friend, ‹Impart this to› if you too desert me, I have nobody I can love but Delawarr. If it were not for his sake, Harrow would be a desart, and I should dislike staying at it. (*BLJ* 1:54–55)

The tease with which my quotation opens privileges the sister by inviting her to request an explanation of his "reason for disliking" Lord Grey, or minimally to promise a receptive ear. It follows a strategically placed prior tease that shows Byron telling "a secret" to Augusta about his mother: it proves him willing to confide, and invites pressure to disburden himself on the more important issue of Lord Grey's behavior toward him. Mrs. Byron's insistence on her son's "reconciliation" with Grey sounds reasonable enough in view of the boy's continuing silence, but it is typical of the maternal torment Byron knew when opposing his mother's will and would have been experienced as an assault. More important, it seeks to make Byron party to his mother's scheme, as he fearfully perceives it, to capture Grey in a relationship that would embarrass and threaten her son. Intimate association between these two figures would bring to bizarre, even nightmarish fruition Byron's fantasy of a reinstated family life, and perhaps exacerbate in him the double-edged jealousy I have hypothesized: Mrs. Byron would no longer be his alone; more troubling, his mother would have replaced him as the object of Grey's desire.

But why should Byron object to the alliance of two persons almost equally abhorrent to him at the moment? Does he fear a doubling of hostility toward himself? The sentence beginning "Now if . . . " suggests as much. Then again, why not suppose their mutuality of interest a diversion from him, an escape for him? Conceivably they might overlook him in attacking each other. If a sexual overture caused the estrangement, does Byron wish to spare his mother the indignity of a match with an impostor? Byron cannot fear exposure by the offender, but he might legitimately suspect use of the mother to come at her son. And yet one wonders again why, with so perfect an answer to his mother's insistence on reconciliation, he does not offer it—unless, of course, as we have speculated, he accepted the overture or felt tempted by it. Interestingly, the issue of pluralization arises again in this passage, although here Mrs. Byron is made to imagine her son's "reasons" for disliking Grey, while Byron himself admits only, and twice, to having an "excellent" reason for doing so. Furthermore, he smuggles in another virtual request for pressure to reveal his "secret" in an ungrammatical but revealing ambiguity: "was my reason known, which it never will be if I can help it, I should be justified in my conduct": that is, justification depends upon utterance of the unspeakable. Effectively, Byron shifts responsibility to Augusta, in what he declares to be an impossible task, for his own moral justification for bad conduct.

At bottom the strategy intends to bond Byron yet more closely to his sister. Betrayed and plagued by mother and friend, now believed conspiratorially allied against him, this lonely adolescent seeks the assuring stability of kinship and friendship in the same person, hoping, perhaps, for a complementary sealing effect. But separation anxiety is never far from Byron's consciousness, and appears here, darkly through its disguise, as a threat: "if you too desert me [i.e., like Mother, like Grey], I have nobody I can love but Delawarr." It is just possible, in other words, that Augusta and Delawarr, respectively, substitute for the *kind* of association represented in Byron's mind by Mrs. Byron on the one hand and Grey on the other. It seems a grotesque suggestion in light of Byron's detestation of the one and affection for the other in both cases, but less so if we anchor Byron's anger at Grey in his age less than in his act. If repulsed by the *older* man more than by his homoerotic gesture, or by the gesture of an older man, Byron may nevertheless count upon Augusta's faithfulness at least to diversify his amorous interests, if not shield him from strangely attractive but recognizably dangerous attachments. Along with the self-pity in Byron's dread, then, we may also hear a quiet but steely warning that Augusta's defection would leave him no alternative but the intimacy of younger boy. Nevertheless, although no erotic implication could have been intended or heard, the statement makes Augusta guardian not merely of Byron's continuing education at Harrow but of his moral character too.

Similarly, when Byron goes on—"You desire me to burn your epistles, indeed I cannot do that, but I will take care that They are invisible. If you burn any of mine, I shall be *monstrous angry* take care of them till we meet" (*BLJ* 1:55)—he makes Augusta's letters the equivalent of his own "secret" about Grey: they will remain "invisible," and yet he knows them, is their custodian, respondent, guarantor. The sentences invite Augusta's guarantee of the invisibility of his great secret and also its preservation. By the same token, for her to burn his letters would amount to precisely the betrayal he fears, for only they tangibly—and fragilely—represent his relationship with a distant half sister rarely seen: they are virtually her only evidence of his existence and regard. Burning them erases him, profanes his love.

One would give much to know whether Byron's next two "crossed out" lines "referring to Delawarr" (*BLJ* 1:55) are a false start on his next sentence, which vindicates his linkage to the schoolmate: "Delawarr and myself are in a manner connected, for one of our forefathers in Charles the 1st time married into their family." Because revisions of this sort are extremely rare in Byron's letters, I suspect, rather, that the retained sentence continues the discourse on Delawarr begun in the effaced lines. Speculation is hazardous, perhaps pointless, particularly in this context; but conceivably an uneasiness about the declared association with Delawarr, elaborated in the blotted lines, prompted Byron to justify and legitimate it through the ancestral connection. That is, his "love" of Delawarr has the authority of kinship to sanction it, and so cannot be impugned or lightly dismissed. Moreover, Byron can almost claim an obligation to care for his relative, although in fact no blood links the boys (see *BLJ* 1:55n). The stipulation of connection very nearly raises Delawarr to the status of Augusta.

About this letter it only remains to note Byron's ever-shadowing concern with betrayal—"Don't betray me to the Dowager," he writes—and its articulation here as another and concluding bonding tactic. The letter closes with the brother's wish to "know your Lady Gertrude, as you and her are so great Friends" (*BLJ* 1:55), a paradigm (with a hint of jealousy?) for the relationship Byron wants with his sister, and model for the blessing upon his with Delawarr that he hopes to receive from her.

"I thought my dear Augusta that your opinion of my *meek mama* would coincide with mine," Byron begins his next letter to his sister a week later (11 November 1804). Almost certainly, despite the ambiguity (their opinions coincide or conflict), Augusta has agreed with Byron's characterization of his mother; but he proceeds to excoriate Mrs. Byron more energetically, and at greater length, than in the previous letter, as though to persuade Augusta to his opinion. But the early attack is pointedly aimed: "She is so very strenuous, and so tormenting in her entreaties and commands, with regard to my reconciliation, with that detestable Lord G[rey] that I suppose she has a penchant for his Lordship, but I am confident that he does not return it, for he rather dislikes her, than otherwise, at least as far as I can judge" (*BLJ* 1:55). If Mrs. Byron really was as persistent as this description suggests, the pressure Byron felt must have been staggering, and his reasons for resisting it imperative. Those reasons here include what appears to be confidence of Grey's indifference to his suitor; but the sources of that assurance are uncertain, for Byron, sensitive to propriety even when challenging it, is not likely to have spoken ill of his parent to his tenant. Presumably, this confidence rests upon Byron's own unhappy experience of Grey's affections, but it may also reflect that ambivalent jealousy we have already noted, an interest in retaining exclusive hold on the mother's attentions despite their aggravation: to be vexatiously engaged is preferable to estrangement. More interesting is the softening of Byron's confidence as the sentence proceeds: does it occur to the writing boy that he had best not, without risking betrayal, assert so strongly his assurance of Grey's "dislike" lest he be challenged to prove it? "At least as far as I can judge" noticeably equivocates, corresponds to the parenthetical "in my opinion" from the previous letter, and provides an escape hatch in the event of inquiry. Just as important, it covertly acknowledges the fundamental and inexpressible anxiety that Grey may *not* be indifferent after all—a deep dread partially accountable for the insistence that he is.

With that Byron drops Grey for the remainder of this letter but cannot be silent on Mrs. Byron, now excused for "foibles" like vanity and age misrepresentation, then pilloried for the more grievous offense of vulgar discipline:

> I am now coming to what must shock you, as much as it does me, when she has occasion to lecture me (not very seldom you will think no doubt) she does not do it in a manner that commands respect, and in an impressive style. no. did she do that I should amend my faults with pleasure, and dread to offend a kind though just mother. But she flies into a fit of phrenzy upbraids me as if I was the most undutiful wretch in existence, rakes up the ashes of my *father,* abuses him, says I shall be a true Byrrone, which is the worst epithet she can invent. (*BLJ* 1:55–56)

Here is the complaint against Mark Drury retargeted. Mrs. Byron has affronted the dignity of her son, dishonored his lordship, by the crudeness of her chastening. The inelegant *style* of her correction confutes it and excuses him from obedience in its wake. The unseemly treatment of a nobleman by his kin would later embarrass and infuriate Byron when the Earl of Carlisle declined to introduce his relation to the House of Lords, but the (nearly) seventeen-year-old lad feels or finds the same insult in his mother's manner of reproach. The "abuse" of Byron's father compounds the injury and solicits Augusta's filial ire and at the same time holds out to the boy in need of one a model for dealing with obstreperous women: the prophecy of "true" Byronhood cannot in the circumstances have seemed to the boy an unwelcome fate. Then follows this remarkable passage:

> Am I to call this woman mother? Because by natures law she has authority over me, am I to be trampled upon in this manner? Am I to be goaded with insult, loaded with obloquy, and suffer my feelings to be outraged on the most trivial occasions? I owe her respect as a Son, But I renounce her as a Friend. (*BLJ* 1:56)

The pose and the attitude are performative, the rhythms oratorical, and—but for the pronounced echoes of *King Lear*—the high-dudgeon manner almost campy with melodrama. I do not suggest insincerity, but the posturing is unmistakable: a histrionic Byron declaims the lines as from a stage, conditioned and enabled by the rhetorically similar lines he is preparing to declaim in the summer. In their measured cadences, however, they model the restrained passion the absence of which in his mother's "phrenzy" renders her own discipline powerless. In whatever degree patterned after Shakespeare, Virgil, and/or eighteenth-century drama, Byron's lines showcase, I believe, the young orator swayed and seduced by a successful performance to practice the rhetorical art in a personal cause, and perhaps as rehearsal for a second or third public offering. Byron will urge Augusta to attend the 1805 Harrow Speech Days; he gives her here a flavor of what she can expect to hear from him. Without doubting the boy's abuse by his mother, I do suggest that the overstatement, swagger, and fustian of these lines draw upon Byron's recent experience as performer and spectator.

Once again, thereafter, Byron plays the "secret" card by assuring Augusta that he knows more than he's told but won't "shock" her female sensibility by retailing other sources of maternal oppression and fractiousness, however entitled to his "confidence" she "as a Sister" may be. It is a tactic Byron polishes to brilliance in *Don Juan,* this withholding of scandalous information, but here it again encourages Augusta's inquiry and discloses Byron's need to vent less the mother's ill-usage than the reason he cannot neutralize its most chafing expression. Indeed, privileging Augusta, Byron practically begs her to ask for more "Scenes" of domestic disturbance, "which to all but you are buried in oblivion" (*BLJ* 1:56): yours, he offers—yours alone—for the asking. And any discourse on Mrs. Byron's current conduct necessarily involves Lord Grey and might lead to the lancing of that poisonous sore. Of those "Scenes . . . buried in oblivion," Byron writes, "Would they were so in my mind. I am afraid they never will." Lord Grey helps to keep them conscious.[7]

"A few short years," Byron continues, "will emancipate me from the Shackles I now wear, and then perhaps she will govern her passion better than at present" (*BLJ* 1:56): toward *me,* does he mean? But, of age, he will then have shed her shackles. What does this fettering have to do with her flammability? Does Byron imagine himself her chief provocateur and his removal a palliative? Or does he think as well of her ungovernable "passion" toward Grey, and by extension of Grey's toward him, which he has also excited: that is, does he here write of unruly adult passion generally and of his own felt physical responsibility for it?

Hoping to "avoid a visit with my mother wherever she is" at the Christmas holiday, Byron goes on: "It is the first duty of a parent, to impress precepts of obedience in their children, but her method is so violent, so capricious, that the patience of Job, the versatility of a member of the House of Commons could not support it" (*BLJ* 1:56). (Ah, yes; but must a [future] member of Lords?) But over against the unacceptable model of parenting is the superior one, to which Byron's mind goes comparatively for comfort after such long and vexed occupation with the bad:

> I revere Dr. Drury much more than I do her, yet he is never violent, never outrageous, I dread offending him, not however through fear, but the respect I bear him, makes me unhappy when I am under his displeasure. My mother's precepts, never convey instruction, never fix upon my mind, to be sure they are calculated, to inculcate obedience, so are chains, and tortures, but though they may restrain for a time the mind revolts from such treatment. [This revolution of the mind from torment becomes, of course, a Promethean theme in Byron's verse.] Not that Mrs. Byron ever injures my *sacred* person.[8] I am rather too old for that, but her words are of that rough texture, which offend more than personal ill usage. (*BLJ* 1:56–57)

Once more Byron protests his mother's crudity in conduct and speech, a crassness unbefitting her station and his, a lumpish heavy-handedness set against Drury's silken thread. But perhaps as much from Mrs. Byron as from Drury's texts has the incipient satirist learned of the wounding power of language: the charge of "rough textured" words—that is, gross utterance and indecorous discourse—aptly anticipates the complaints leveled against Byron's satires by reviewers and his fellow aristocrats alike. (At its worst, such verse never replicated the disorder of the maternal passion that taught him to restrain it.)

But however disagreeable his mother's company, Byron does not "wish to be separated from *her* entirely" (the emphasis desires complete separation from Lord Grey), he writes to Augusta from Harrow on 17 November, "for I do believe she likes me, she manifests that in many instances, particularly with regard to money, which I never want, and I have as much as I desire" (*BLJ* 1:57). If Byron's slight backtracking is economically motivated, it also credits Mrs. Byron with the good sense to find him likable and records an unusual sense of financial well-being for a sixteen-year-old. One can scarcely help but feel, however, that Byron himself, in this redundant iteration of his mother's liberality, senses the substitutive character of it, even the excess of it, as payoff or bribe, emotionally and qualitatively unsatisfactory in expressing the "like" of mother for son: the verb is notable for its mildness as descriptive of maternal affection. That credit (or debt) awarded, he rehearses again the "caprice" and "passion" that render her company insufferable, and remembers yet another defect: "I forgot to mention a most *ungovernable appetite* for Scandal, which she never can govern, and employs most of her time abroad, in displaying the faults, and censuring the foibles, of her acquaintance" (*BLJ* 1:57). The redundancy underscores another inhibiting anxiety, for having already sustained Mrs. Byron's publicity of his failure with Mary Duff, and probably with Mary Ann Chaworth too, Byron would be particularly reluctant to provide her with so delicious a tale as Grey's indiscretion, however helpful to his own interests in parting the mother from the tenant. Whether or not he had succumbed to Grey, or confessed it, circulation of the story might invite legal action from Grey and would certainly further damage the boy's reputation, already under skeptical scrutiny.

Offered against his mother's example is, again, Dr. Drury's: to her insistence that "what little accomplishments I possess either in mind or body are derived from her and her alone," Byron in neat antithesis answers, "what little I have learnt I owe to him [Drury] alone" (*BLJ* 1:58), especially, he implies, about amiability, gentlemanliness, scholarship without pedantry or affectation, self-instruction; and he admits a desire "to repay the numerous obligations, I am under, to him or some of his family" (*BLJ* 1:58). The contrast between two modes of "parenting" and teaching could hardly be more stark, or more distinct the boy's respect and sense of indebtedness for each. For all of his brave talk, however, Byron's closure plays the "secret" card once more, drawing Augusta close in a confidential conspiracy to keep Mrs. Byron ignorant of his "wish to be absent" from her for the duration of the Christmas holidays and perhaps for "some time to come" (*BLJ* 1:58). The persona mixes the bold, cunning rebel with the cowed, uncertain boy: "*if I can* I shall continue to evade going to Southwell, depend upon it I will not approach her for some time to come, *if It is in my power to avoid it*" (my emphasis). As a shared secret between siblings, the intention begs Augusta's sympathy and support.

Four days later Byron reveals his strategy to Augusta, in effect implicating her in it and so aligning her with himself in the event of future difficulties with Mrs. Byron. The attorney Hanson will provide cover and refuge by reissuing an invitation Byron had declined for the previous holiday, to the acceptance of which, now, Mrs. Byron "surely can make no objections" (*BLJ* 1:58); and Hanson is charged with informing Mrs. Byron that her son prefers his solicitor's to her own company at Christmas. Byron has learned well the advantage of mediated communication, but he appears unconscious of his duplication of Henry and Mark Drury's offenses against him.

More surprising, in light of Byron's recent admission of liking Harrow, is his consideration of leaving it. His implied reason is telling: "I have some idea that I leave Harrow these holidays. The Dr. whose character I gave you in my last leaves the mastership at Easter [;] who his successor may be I know not, but he will not be better I am confident" (*BLJ* 1:59). This abrupt announcement appropriates the abandoning prerogative: Byron will leave the kingdom of a beloved father surrogate before that figure can forsake him. The passage shows Byron refusing to suffer another desertion, another betrayal, and, under the threat of it, usurping the separative option—a recurrent tactic in Byron's poetry, where audience is often the partner under threat of separation. In the event, as we shall see, he stayed for Drury's departure, but the desire to avoid it partially explains this declaration. On the other hand, the "bad parent" who does *not* leave her post once more passes under Byron's review, now with recognition of her good intentions, but whose "*manners are not the most conciliating*" (*BLJ* 1:59; my emphasis); and meanspiritedly, the brother, still eager to seal the sibling pact of solidarity against the mother, cites Mrs. Byron's objection to Augusta's marriage and to the younger woman's negligence of her. Then this: "How far her opinion of your love for her is well grounded you best know." That is, perhaps she is right and it isn't. The statement almost encourages an affirmation of Augusta's indifference, and in any case wants her vigilance of and agreement on the mother's character and conduct during her upcoming visit to Southwell.

Moreover, if Augusta can confirm Mrs. Byron's indecorous conduct, Byron will have secured another ally in the battle against Grey, to whose corresponding defect he now returns: "I have more reasons than one, to wish to avoid going to Notts, for there I should be obliged to associate with Lord G[rey] whom I detest, *his manners being unlike those of a Gentleman* [my emphasis], and the information to be derived from him but little except about shooting, which I do not intend to devote my life to. Besides, I have a particular reason for not liking him" (*BLJ* 1:59). Gauche, tedious, unmannerly, fixated like Mrs. Byron, Grey is further handicapped by the unutterable offense, about which Byron is equally obsessive, but the young man domesticates it with every iteration, every flirtation with disclosure. Out of this one, however, emerges clarification on the question of reason or reasons for his avoiding Newstead. It is as though Byron hands Augusta a brief, an outline of his rationale:

I. Obligatory association with Grey
   A. Manners unbefitting a gentleman
   B. Narrow interests
   C.

"C" is the tease, begging Augusta's follow-up. These remarks to her attempt to disqualify Grey as host on general *and* individual grounds for faults offensive to anyone, especially to members of his own social class, and so render less eccentric Byron's decision to eschew Newstead. The hierarchical arrangement of the sentences privileges Grey's social failures—the bad manners, the boring, single-minded conversation—and subordinates the "particular reason" at the same time that silence on "C" encourages, excuses, and dismisses inquiry. I have three good reasons for avoiding Newstead, Byron in effect writes, all of them implicating Grey. With two, both *sufficiently disenfranchising by themselves,* everybody would agree; but the third reason is unique to me. In a context of such compelling reasonableness, who could doubt the legitimacy of his claim—or restrain speculation about its bases? But the logical orderliness of Byron's remarks finally betrays him: the very tone of calm assurance that stabilizes the argument also satisfies us with the given: this voice of reason, we conclude, must be justified in its final silence. It knows what it is about, and needn't countenance dispute. Contextually, it neutralizes—in Augusta, anyhow—the curiosity it has aroused. And we know, at this point, that all of Byron's "reason*s*" for avoiding Newstead originate in Grey's presence there.

He is even less forthcoming to Hanson, however, on 1 December, when, finally inviting himself for the holidays, he gives among his reasons for avoiding Southwell the continuing tenancy of Grey at nearby Newstead: "[Grey] is still more disagreeable to be with [than "the edifying conversations of old maids"], I presume he goes on in the old way, quarreling with the farmers, and stretching his *Judicial* powers (he being now in the Commission) to the utmost, becoming a torment to himself, and a pest to all around him" (*BLJ* 1:60). Apart from the reference to Grey's official capacity as justice of the peace, Byron's complaint might describe his mother's harassment of himself, but may in its final phrase sanitize the tenant's personal affront, while the expectation of self-torment projects onto Grey a habit of the mind desiring it. But following this censure, Byron lavishly, fulsomely compliments Hanson on his sportsmanship as a hunter who has also approved of Byron's weapon ("my Gun"). The tone is light, bantering, even cozy, and yet the apparent endorsement of a genteel pastime practiced by his attorney is startling after Byron's condemnation of it in the hands of Grey. At the very least we can remark the diplomatic absence of reference to Grey's obsession with shooting in Byron's complaints of him to Hanson.

Nearly two months elapse between letters to Augusta, Byron's next coming on 30 January 1805, stating his intention to return to Harrow "until June," then to make for "the university," and inviting his sister to visit her stepmother at Southwell for a "raising" of spirits. Out of his own unhappy experience, however, he warns her against confiding in Mrs. Byron, who "might very possibly divulge" any secret, including and especially any, I expect he means, trusted to Augusta by himself. Additionally, he scrambles to cover himself for any detected discrepancy between his reports of Mrs. Byron's conduct and Augusta's observation of it by anticipating maternal duplicity: "I daresay she would behave very well to *you*, for you do not know her disposition so well as I do" (*BLJ* 1:61), as though knowledge of a witch activates her. And yet so eager is he for confirmation of his mother's instability, he risks being thought deluded in his representation of it by inviting Augusta's inspection. But Augusta must also withhold as much as she can— that is, misrepresent herself on so critical a matter as her own marriage, and perhaps on subjects equally sensitive to her brother—when conversing with Mrs. Byron. These issues of representation and self-representation, of secrecy and disclosure, of dissimulation and prevarication, even as marks of adolescent anxiety, acquire considerable weight as constituents in the making of an autobiographical poet.

3 : William Henry West Betty

BACK IN DECEMBER, at about the time that Byron was inviting himself to Hanson's, Dr. Drury was disinviting him, through Mrs. Byron, from returning to Harrow. Mrs. Byron informed Hanson, who informed Augusta, who brought Lord Carlisle into the conversation, whereupon Hanson inquired of the headmaster, who carefully replied:

> During his [Byron's] last residence at Harrow his conduct gave me much trouble and uneasiness; and as two of his Associates were leaving me at Christmas, I certainly suggested to him *my wish* that he might be placed under the care of some private Tutor previously to his admission to either of the Universities. This I did no less with a view to the forming of his mind and manners, than to my own comfort. (Marchand 1:92)

Apart from the probably inadvertent suggestion of a wholesale housecleaning of troublesome boys, Drury must have exercised as much tact in expressing this wish to Byron as in reporting it to the family, for the boy appears not to have responded dramatically to what amounts to, and must have felt like, dismissal by a respected, even loved mentor and authority figure, no matter how sugar-coated the notice. On the other hand, perhaps at the moment Byron was content to leave a site only moderately loved where an indifferent scholastic record, habitual "rebelling, *rowing*, and ... all manner of mischief" (Byron's self-description, quoted in Moore, 1:50), overheated friendships "fraught with jealousies, heartaches, and sometimes ruptures" (Marchand 1:91), and recent hostility to his unorthodox religious opinions conspired to make life difficult. The imminent abandonment of the retiring Dr. Drury, and Drury's figurative abandonment of Byron in the wish for his reassignment, cannot have brightened the boy's Harrow prospects. So he temporarily yields to Drury's wish and takes his farewell of the school when departing for the Christmas holidays, and in a lordly gesture perhaps tinctured with spite he leaves behind all his books, although bequeathing a few to the library (the facts are Marchand's, 1:92, the speculation on motive, mine).

But by February he was back, and writing to Augusta that he would remain at Harrow until June (*BLJ* 1:61). What changed, or changed his mind? Much of the interim—perhaps all of it—Byron had spent in London, at the Hansons' home. Among other entertainments, he dined pleasantly with Lord Carlisle on 26 January (a long-delayed event sending Augusta into raptures); while no record of the visit exists, it seems reasonable to assume that Byron's future in the House of Lords, where his recently discovered gifts for oratory would be useful, might have been discussed. Given the interest he expressed to Augusta, three months later, in hearing the Houses debate, and delaying his departure from London in order to do so (*BLJ* 1:67), he may have attended sessions in December/January as well, possibly for instruction in speechmaking (cf. Marchand 1:95). But a spectacular London attraction, I suspect, also encouraged reassessment of his concession to Drury's wish.

The theatrical sensation of the day was the thirteen-year-old actor William Henry West Betty, "Master Betty" at Covent Garden, "Young Roscius" (after the first-century B.C. Roman actor, his surname as epithet for thespian excellence most recently attached to David Garrick) at Drury Lane. This boy's wildly successful tours of the provinces—Cork, Londonderry, Glasgow, Liverpool, Stockport, Manchester, Birmingham—had hyped the London public, by press, word of mouth, and strategic puffing, to feverish anticipation of his City opening. Following it, Master Betty awoke to find himself famous at the palace, at Carlton House, at the House of Commons, in clubs and parlors across the metropolis, the object of fascinated talk and scrutiny by women and men alike. Byron attended several performances by this prodigy during the 1804–5 season and deemed him "tolerable in some characters but by no means equal to the ridiculous praises showered upon him by *John Bull*" (*BLJ* 1:67; 25 April 1805 letter to Augusta), this latter shot being precisely the charge he brought against the sycophantic Robert Southey and others in *The Vision of Judgment* eighteen years later. But if Roscius was only a "tolerable" actor, why did Byron return "several times at hazard of my life" to see him perform?

He does not much, if any, exaggerate the risk of doing so. By mid-morning of 1 December 1804, the day of Master Betty's London premiere, crowds had gathered outside Covent Garden, swelling to thousands by mid-afternoon in "long, thick-wedged, impenetrable columns" (*Daily Advertiser*, 2 December 1804). An anxious management summoned a detachment of guards for crowd control and posted peace officers inside in hopes of preserving order and property. When the doors opened, "the rush was terrific":

> In the space of a few minutes the two galleries . . . seemed as one solid mass: Gentlemen who knew there were no places untaken in the boxes, paid for admission and poured from the front boxes into the pit in twenties and thirties at a time. . . . [I]n spite of the ventilators the heat was so terrific that men and women fainted . . . The Ladies in one or two boxes were employed almost the whole night in fanning the Gentlemen beneath them in the pit. Upward of twenty gentlemen who . . . fainted were dragged up into the boxes; we observed several more raising their hands, as if in the act of supplication for mercy and pity.[1]

Seeing danger from trampling, soldiers encircling the Garden struggled to clear the entrances and streets, and evidently prevented repetition of the fatal stampede marring Master Betty's command performance in Liverpool.[2] But the next night, violence erupted among impatient patrons, with considerable damage resulting to persons and property, as part of the Garden itself collapsed under the crush,[3] and spectators again swooned, perhaps as much from delirium as from the heat and press. On 10 December Young Roscius opened at the Old Drury (Lane) to a packed, but apparently orderly, house, but on the eleventh the masses awaiting entrance "broke most of the windows within their reach on the vinegar-yard side of the theater; and by the impetuosity of their movements, when the passages were thrown open, the balustrades, on both sides of the staircase which leads to the boxes, were entirely demolished" (*Memoir* 12).[4]

Reviews competed for superlatives: The *Times* proclaimed Master Betty's premiere *itself* "a remarkable epoch" in the English theater; Garrick was said returned, and Kemble equaled or excelled. James Northcote, the painter who would render the boy's portrait, told his diary that Betty and Napoleon "now divide the world"—although in inches of newsprint the Infant Phenomenon's opening far surpassed coverage of Napoleon's Coronation on 2 December.[5] Similarly, one source reported that "an Empire [is] occupied by a boy of thirteen."[6] Memorial medals were struck; daily bulletins during a brief illness reported Betty's status—a serious and offensive breach of decorum, for such privilege belonged exclusively to royalty.[7] He was found to be "a perfect master."

There is something in his whisper like the under-notes of the Kembles. . . . The oldest actor is not equal to him, he never loses sight of the scene. . . . His judgment seems to be extremely correct. . . . Nature has endowed him with genius which we shall vainly attempt to find in any of the actors of the present day: . . . their Majesties were charmed by their new "servant," royalty received him in its London palace, and to the Count d'Artois [future king of France] and an August party at Lady Percivale's, the small-eyed and plump-faced boy shook his luxuriant curls. . . . The philosophers went as mad as the "quality" and critics. *Quid noster Roscius egit* was given by Cambridge University as the subject for Sir William Brown's prize-medal. Old "Gentleman Smith," the original Charles Surface . . . presented Young Betty with a seal bearing the likeness of Garrick, and which Garrick, in his last illness, had charged him to keep only till he should "meet with a player who acted from *nature* and from *feeling.*" Having found such an actor, Smith consigned to him the keeping of the precious relic![8]

"In short," wrote the Duchess of Devonshire to her son, "He [Master Betty] has changed the life of London" (Playfair 72). Such mass hysteria as these extracts indicate—too familiar in the age of Michael Jackson but extraordinary, not to say unprecedented, as awarded to a boy in turn-of-the-century London—had begun to subside when Master Betty's London run ended for the season in May, but all accounts agree that it typified theatrical patronage during Byron's London holiday. Was mediocre performance by an inexperienced child the liveliest entertainment on offer for him?

Unlikely enough except for the associated pandemonium. While we should credit Byron with more perspicacious judgment and the courage to articulate it, if in a private letter, than the public and most reviewers took away from Master Betty's performances, he is almost certainly masking an interest in Roscius with the mildly critical appraisal. He went public only a little later, but background is necessary to that discussion. Having caught the thespian fever at Harrow and the Theatres Royal, Byron enthusiastically participated in amateur performances in the Leacrofts' drawing room, at Southwell, during October 1806 before going up to Cambridge, and again in January 1807. En route to Southwell with John Pigot in September, he set down "An Occasional Prologue, Delivered Previous to the Performance of 'The Wheel of Fortune,' at a Private Theatre," which included the ironic, self-exonerating disclaimer, "To night, no vet'ran Rocsii you behold, / In all the arts of scenic action old" (ll. 11–12; *CPW* 1:365). But this criticism targets less the gift than the age and experience of Master Betty, and, in its multiplication of the phenomenon, the cultural fashion that he inaugurated. Similarly, if with a slightly sharper quill, *English Bards and Scotch Reviewers* sketches Betty third in its gallery of dramatic miscreants (ll. 560–607)—"Though now, thank Heaven! The Rosciomania's o'er, / And full-grown actors are endured once more" (ll. 563–64)—but again Byron bypasses an opening for the sort of excoriation on full display elsewhere in the satire. That the mania *has* subsided, that Betty is not hot news, may restrain him, although this deterrent is not always operative elsewhere in *English Bards* or other works. I suspect that an unacknowledged or grudging and emulous respect, a mysterious and nagging fascination, an unwelcome but irresistible magnetism, and a disconcerting identification checked any conscious impulse to decry at length.

For the passing of another year finds Byron conceding agility to Master Betty in a lively satire written, says McGann, "partly for the amusement of his friend John Pigot" (*CPW* 1:386), a medium practically inviting irreverence, and getting it in most other connections. This is "The Edinburgh Ladies' Petition to Doctor Mayes, and his Reply" of 1807. "The Reply" portion expands upon "The Moderns' " discontent "with common things," out of which springs "some daily wonder,"

> An Infant Billington, or Banti,
> Squalls out Adagio, or Andante.
> The Town to view the veteran Kemble,
> In nightly crowds no more assemble;
> The House is crammed in every place full
> To see the Boy, of action Graceful;
> While Roscius lends his name to Betty
> Tully must yield the palm to Petty (ll. 22–30)—

that is, Henry Petty, who entered Commons at twenty-two and became chancellor of the exchequer only three years later (*CPW* 1:387). Byron may have confused or conflated Elizabeth Billington, veteran soprano, and Brigitta Banti, of London opera, with "the Infant Billington, who had made its mark strutting about the stages of Brighton and Worthing," but not as a singer.[9] But then follows this delightful surprise:

> And last though not the least in Crime,
> A sucking *Peer* pretends to rhyme—
> Though many think the noble Fool
> Had better far return to School,
> And there improve in Learning faster,
> Instead of *libeling* his Master.
> Such Trifles now amuse the Age,
> Infant Attempts are all the Rage. (ll. 32–38)

Among such attempts is of course the *Hours of Idleness* of *this* "sucking *Peer,*" to be published the last week of June, the preface to which would highlight, as excuse, and to Byron's everlasting embarrassment, the author's youth. The lines in question were a late addition to "The Reply," and are accompanied on the holograph copy by a note from Elizabeth Pigot dated "March 1807," directing their insertion into the existing text (*CPW* 1:386). In other words, long before reviewers seized upon Byron's plea of minority in his preface to *Hours of Idleness,* he himself appears to have understood the folly of the defense he would mount, and in a witty anticipation associates it with the cult of infantilism that swept the kingdom in the wake of Master Betty's success, even using some of the language his preface would adopt in confessing the "Crime" to be denied there ("To the dictates of young ambition, may be ascribed many actions more criminal, and equally absurd" [*CPW* 1:34]). It is of course possible that Byron has already written the preface, in which case he borrows from rather than anticipates it. In either event, he appears to have proceeded with a plea recognized to be risky. One wonders if that decision might have been driven by Byron's wishful suspicion, in light of the mania for youthful performance inspired by the Prodigy, that the public's forgiveness of other artistic sins in the name of youth might extend to him. Moreover, the self-association with Betty, albeit here in absurdity, helps to explain Byron's moderation on the boy elsewhere, and reinforces the hints of identification and competition with him noticed in my argument. Verse making, like speechmaking, was for the early (and perhaps the later) Byron the practice of rivalry, a verbal form of the physical sparring at which he also distinguished himself. A chief spur in the exercise of that competitive exigence was Young Roscius. (On the "*libeling* his Master," see below.)

Byron, then, was intrigued, wary, distrustful of his own interest and careful to disguise it but unable to withhold the report of his repeated attendance at the Theatres Royal for sight of "Infant Roscius." The risk to life and limb, advertised in the letter to Augusta, glamorizes the visits as adventures—a heightening of color to which Byron was rarely adverse. But inasmuch as royalty, nobility, statesmen, journalists/critics, and common folk had all lost their heads to Master Betty (and, indecently, it would appear in some cases, their hearts and glands, too), Byron's critical review aligned him against most representatives of the establishment, save only some prominent actors—a surly Kemble and a stiff Mrs. Siddons among them—who, envious of and feeling, if not literally, threatened by the boy's success, and fearing offense to their own partisans, quietly descried his inexperience and unfitness for the adult roles he attempted. In other words, the very popularity of Roscius excited the rebellious instincts that so frequently led Byron to strike an oppositional stance.

And yet he returned "several times" to see the actor he thought— or said he thought—only moderately gifted. Master Betty—Byron could not have been deaf to the punning potential of the name, although no example of his exploiting it has to my knowledge surfaced, an absence so conspicuous as itself to indicate conscious suppression— Master Betty at thirteen was "prepossessing in a very great degree";[10] "slight, but elegant, and extremely youthful" in appearance, according to *The Infant Roscius* of Messrs. Jackson, Bisset, Merrit, and Harley,[11] weighing in at eighty-seven pounds on a frame of four feet, ten inches, said to be tall for his age. "His features," the *Daily Telegraph* reported, "were delicate, but somewhat feminine, his eyes were a full, bright and shining blue, his fair hair was long, and hung in ringlets over his shoulder." *Infant Roscius* elaborated: "His complexion is fair . . . his face sweetly interesting. . . . His features are not strongly marked, yet his countenance is capable of considerable expression" (33). Assessments of the voice ranged from admiration of its depth and power to mild criticism of its monotony, harshness, and adolescent "cracking," to the sharply censorious observation that it "was very bad, and his mode of managing it peculiarly exceptionable . . . a revival of that [1710–1740] unnatural way of speaking on the stage."[12] But the author of *Critique* is undisturbed: "From the breaking of his voice, as is natural at his time of life, it may be presumed to be deficient in sweetness and variety of tone. We perceived no such defect in this speech [from *Barbarossa*]. His voice was finely modulated and varied" (17). Whatever we make of these judgments, the attribution of "power"—that is, the capacity for great volume—must be true, for the 1804 Old Drury (Lane) theater housed at least twice as many spectators as does the current one (Playfair 78).

William Hazlitt's raptures soared off the charts:

> Master Betty's acting was a singular phenomenon, but it was also as beautiful as it was singular. I saw him in the part of Douglas and he seemed almost like "some gay creature of the element," moving about gracefully, with all the flexibility of youth and murmuring Aeolian sounds with plaintive tenderness. I shall never forget the way in which he repeated the line in which Young Norval says, speaking of the fate of the brothers: "And in my mind happy was he that died!" The tones fell and seemed to linger prophetic on my ear.[13]

So, too, Lord Campbell, recalling his own "critical reign":

> I must confess that I was one of those who enthusiastically admired him, and who thought not only that his performances were wonderful for a boy of his years, but that the characters he undertook were most beautifully portrayed. Some more fastidious critics rather thought him one of the "aery of children, little eyases, that cry out on the top of the question, and are most tyrannically clapped for't" [Hamlet 2.2]; but if I erred I need not be ashamed, for night after night, as often as he acted, there was Charles James Fox in the stage box, hanging on the boy's lips and rapturously applauding him. John Kemble in "Hamlet" or "Coriolanus" no doubt was a better study for the judgment, but I confess he could never so powerfully touch in my breast the chords of terror and of pity[14]

Fox[15] remarked to Samuel Rogers as they, together with Pitt (who allegedly wept over Betty's *Douglas*), Canning, and other notables, viewed Roscius's *Hamlet* on 14 March 1805: "This is finer than Garrick,"[16] and the Marquis of Wellesley, brother of Wellington, declared Betty "an angel from heaven, for that nothing on earth was like him."[17] Nor is this his only association with the sacred: the anonymous author of *Critique* writes: "He seemed inspired with a holy devotion . . . every feature is lighted up with the holy frenzy of one inspired. . . . Viewing him . . . as a heaven-born Actor, we must deprecate all invidious comparisons" (17–18, 24).

James Northcote, who would paint the boy, spoke of his acting as "a beautiful effusion of natural sensibility; and then that graceful play of the limbs in youth gave such an advantage over every one about him."[18] On his stage craft, *Infant Roscius* is only slightly less encomiastic: "His action is graceful, chaste, and varied. . . . He appears to possess a complete knowledge of stage business; treads the boards with firmness and dignity; pays the most critical attention to his brother actors; and, with the exception of Kemble, is, perhaps, the most perfect master of attitudes of any performer at the London theatres" (33). If to some eyes of a "deportment and address . . . completely those of a man" on stage, off it Master Betty "is more than commonly childish. All his amusements and sports are infantile, even beyond his years. . . . [H]e is sportive and boyish; his usual manner is serious and pensive. Sometimes he appears restrained and timid, at others he seems indifferent to every thing around him. . . . But his fondness for . . . everything else, instantly goes away, when his favourite pursuit is in question. His attachment to his art is paramount" (*Infant Roscius* 37). That Master Betty *was* in some degree genuinely artistic, even if, as some thought, his art was "mimic" in mere duplication of "tricks and speech drilled into him by the 'theatric tutor Hough,' " his manager,[19] is corroborated by the skeptically inclined authors of *Infant Roscius* upon first seeing Betty perform: "We trembled for a moment [after he muffed a line], lest all the vaunted fire and discrimination of Roscius should terminate in schoolboy rant and declamation. But we were agreeably undeceived" (25).

Byron did not, then, find in Master Betty mere recitation of the sort familiar from speech days, although he might very well have discovered in him strategies for lifting his own performance above the routine level. What he also found, beyond the "tolerable" actor, was a lad of about the age, size, and (im)maturity of Harrow boys who had inspired his own interest, defense, and devotion. William Harness, for example, at twelve, was two years younger than Byron when honored by the poet's first verses, and we have already heard Byron on his own age difference from Delawarr. In his journal Byron identified four "principal friends" of his Harrow years (Peter Hunter, Hon. George Augustus William Curzon, Edward Noel Long, and John Cecil Tattersall), but also six younger men as "my juniors and favourites, whom I spoilt with indulgence" (John, Earl of Clare, George John Frederick, Duke of Dorset, Charles David Gordon, D. Bath, George *or* John Thomas Claridge [it is not clear which of the Claridge brothers Byron favored], and John Wingfield) (Moore 1:38), three of whom appear more frequently in Byron's discourse than any of the first group except Long;[20] and within a year Byron would find himself strongly attracted— first by the voice—to the fifteen-year-old Cambridge choirboy John

Edleston, for a while his intimate. Four years earlier, himself thirteen, Byron had entered Harrow scholastically behind his fellows, as a partial consequence of which the grand achievement and fame of the theatrical phenomenon "Young Roscius" must have registered itself all the more forcefully upon him. For there, commanding the London stage and from it all London society and the royal family itself, was a mere boy undeterred, evidently unintimidated by his physical difference from other actors. Genest (7:60) notes that "some little addition to Master Betty's height was made by art, but his figure was still such as disqualified him from playing with men and women without a manifest breach of propriety—if indeed a company of young persons of his own age could have been formed, he would have been seen to more advantage—he would then have appeared to be what he really was, 'the Triton of Minnows.'" But this comment rather misses the point that the aberration, the physical incompatibility between Betty and his fellow actors *is* his advantage, is precisely part of his drawing power on the public; indeed, he and his managers capitalized upon the "difference" that made him, because a gorgeous novelty, the toast of two seasons. What Byron returned "several times" to see was a boy-star resembling his Harrow favorites, a boy who had surmounted the perceived "handicaps" of physical and professional immaturity to triumph by speaking— by acting out—dramatic lines. Byron saw, I believe, possibility for himself, if immediately on a reduced scale, perhaps on a more spacious stage down the years.

But Byron also saw himself in a less visionary sense. If the extant portraits and sketches are reliable, he would have observed at the Theatres Royal an actor bearing resemblance to himself, and *startlingly* like himself at thirteen, although unimpaired in limb and graceful of movement. I am not sure that this likeness has been previously observed, but it seems to me a significant factor in accounting for Byron's relatively sustained attention to Master Betty, for such (even subliminally) recognized similarity would have even more graphically represented to him the possibilities of early fame not despite "difference" but by smart exploitation of it—by capitalization upon aberration, which is, after all, only individuality *in extremis*. The portrait of the boys at thirteen—of Byron a pencil sketch signed "T.W." now lost[21], of Master Betty in theatrical dress by James Northcote and a mezzotint by J. Ward after H. Burch—show conspicuous resemblances between high foreheads

under profuse light curls tumbling past ears onto the necks; large eyes, somewhat protuberant pupils, puffy lids under gracefully arched brows (Betty's cosmetically enhanced), long, narrow noses, pouty, cupid-bow lips (more pronounced in later renderings of Byron), discreetly cleft chins, a soft, pudgy fleshiness in the oval faces predictive of corpulence. Under a schoolboy jacket and knotted scarf, Byron sports a modest version of the open, flared collar he was to make famous, and so reveals a fair amount of throat, but nothing like as much as Betty in the mezzotint, where the edges of a very wide, fringed collar expose a well-proportioned throat and a smooth upper chest before plunging to what one might almost call a décolletage where the folds of his blouse suggestively hint of breasts beneath them. A higher lace collar frames the neck and chin in the Northcote portrait of Betty, where the face is fuller, with shadowy anticipations of a double chin suggestive of indulgence.

Both portraits of Betty are staged, an effect heightened by Ward's backdrop of dark, roiling clouds, and in the Northcote by the dress of a dramatic character; but from our historic perspective we can recognize them, without minimizing the real physical similarity of feature, as *Byronically* stagy, so to speak, as part of that convention of sensational self-representation to which he gave his name, thus completely trumping Master Betty, his model! In the pencil sketch, Byron looks just younger, perhaps because of the schoolboy apparel. Exchange the dress, however, and the boys could pass for each other.

And not only the boys. Arresting, too, is the resemblance between Ward's Betty and the famous, anonymous miniature of Lady Caroline Lamb outfitted as a page. Just after Young Roscius's London opening, the Countess of Bessborough wrote to Lord Granville Leveson Gower, British ambassador to St. Petersburg, about the future Lady Caroline Lamb's "raving wild with Master Betty" upon seeing him perform (Playfair 73). Looking at that portrait, one can hardly help wondering whether recollection of Betty, and awareness of her own facial resemblance to him, might have inspired Lady Caroline's choice of costumes with which to interest Byron. She was savvy and cunning enough to have capitalized upon the similarity. But the resemblance need not be as close as the portraits suggest for a narcissistic dynamic to have acted in Byron's repeated observations of the "Infant Prodigy." I am positing, in other words, in his perception of Master Betty, an attraction to the self he imagines he might have been in success, acceptance, popularity, fame, *and* to a possible future identity. Self-recognized as such or not, Byron's spectatorship was definably motivated, and motivational.

But he was hardly immune to another attraction, most obvious in the androgyny of the Ward depiction but clear enough in contemporaneous written accounts of Young Roscius. Unmistakably to the British populace, he was a stunningly beautiful youth, "the little Apollo off the pedestal," in the opinion of the painter Humphrey (Playfair 78), and his appeal is in considerable measure sexual for both genders. His contemporary biographer calls "Bettymania" basically a sexual phenomenon, and from the beginning the suspicion has persisted that the touted theatrical art of Master Betty provided a respectable cover for adoration of a pretty boy (Playfair 76–77). "Female beauty," the *British Press* reported of Betty's Covent Garden debut, "cannot afford any thing more sweet than his smile" (3 December 1804); the anonymous author of a memoir recalled "the hair of Roscius . . . [as] not only luxuriant but of a most beautiful hue. . . . He displayed his ringlets on critical occasions with much effect"—as though tossing, stroking, or toying with them (*Memoir* 12). We have already heard the *Daily Telegraph* on the "delicate . . . somewhat feminine" features of the boy, but it went on to remark that Betty's "abundant tresses confined with a comb [in daytime, off stage] . . . still more gave the idea of a female in male costume." Cosmetics enhanced a "young and girlish beauty" mistaken by professional actors as the creation of female drag; the *Times* correspondent, in a happily androgynous phrase, thought Roscius's "features handsome and rather feminine" (Playfair 76).

The emphasis in many accounts on the femininity in Betty's countenance hint at the sexual component in his appeal, but Northcote is bolder, blunter. He recalled the boy's theater dressing room: "as full as it could contain of all the court of England, and happy were those who could get in at the time his father was rubbing his naked body from the perspiration after the exertion in performing his part on the stage."[22] Not, notice, "rubbing the perspiration from his naked body" but vice versa: the body focuses the activity and the description of it. If this passage reveals as much about Northcote as about the dressing room, such an experience must have inscribed itself in the painter's portrait, where Betty's face does express more sensuality than in Ward's innocent if also more provocative version. Mrs. Charles Matthews corroborates Northcote's sense of the dressing room as idolatrous shrine for voyeuristic patronage: "It was offensively amusing . . . to listen to the enthusiastic ecstasies of the noble visitors who came nightly to the green room to gaze upon the Boy-wonder, and haply to kiss the garment-hem of the Betty, who, had his person been as feminine as his name, could not have had more fervent male adorers, some of whom were [in any case] almost impious in their enthusiasm" (Playfair 86). Playfair himself remarks upon the extraordinarily pervasive and ardent *male* attention (twenty to one) at Master Betty's London opening (81ff.), with peers of the realm and its leading statesmen virtually dancing attendance upon the boy thereafter. And while the predominance of men in these early audiences is partly attributable to the perceived risk of injury to women braving the throngs, the national enthusiasm of men for young Betty appears to bespeak a highly charged erotic magnetism perhaps innocently projected by the boy (or perhaps not so innocently; see Playfair's speculations) and certainly fostered by his managers. The *Times* did not scruple to mince words: "Master Betty's success is very naturally the cause of much envy and heart-breaking amongst the Master Polly's and Master Jenny's of Bond Street and Cheapside, who in all their attempts to distinguish their pretty persons and effeminate airs, have only miscarried" (5 December 1804). I do not, of course, impute conscious pederastic lust to the entire male theater-going patronage of the British Isles, but the flushed, panting excess of men's approbation of Master Betty's appearance and stagecraft insinuates more or other than merely aesthetic or Platonic interest, although evidence of sexual pursuit of the boy is slim and except in two cases questionable (see Playfair 87), the more plausible one involving Betty's tutor and manager, William Hough, who may have been almost as interested in the boy's body as in his earnings. In an effort to deny or conceal his own homoerotic attraction, I suspect, Byron disapproved of Betty's performances in his brief review for Augusta. But he could not, though the crowds would have helped him, stay away.[23]

4: Villain : *6 June 1805*

WITH SPEECH DAY SCHEDULED for June, Byron changed his mind about returning to Harrow, at least in part, I believe, because inspired by William Betty to strut and fret upon the available stage. His successful avoidance of Southwell and of his mother for the entirety of a holiday that included Christmas and his own seventeenth birthday must have empowered a determination to preserve distance between himself and the domestic war zone. But if not then at Harrow, where could he find "home"? He literally had no other options for safe and long-term refuge. Better school discipline among friends, perhaps, than combat with family. That Byron frankly regarded Harrow as home, at least in the months after leaving the school, is manifest in lines already quoted from "Childish Recollections" (ll. 213–42).

Besides, the appearance, the effect, and the possible interpretations of his school-leaving had belatedly dawned upon him, probably with Hanson's assistance. The attorney wrote on 29 January: "[Byron] seems now to think that his not returning to Harrow would after what has been said amount in the opinion of his Friends to an Expulsion and as that idea hurts him very much and he has a great wish to speak in the Summer he seems bent upon his returning" (Nathan Hanson narrative; quoted in Marchand, 1:93). That his friends should have perceived his December departure as ignominious expulsion is insufferable, but one wonders how Byron explained it—or expected it to be explained—at the time, since tactful expulsion it unmistakably was. And what *has* been said in the interim, and by whom? A leak of the truth seems likeliest. Although he certainly has other motives, Byron also opts for return to recuperate a reputation he fears damaged by rumors of truth, all of which can be scotched by his reappearance on the site. Further, to feel the stings of ignominy and disrepute while admiring and in part identifying with a young man worshiped by all London must have fed the will for self-rehabilitation, and in the most public place and manner possible. Only the reverse could happen at home. Through Hanson's intervention, then, Byron received Dr. Drury's permission to return and complete the Harrow year.

But a disturbance not of his making was brewing at the school, and in the event may have produced as much strife as Byron sought to escape at Southwell. Dr. Drury had announced to the governors on 25 November 1804 his intention to retire, for domestic reasons involving the health of his wife, at Easter in March of 1805, at the height of his successes after twenty years in the headmastership. But Byron knew of these supposedly confidential plans no later than 21 November 1804 (Tyerman 35)—intelligence suggesting either his intimacy with Dr. Drury (or his associates) or the porous character of Harrow security. This double abandonment by a revered master, in effect a virtually simultaneous expulsion and resignation, proved all the more troubling and disorienting because its early delivery evidently sanctioned Byron as a privileged party, honored by the authority who in the announced intention yet forsakes him. Here is another version of the mixed affectional signals that Byron has received since infancy, from parents, nurse, relatives, tenants, women, and of the sign he will send to numerous mates and friends throughout his life, the same one, infinitely varied, marking relationships in his lyric, dramatic, and satiric poetry. Its sting would have been especially piercing in 1804, because, as we have seen, Dr. Drury had upon Byron's arrival at Harrow treated him kindly, before the blowup with his first tutor, almost as a family member, placing him for special oversight in Henry's boardinghouse.

The same could not be said for Mark Drury, of course, who enjoyed his brother's favor for the headmastership. But Benjamin Evans, the replacement for Henry as Byron's tutor in 1803, also declared for the post in late November, as did Dr. George Butler, tutor of Sidney Sussex College, Cambridge, in January 1805. With Dr. Drury's endorsement, Mark also proved the boys' favorite, but probably because of his unhappy interactions with Mark, Byron declined active campaigning until Tom Wildman, chief of the Drury faction and later purchaser of Newstead Abbey, surrendered the leadership to Byron in exchange for his active backing. One can imagine the self-righteousness with which the young nobleman may have suppressed his sense of injury in the interests of a Drury succession, doubtless in loyalty to the headmaster; but the political maneuvering is noteworthy—the bold, self-serving trade-off by this formerly shy boy now bent on visible prominence. On the other hand, it is possible that Byron remembered his former epistolary promise to Augusta to repay the headmaster and his family for all of Dr. Drury's kindness; this support of a man once experienced as foe may express an admirably unselfish large-heartedness. But why, on the eve of Byron's permanent departure, take an interest at all, particularly to promote the cause of a once-friendly family that had insulted and now expelled him? Can we interpret Byron's negotiation with Wildman as the disinterested effort of a lad with nothing to lose strategically positioning himself to take the blame in the event of failure and retaliation? Because sent down, he stood to gain nothing in the event of success. In all of the pre-election debate and excitement, Byron may have found the invitation to leave more liberating than demeaning. Well might we see in the detached will of the disenfranchised boy to guard the front against the invasion from Cambridge the seed and shape of the 1820 defender of Greece.

The Harrow board of governors distributed its votes evenly among the three contenders, throwing the decision to the Archbishop of Canterbury, who chose Butler, as a consequence of which, for the second time in its history, Harrow mutinied over the headmastership appointment, although at least one historian (Tyerman) believes the energy of the demonstrations wildly exaggerated in other accounts.[1] Predictably, Byron plays a conspicuous and colorful role in the legends. He is said to have ripped away the window gratings from the headmaster's residence, plotted to lay a gunpowder trail for blowing up Butler, haughtily refused dinner with Butler on the grounds that he himself would never, were Butler in the Newstead vicinity, invite *him* to dine (this last surely the most authentic-*sounding,* the most in-character, of the Byronic anecdotes emerging from the event). The boys realizing in the nick of time—possibly with Byron's help—that the planned explosion and fire imperiled the fourth form room, whose walls sanctuaried the carved names of their predecessors and would soon enshrine their own, the gunpowder plot fizzled.[2] The scale of this rebellion, and the degree of Byron's participation in it, remain in dispute. Notably, however, Harrow village chancery records, unusually faithful in naming participants in all local disturbances, say nothing of a school rebellion at this time, or of Byron's fabled rowdiness over the Butler succession.[3] What isn't contested, however, is his scurrilous poetic attacks upon the new headmaster, circulated to admiration at the time and later published, although the young poet shortly made it up with Butler as he had with Henry Drury and remained a friend. Meanwhile, Byron's anxiety about his continuance at Harrow is clear in a letter to Hanson of 2 March 1805 (*BLJ* 1:62), expressing hope that Mrs. Byron will refrain from attacking Dr. Drury, since "inevitably [my] expulsion would be the consequence." At the same time, he expects to contribute through her to a farewell gift for Drury, a liberal mark of the boys' affection worth 330 guineas.

Obliged by the seven-month lapse between visits to his mother, Byron reluctantly left Harrow for a Southwell spring holiday on 3 April but dallied for three days in London, at the Hansons' again, en route. On the first day, he wrote to Augusta "in very bad spirits, out of humor with myself, and all the *world* except *you*" (*BLJ* 1:62), so fierce was his dread of more domestic turbulence, which in fact erupted. As antidote he anticipated better times: university matriculation, a London reunion with Augusta, and her possible appearance at Harrow: "If you stay [in London] till the middle of next month, you may have the opportunity of hearing me speak, as the first day of our *Harrow orations* occurs in May" (*BLJ* 1:63). In fact, it occurred in June and Augusta missed it, but Byron's eagerness to have her there witnesses both his confidence in his skills and his pride in a family member he might without shame display among peers. But such expectations were weak tonic: "I hope you will excuse this *Hypochondriac* epistle as I never was in such low spirits in my life" (*BLJ* 1:63). After all, the good "parent" was gone, replaced by an unsatisfactory alternative, the bad parent awaited, and prospects for interesting occupation seemed bleak, in the middle space between equally unacceptable options.[4]

On the other hand, Byron is already planning his return to the stage, and, according to Marchand, *has* been preparing himself since February, when he selected for his second public recitation the speech of Zanga over the corpse of Alonzo from Edward Young's *The Revenge* (Marchand 1:96). I shall later suggest reasons for this choice. For the moment, I explore a possible motivational connection in Byron's mind between the upcoming Speech Day and another, apparently unrelated episode.

With no break in his text, Byron follows the invitation to Speech Day quoted above with this sentence: "My friend Delawarr (as you observed) danced with the little princess, nor did I in the least *envy* him the honour" (*BLJ* 1:63). Marchand identifies the "little princess" as Charlotte of Wales, and the occasion as a "house warming" at Windsor Castle on 25 February 1805 (*BLJ* 1:63n). Although Byron was in London at the time and dined at Carlisle's the next day, he almost certainly refers to Augusta's epistolary "observation," or perhaps to a newspaper account of the event that she had read and alluded to in her letter, not to her or their presence at the Windsor event. More interesting is Byron's denial of envy toward Delawarr: it is hardly necessary to deny envy unless the suspicion—possibly the certainty—of envy exists. Byron declines to envy the "*honour*" of dancing with Charlotte, not—explicitly— the *ability* to do so, but his compensatory qualifier and italics point to envy of the "honour" as well, for Byron is jealous both of his friend's physical agility and of his attentions to the "little princess," an epithet not entirely free of scorn. Delawarr is, after all, the last time we heard of him, Byron's best loved friend, after Augusta.

But what makes this passage particularly intriguing is a fact of Harrow architectural history. Until about 1840, dancing was taught at Harrow after regular hours as an essential component of a gentleman's education, but usually as an extracurricular activity, along with modern languages (French and German), fencing and boxing, penmanship, drawing and painting (Tyerman 29; Hawkyard, conversation, 24 May 1996). So popular had it become by 1770 that the dancing master at the time, Anthony Tassoni, acquired on lease a plot of ground from the governors and at personal expense erected a dancing school building just north of the chapel.[5] Until the present Old Speech Room was completed in 1820 (to be replaced in 1877 by the current Speech Room), the Speech Day festivals were staged in the dancing school (Hawson and Townsend 202), site also of the balls that concluded the Shooting Day archery competition until Dr. Heath abolished the custom in 1772, as we have seen, because it excused absenteeism for the boys and attracted riffraff from the city. Aspiring orators, then, recited their declamations in a ballroom presumably refitted to accommodate the substantial audience of relatives usually drawn by the Speech Day event.

One clause in Byron's lyric "On a Distant View of the Village and School, of Harrow, on the Hill," taken literally, appears to describe the position of Harrow speakers vis-à-vis audience in the dancing school setting, however we read the grammatical ambiguity: "I once more view the room, with spectators surrounded" (l. 17). Such enclosure seems likely to have increased (over, say, proscenium framing) the sensation of spotlighted centrality, and thus the tension or pride or both, depending upon the boy, experienced by Speech Day performers. On the other hand, an unsigned etching I have acquired of Harrow Speech Day from about 1880, with the artist looking from deep stage right across a platform defined along its rear by a long crescent of boys awaiting their turns, a single boy holding forth stage front center, *does* create the feeling—almost claustrophobic—of circumscription by an audience of individualized faces packed into tiers out front.

In 1804–5, the Speech Day space at the dancing school in its normal configuration would of course have been largely foreign territory to the hobbled Byron.[6] But the serendipitous opportunity fell in his way to compete on a court otherwise forbidden him, before parents, peers, peerage, and (other) prestigious alumni returned to Harrow for the occasion. Because of its principal identity, the location gave Byron symbolic entry into a communal space where forensic elegance legitimately substituted for the graceful athleticism of the dance in a respected, honorable competition. Speech Day literally opened another Harrow door for Byron into that rivalry foundational to schoolboy reputation, and onto another social arena where gentlemen shone. Almost as equalizing as "Ducker" the school pond, the dancing school, reinvented for Speech Day, forgave Byron's physical liability, nearly leveled the playing field. That he may have understood it in such terms, consciously or not, is suggested by his apparent association of Augusta's possible Speech Day visit with Delawarr's dancing fortunes. His own pride in the *"Harrow orations"*—an inflating epithet—subordinates any to which Byron imagines Delawarr might feel entitled for squiring the princess, and very nearly offers himself as an object of his friend's envy.[7]

The degree of Byron's preoccupation with his approaching opportunity may be measured in the language of other letters. A postscript to Hanson complains of dull Southwell and "the eloquence of a *near relation* of mine" (*BLJ* 1:64; 20 April 1805), a lightly ironic ennobling of Mrs. Byron's tirades that points to one source of his own gifts for passionate expression. Three days later, he reported to Augusta an imprudent slight of Southwell—"*sweet town*" that, for all he cared, might be "swallowed up by an Earthquake, provided my *Eloquent mother* was not in it." His "unlucky sentence" prompted from Mrs. Byron "an Oration in the *ancient style,* which I have often so *pathetically* described to you, unequaled by any thing of *modern* or *antique* date; nay the Phillippics against Ld. Melville were nothing to it" (*BLJ* 1:65–66; 23 April 1805). Byron's fantasy of a tiresome Southwell vanishing down the throat of fissured earth, in the context of complaints about a clamorous mother whom he nevertheless wishes spared the catastrophe, is surely suggestive, particularly when the author's own tongue, pricked by his "evil

Genius," produced the maternal eruption. The stylistic classification of Mrs. Byron's harangue boasts the schoolboy's rhetorical training, as does the technical descriptive "Phillippics," although whether of a Ciceronian or Demonsthenean stamp would be a distinction lost upon Augusta and probably of no consequence to the boy content to show off his linguistic range: what Mrs. Byron's Philippics amount to is perfectly clear from the context. Byron would have known from the *Morning Chronicle* and other journalistic reports about Henry Dundas, Viscount Melville's concurrent trial in the House of Commons for the mishandling of naval accounts (*BLJ* 1:66n); but the comparison of himself as his mother's verbal victim to the assailed Lord Melville not only, as Byron quickly points out, confers upon himself the status of "a most *treasonable Culprit*" (*BLJ* 1:66)—a role he fancies; more subtly it figuratively positions him *in* Parliament, already situated to hear and deliver speeches, where neither "*ancient style*" orations nor modern philippics need be silently endured, as is the case at Burgage Manor against Mrs. Byron's invective. Probably, Byron's exposure to newspaper stories of the parliamentary trial helped to shape his resolve, announced in the next letter to Augusta, to visit "Both Houses" (*BLJ* 1:67) for firsthand experience of the debates. Speechmaking and its power are in any event embedded in Byron's consciousness during the spring of 1805, with his own "declamation" scheduled for 6 June.

But his association of oratory with Mrs. Byron's vilification also suggests that Byron's interest in public address partially originates in a wish to retaliate against his mother's unremitting, unanswerable diatribes; in some sense, she models philippic discourse, teaches him by example, but in repressing response drives him to discover other channels for talking back (including, of course, eventually, his satiric verse lampooning her). His Harrow experiments in recitation imitate maternal jeremiad but relocate the battle site to his advantage in eliding her. Augusta, however, should be present to witness proof, as it were, of the allegations Byron has for months lodged against his mother in confidential correspondence: he wants validation of his charges and vindication of himself. His Harrow declamation, in other words, will reflect the imprint of maternal invective, avenge it through the surrogate figure Augusta, and ratify for her the justice of Byron's running litany of accusations against his mother. That this is a family affair is plain from the way Byron's thinking unfolds as the letter continues:

> I have never been so *scurrilously* and *violently* abused by any person, as by that woman, whom I think, I am to call mother, by that being who gave me birth, to whom I ought to look up with veneration and respect, but whom I cannot love or admire. Within one little hour, I have not only [heard] myself, but have heard my *whole family* by the fathers side, *stigmatized* in terms that the *blackest malevolence* would [perhaps] shrink from, and that too in words [you] would be shocked to hear. Such, Augusta, such is my mother; *my mother.* I disclaim her from this time, and although I cannot help treating her with respect, I cannot reverence as I ought to do, that parent who by her outrageous conduct forfeits all title to filial affection. (*BLJ* 1:66)

The half sister's surrogate role then becomes almost explicit:

> To you Augusta, I must look up, as my nearest relation, to you I must confide what I cannot mention to others, and I am sure you will pity me, but I entreat you to keep this a secret, nor expose that unhappy failing of this woman, which I must bear with patience. I would be very sorry to have it discovered, as I have only one week more, for the present. (*BLJ* 1:66)

We have heard something very like this before, of course, directed to the same audience out of similar circumstances. Here again the stately, impassioned cadences and rising crescendo of the first half of this passage are oratorical and performative, the characterization of Mrs. Byron's discourse melodramatic, the strategic repetitions and the disclaimer of the mother downright theatrical, although not for all that necessarily inaccurate or insincere. The quotation represents the boy rehearsing for Augusta the retaliatory dynamics to be more subtly played out on Speech Day. Mrs. Byron attacks the boy and his paternity; the boy strikes back with dignified repudiation; the boy replaces the mother with a trustworthy sister meriting "reverence" ("I must look up"), and confides to her the mother's disgrace, in effect substituting Mrs. Byron for the father she has so acidly "*stigmatized.*" Byron's insistence upon secrecy does appear designed to conceal the dirty little scandal of his mother's pathology and instability, but one can scarcely help wondering whether it is not as severe as all his accounts maintain. Is his intent wholly or principally to protect the remaining shards of family honor? Or does he dread a leak from Augusta that would effect intensification of his misery? Byron poses here as the silent, loyal, long-suffering scion of a noble line (while whimpering away in Augusta's ear). But if he is unwilling to have Mrs. Byron's "failing discovered" *because* he has "only one week more" at home with her, his motives for pleading confidentiality are less high-minded than we might have supposed them. In any event, the effort proceeds to thicken the sibling conspiracy in Byron's closing assurances that Augusta may write "with the greatest safety" to him at Burgage, "as she [Mrs. Byron] would not open any of my letters, even from you"—a confidence calling into question the subjugated status he has professed to suffer at home.

Buoyed by the prospect of relief from "those *agreeable amusements*" at Mrs. Byron's Burgage Manor, Byron writes merrily to Augusta on 25 April, declining to respond in kind to the "benediction" of his "Angelic" sister and her friend, since his "*profane blessing* would but expedite your road to Purgatory . . . the *unhallowed adjurations* of a mere mortal" being "of no effect" (*BLJ* 1:67). This is of course Byron playing the diabolic role out of which he would eventually make so much literary capital, and it humorously exploits his incipient, melancholy sense of the ancestral and inherited doom from which Augusta has luckily escaped. But his language appears also to reflect shades of the villainous character he will personify on 6 June at Harrow, whose dark plot of revenge gives Edward Young's play its title, and whose lines Byron had already begun to rehearse. That expectation, together with Augusta's remark upon a Windsor Castle spectacle, prompts Byron's report of having seen, with only moderate pleasure, "this young Roscius[8] several times at the hazard of my life from the *affectionate squeezes* of the surrounding crowd" (*BLJ* 1:67); indeed, his demonstrative adjective certainly condescends and nearly sneers. On the other hand, the mild irony of the italicized phrase yields in interest to its subtle suggestion of affection displaced from the boy on the stage to the boy in the crowd—its situation of Byron as rival to the performer he scuffles to see. And as we have observed, he repeats the risk at least twice, perhaps more.

It is difficult not to suspect dissemblance in Byron's critique, especially in light of a later appraisal. Writing to Lord Holland on 10 September 1812, Byron deplores the present shape, voice, and acting style of the aging Roscius (at all of twenty-one years), but then adds: "When I last saw him, I was in raptures with his performance, but then I was sixteen—an age to which all London then condescended to subside—after all much better judges have admired & may again" (*BLJ* 2:192). Possibly

Byron misremembered his earlier reaction; possibly he forgot that he had misrepresented it. But a more secure, more mature 1812 Byron had already largely satisfied his need assertively, defiantly to establish an identity by differentiation. The sixteen-year-old, "*squeezed*" by more than the literal crush at the Theatres Royal, may have challenged the party line on Young Roscius for psychological as much as for aesthetic reasons. To cut against the grain, particularly if Master Betty excited any sense of competition, envy, jealousy, hero-worship, or desire in Byron, as I think likely, would have been consistent with and expressive of his generally mutinous temper at the time. And yet it is curious that he saw the "Infant Phenomenon" at least thrice before mentioning him to Augusta, insofar as we can surmise from surviving correspondence.

But when, and in what roles? Master Betty opened in London on Saturday, 1 December 1804 at Covent Garden as Selim in the old tragedy *Barbarossa* by the Reverend Doctor John Brown, modeled after Voltaire's *Merope;* that Garrick had memorably performed the role probably influenced the managerial choice of it for Betty's debut.[9] The terms of a compromise worked out between the rival theaters required Betty to move over to Drury Lane on 10 December, where he remained through the 18th, returning to Covent Garden for seven performances beginning on 28 January 1805, then shuttling back to Drury Lane on 13 February for a long run of twenty performances followed by one at the Garden, four more at Drury Lane, another at the Garden and one at Drury, then four at the Garden and one at Drury before closing his season with eleven at the Garden. Byron relocated to the Hansons' in London for the Christmas holiday four days after Master Betty opened at Covent Garden—i.e., on Wednesday, 5 December 1804—intent on taking maximum advantage of his freedom in whatever entertainment the city afforded. But he could scarcely not have already known, from Harrow or virtually anywhere else in the kingdom, of the Betty phenomenon, and might have seen the boy perform even before arriving at the Hansons', where he remained until "early in February," according to Marchand's calculation (1:93).

On 3 April, Byron returned to London and the Hansons' at the beginning of another school holiday and stayed "as long as he dared," says Marchand (1:94), before undertaking the obligatory and overdue visit to his mother in Southwell, from where he wrote to Augusta on 25 April of having seen Young Roscius. Back in London for 1–7 May, Byron would have heard much of the prodigy and might have seen him again. Even if he did not return to London for theater after resuming Harrow residence in February and May, Byron had ample opportunity to see Master Betty in both of the boy's featured roles of the season—Norval in John Home's *Douglas* (his signature role, with fourteen performances),[10] and Selim in *Barbarossa* (seven performances)—and, depending upon when "early in February" Byron returned to Harrow, in at least two and possibly as many as five of Betty's other parts: Frederick in Mrs. Elizabeth Inchbald's *Lovers' Vows* (from August Kotzebue) (six performances on the season); Octavian in John Coleman's *The Mountaineers* (two performances); Romeo (three performances); and Tancred in James Thomson's *Tancred and Sigismunda* (three performances). In addition to *Douglas* and *Tancred and Sigismunda,* Master Betty also played the king in *Richard III* during Byron's May sojourn in London, after he had mentioned the Infant Phenomenon to Augusta; nor can we absolutely rule out the possibility that Byron saw Betty's *Hamlet,* performed five times at Drury Lane during Byron's March schooltime. But statistical, geographical, and psychological factors favor *Barbarossa* and *Douglas,* with *Lovers' Vows* a strong third, as the plays in which Byron saw Master Betty act, in one of them perhaps more than once (my guess: *Douglas*).[11]

His reference to "Young Roscius" in the letter of 25 April may then reply to a query from Augusta (its context is responsive) or anticipate seeing Master Betty again, or reflect preoccupation with his own upcoming performance if, as I have speculated, it is in part influenced by the young actor's triumphs. Or all of these hypotheses may be true and relevant. Revealingly, I think, the allusion to "Roscius" leads in the letter directly to Byron's explanation of his extension into truancy of his London stay: "I should not continue it so long [until the 10th], as we meet [i.e., reconvene] on the 8th at Harrow, But, I remain on purpose to hear our *Sapient* and *noble Legislators* of Both Houses debate on the Catholic Question, as I have no doubt there will be many *nonsensical,* and some *Clever* things said on the occasion" (*BLJ* 1:67). The ruse is only partial: Byron does anticipate entertainment by Parliament—after all, schoolboys no less than their elders *want* political speeches seasoned with clever and nonsensical utterance—but he is probably also still on the hunt for serviceable oratorical tips, and in search of any close-up experience of legislative process, for, as Marchand reminds us, he already contemplated a parliamentary career.

What he heard on 10 May (Marchand says that he "apparently attended the session" [*BLJ* 1:67n]) was a motion in the House of Lords to consider remedial action on behalf of the Catholics, a disenfranchised minority, with whom Byron, in his own marginalization on various grounds, would have had some sympathy; indeed, he later spoke on their behalf in Lords (21 April 1812). It must have been gratifying and affirming for him to observe in that historic chamber the kind of defense of the oppressed that he himself sometimes practiced in the Harrow schoolyard. That the instruments of such championship were linguistic, not physical, would have reassured and encouraged the young author who was nevertheless no slouch at fisticuffs, particularly as he imagined himself, while watching the debate, speaking to Harrow crowds and, soon enough, from the benches. At the moment, however, such fantasies cannot hold their shape under the verbal barrage of "my *wise* and *Good* mother, (who is at this minute thundering against Somebody or other below in the Dining Room)"—a mother whose threatened "malediction" prevented her son's attendance upon Lord Carlisle because of that guardian's alleged—and for Byron suspect—ill-treatment of her. The letter ends, then, by returning to the "*agreeable amusements*" of Mrs. Byron with which it opened, although they are now made wicked in the mouth of a figure not unlike the stage villain whose cloak Byron is about to assume.

IT IS IMPORTANT TO INQUIRE whether the plays themselves, as well as or more forcefully than Master Betty's performances in them, may have drawn Byron back to the theaters "several times." Two styled themselves "tragedies," *Lovers' Vows* calls itself "a play," and all three ring melodramatic changes on the themes of betrayal and revenge. *Barbarossa* and *Douglas* are in some degree mistitled, for each features less the eponymous "hero" than the strong if baffled relationship between a mother and her son, as, indeed, does Mrs. Inchbald's adaptation, "Roscius" playing the son in all three dramas. Barbarossa, having murdered the king of Algiers, presses his unwelcome suit on the widowed Queen Zaphira, and "With ceaseless hate her exil'd son pursues, / The virtuous youth" (act 1; text lines are not numbered). The son Selim's responsibility, as he understands it, is to protect his beloved mother from the beastly lust of this usurper, avenge the regicide, and restore royal and familial honor. But the first of these aims seems paramount, in part because of the stage time given Zaphira, in part because of her ferocious rhetoric against Barbarossa, as bitterly disdainful as anything that Byron would have heard at home. Selim's Hamletian mission is to guard his mother from the intruder who also pursues him. The parallel with Byron's domestic situation is loose, but Lord Grey does presently occupy Newstead as interloper, from where he has launched offensives, in Byron's view, against both the heir and the widowed mother. Barbarossa has in fact "courted" Selim "in vain" "to meet my kindness" since "the down / Cover'd his manly cheek"—that is, since Selim turned thirteen, seven years earlier.

The match here with Master Betty's present age might have challenged dramatic illusion for contemporaneous audiences, and the language would certainly alert modern spectators to predatory idiom. But Byron, I believe, was already experientially sensitized to it. And in light of his (presumed or attempted) victimization by Grey, he could scarcely have heard such phrases and remained deaf to the sexual innuendos probably not a part of the Reverend Doctor Brown's conscious imaginative conception. Those lines, along with the threat to the solidarity of the mother-son alliance by the betraying and rapacious agent, must have brought vividly before a worried Byron, as though through a palimpsest, the triangulation in which he felt caught and abused. Observation of satisfactory resolution on the stage might have been psychically worth the physical risk of repeated attendance at a mobbed theater. Additionally, Barbarossa's daughter Irene focuses a subplot of greater psychological complexity than the principal one, for she is trapped between conflicting loyalties, to her own father the usurper, and to Selim's surviving parent, whom he, upon rescuing her from kidnappers, has commissioned her, as she loves him, to protect. In short, Irene is torn between the present and the desired parent (-in-law), the bad and the good authority figures, not unlike (with gender reversal) Byron's conflict between the acceptable Drury and the oppressive mother (or between the two opposing sides of his mother's character).

MRS. ELIZABETH INCHBALD'S 1798 *Lovers' Vows,* adapted from *Child of Love* by August Kotzebue (1791) and familiar to modern readers through Jane Austen's sport with it in *Mansfield Park,* refined somewhat for English taste the "Jacobinical feelings" that Robert Southey found in all of Kotzebue's dramas, a recurring attack "on some old prejudice or old principle."[12] Mrs. Inchbald, too, if more politely, thought the German original "discordant with the English stage," particularly because of the "indelicately blunt" representation of Amelia's love for her tutor/chaplain. But Mrs. Inchbald's authorial integrity trumps her respect for

British dramatic propriety, for although tamer, milder than its original, *Lovers' Vows* is by no means purged of Jacobinical tendencies. And its timely subversive politics would have caught Byron's imagination especially because they are played out in domestic situations and they debate ideologies over which he was himself conflicted.

Lovers' Vows, in a word, pits birth and fortune against head and heart. Baron Wildenhaim, himself delivered, by an ambitious mother whom he feared, out of a liaison with the commoner Agatha into unhappy marriage with a proud, imperious woman (now recently dead), wishes to match the fruit of that union, Amelia, with the wealthy, fatuous Count Cassel, although never against her will. Having long ago (with apparently token resistance) abandoned Agatha, he knows nothing, despite the commissioned searches of Anhalt, of his son by her or of her whereabouts, although these two coincidentally and by separate routes joyously reunite nearby, Frederick from military service, Agatha outcast and impoverished. As these principals and their histories become known to each other, the plot thickens with the younger set, empowered by a gracious but forceful, strong-minded, sure-handed Amelia, who successfully asserts individual will against convention, propriety, and expectation. Defying her (albeit amenable) father the Baron, Amelia engineers her own engagement to the class-conscious tutor-chaplain Anhalt (from the German for "basis" or "support"; vb: *anhalten* = to stop, draw up; but also to persevere, persist), himself torn between love for her and loyalty to his employer. Frederick, become a voluntary beggar on his mother's behalf, attacks the Baron for the meagerness of a contribution unworthy of his means, for which the young man, still unknown to the Baron, is imprisoned in his father's tower. Amelia continues her campaign against "old fashioned things": partially through her mediation, her half brother Frederick is granted an interview with his captor, wherein, seconded by Anhalt, he reveals his identity and dictates the act and terms of the Baron's restitution to Agatha; Anhalt elicits by virtual interrogation what amounts to a confession of the Baron's wrongs against his early lover; and the Baron, after some squirming casuistry, happily agrees to wed Agatha at a public ceremony—a marriage radically beneath his station, as will be Amelia's to Anhalt. That women control the action in this play, directly by rebellious or unorthodox or extreme praxis, or by subtle suggestion or example, is manifest—from Frederick's mother's and Amelia's orchestrations of marriages, to Agatha's absentee creative management of her son's conduct. The subversiveness of that action would certainly have appealed to the Harrow revolutionist, although the object of it—a baronage—and the gender of its principal author might have unsettled him, but probably not much, as he was himself a youngster with singular romantic interests. In its challenge to authority, in any case, and its promotion of individual will over custom and established values, *Lovers' Vows* would have found sympathetic hearing in the malcontented Byron. (Still, it must be said that he defended the status quo at Harrow and the prospect of a Drury dynasty.)

But another dimension of the play may have appealed even more strongly if subtly to him. Absent from the neatly structured climax I sketch above is Frederick, a fifth wheel among the lovers but a star of the play's final tableau and awarded its last lines. *Lovers' Vows* opens with a quadruple rejection, as the destitute Agatha's repudiation by her landlord replays the abandonment of her seducer twenty years earlier, and her autobiographical narrative to her furloughed son of that union reports the consequential spurning by her own and her lovers' parents. Rejoined after his five military years, Frederick and Agatha model a self-sacrificing loyalty (even if hers seems faintly, and of course unconsciously, manipulative) notably absent from other relationships in this drama, excepting only the lowly cottagers who shelter her (as welcome opportunity, not for fees).

If forsworn oaths and broken promises give the play its sanitized English title (and circumspectly avert focus from the bastard Frederick), its prominent secondary subject is the search for a family by the impecunious heir of a baron, and by the sire who abandoned him and his mother in fear of his own parent and her respect for social stratification: i.e., Frederick's quest for a biological and the Baron's for a moral legitimacy, in the parallel courses of which the son gains a father and a half sister, the father a son and a wife, the jilted woman a husband and a (step)daughter, and the daughter a (step)mother, half brother, and bridegroom. Of this last figure's abandonment, Amelia fearfully dreams before the Baron, under her coaching, surrenders plans to match her with the well-born, well-heeled, but (it turns out) morally bankrupt Count, whom the tutor Anhalt has been instructed, by a Baron blind to opportunity, to "make . . . something like yourself" and thus a suitable mate and son(-in-law).

The tutorial motif is pronounced in a drama whose ultimate moral orthodoxy and even vapidity, despite the originating sexual indiscretion, might be supposed to have bored Byron, and whose inane humor would have sickened him. (He may nevertheless have called upon the butler Verdun's eagerness to rhyme [horribly] on any and all occasions when pillorying Southey for like zeal in *The Vision of Judgment*.) Redeeming it from such fate, however, are the *social unorthodoxy* which plot and character develop; the high incidence of dispossession, particularly by a maternally intimidated scion; and his victims' searches for certification, social legitimacy, and acceptance despite an obvious and disabling embarrassment of fortune—circumstances, even without minimal reconfiguration, recognizable as Byron's own. His stewardship of less privileged boys at Harrow may have seen itself reflected in Mrs. Inchbald's sympathy for the have-nots—another subversive motif—particularly in Frederick's cheeky refusal of less than sufficient philanthropy, a lordly gesture egregiously insulting to the proudly charitable Baron. Moreover, the sacrifice of true love on the altar of rank and fortune would have fueled the brooding of the sentimental boy recovering from amorous disappointment; and Mrs. Inchbald's mild flirtation with incest, as heretofore separated half siblings are positioned to fall in love before learning of kinship, could have peculiarly intrigued a half brother strengthening ties to his newly known sister.

But the apparently virtual inversion, in the Frederick-Agatha relationship, of Byron's affective transactions with his mother would have rendered the play memorable to him, given the centrality and force of its representation. No child in so vexed a maternal relationship as Byron's could have witnessed without pangs (and perhaps disbelief) the mutually doting, compassionate, sacrificing (Byron might have said "treacly"), at times almost spousal attentiveness of Agatha and Frederick; and that Agatha is given into an overdue marriage with the reformed aristocrat on terms stipulated by the still loyal son vowing never to part from her, would not have been lost upon a Byron troubled by his mother's courtship of a reprobate occupying his own baron's castle.[13] And yet a fundamental reason for Byron's probable interest in the Agatha-Frederick relationship is not so much its real difference from as its similarity to the association he usually and superficially keeps up with Mrs. Byron, although out of obligation not unselfish love, and enabled by his vetting of complaints about it to trusted confidants Augusta and Hanson. Would anyone at Southwell not privy to Byron's epistolary opinions of his mother suppose him other than a reasonably dutiful son, honoring the proprieties with her, dutifully at home or disposed at her will on school holidays? Frederick and Agatha sincerely perform the act that Byron and his mother sham. Mrs. Inchbald's characters point out, to the self-interested young spectator, Byron's hypocrisy at the same time that her conclusion realizes a familial completeness unknown to him except, perhaps, as approximated at the Drurys' and the Pigots' houses.

Kotzebue and Inchbald construct the concluding tableau of the play with fuller, more detailed stage directions than appear elsewhere in it. Here they are, from the Baron's uneasy declaration of readiness to see Agatha after their long separation:

> [*He looks steadfastly at the door* (of her expected entrance)— ANHALT *leads in* AGATHA—THE BARON *runs and clasps her in his arms—Supported by him, she sinks on a chair which* AMELIA *places in the middle of the stage*—THE BARON *kneels by her side, holding her hand.*]
>
> THE BARON: Agatha, Agatha; do you know this voice?
>
> AGATHA: Wildenhaim.
>
> THE BARON: Can you forgive me?
>
> AGATHA: I forgive you. [*embracing him*]
>
> FREDERICK [*as he enters*]: I hear the voice of my mother! —Ha! mother! father!
>
> [FREDERICK *throws himself on his knees by the other side of his mother—She clasps him in her arms.*—AMELIA *is placed on the side of her father attentively viewing* AGATHA—ANHALT *stands on the side of* FREDERICK *with his hand gratefully raised to Heaven.*] *The curtain slowly drops.*

Feeble as she is, Agatha commands center stage, inverting her entrance in act I as the rejected tenant of the heartless landlord. There, he led her on; here, assisted by the lord of the estate, she accepts the seat of honor positioned by her stepdaughter and first lady of the new order. Flanking her are the two beloved men, son and spouse-to-be, in positions and postures suggesting social equivalence as well as supplication, reverence, and love. Embracing both, she privileges neither; or, if she continues to hold Frederick while the curtain descends, she repays the Baron's abandonment in kind, despite her just granted forgiveness of him, with a slight, a marginalization that favors his "rival." For Agatha to turn from the Baron's embrace into Frederick's arms and remain there would effectively isolate the Baron in the tableau, and skew its moral symmetry. But in any case Agatha will have had to release herself from the Baron's hand and embrace to "clasp [Frederick] in her arms" (my emphasis). Standing, Amelia and Anhalt also subordinate the Baron and Frederick, and thus signal their political and social empowerment, their triumph in the conflict between old principle and new, in the gentle revolution of values and courtesies at the Wildenhaim castle.

Precisely who intently views Agatha is grammatically uncertain: if "father," the Baron, presumably in rapturous devotion. But if Amelia? More interestingly, Amelia's intent gaze upon Agatha would remind us again of that second concern of the play, as do Frederick's final lines: she too acknowledges a parent and proves herself a deserving sibling for the attentive Frederick, as well as recalling for us the attention denied him by the faithless Baron. Familial—extended familial—relationships restored and launched, Anhalt as chaplain (and betrothed) gestures "gratefully" (however that may be done!) to a "Heaven" presumably as attentive as Amelia and the Baron to the human family of its creation. Again, similarities to Byron's experiences are inexact but suggestive of his more than passing and even personal interest in *Lovers' Vows:* like the other plays he may have seen Master Betty perform, it touches on issues close to the bone for him—abandonment, betrayal, maternal dominion and pressure, rebellion, individual expression, lost love, and so on. But it also, and more engagingly, interrogates the role, position, and authority of aristocracy in a rapidly evolving ideology contesting the sacredness of "old principle" and "old prejudice," as Southey said. If the play fed Byron's rebellious, democratic instincts, it must also have probed his aristocratic pride.[14]

The epilogue of John Home's *Douglas* adjures witty closure lest it dissipate the "celestial melancholy" in which the drama has enveloped us—a typically Byronic emotion, one might say, anticipating by a half century the poet who gave it Regency fashion (after, of course, its exploitation by the graveyard poets). In fact, one commentator *did* say it: "Lady Randolph," writes Robertson Davies, "is almost Byronic in the sense she gives of an introverted nature feeding upon itself: she contains . . . much of her own contrary destiny" and is, like her creator, "troubled by intimations of mingled and inadmissible" feelings. The play, he goes on, dabbles "with unexpressed, dangerous emotions"—the hinted attractions of incest among them; it inspires "dark fascination" and foregrounds "not pity, but its seductive bastard, self-pity" in "the twilight world of the psyche."¹⁵ The impact of this play upon gothic drama and fiction, and upon Byron's peculiar reformulation of "heroic" melancholy, is for others to map. I want to suggest additional and immediate reasons why the seventeen-year-old Byron may have found the drama riveting and memorable, particularly with "Roscius" as star, and perhaps deserving of a second look.¹⁶

For one thing, it opens with a valedictory, and subsequently puts into Lady Randolph's mouth a recollected farewell that the young spectator hearing it would make famous: "When we two parted. . . ." Now, Byron's practice of intimacy was always conditioned by the accessibility of escape; by the same token, the prospect of loss always increased for him the value of the threatened intimate (including, of course, his spouse). His growing reluctance to leave Harrow as his departure date approached, his early return visits, and his nostalgic longings, once away, for its idealized companionships, pleasures, and prestige, are consistent with the associational dynamics of his other relationships—with lovers, poems, and audiences. This psychic predisposition is presently germane because a number of public schools, and eventually Harrow, included *plays* in institutional rituals of closure—sometimes at Christmas, inaugurating the holiday, more often as a component of "school leaving" ceremonies in June, at the onset of the long vacation, either together with or in place of speech programs. Departure itself, in other words, encourages its own theatricalization, invites and accommodates texts and other structures that exploit its own inherent drama.

As a year-ending event, Speech Day draws upon dramatic capital already invested in a recognized closural procedure dividing student from friend, tutor, and site. That such occasions were always already cathected for Byron ensured his sensitivity and attraction to Speech Day, even his willingness to explore what we may now see as the therapeutic opportunities it afforded him. Whatever else it may do, Speech Day grants Byron the chance to be theatrically but surreptitiously valedictory, to withdraw, under cover, from those very intimacies which had begun to make Harrow dear (and therefore threatening) to him, but without risk of hurt to others or himself. Sanctioned by the sponsoring institution, the separation that Speech Day initiates scars nobody with guilt or irresponsibility. But powerful, theatricalized Speech Day oratory denies the division it helps to effect both by disguising itself and by empowering the mnemonic negation of that division: orator speaks and audience hears something else than a farewell, and both carry away impressions of each other in tight, dramatic if static relationship. As a trope the Speech Day connection between the boy and his audience figures a habitual affiliation in Byron—an act, often in verse, frequently staged, that simultaneously unites and disjoins in exquisite tension.

Within months of leaving the Harrow site he has at last come to love (precisely because he must leave it, in an apt forecast, then, of subsequent associational rhythms in his life and art), Byron's mood and mode are valedictory. Indeed, three of the six poems that McGann's table of contents assigns to the 1804–5 years treat separation, all of them on Mary Ann Chaworth (the others are an epigram, a quatrain, and a translation); "[Then Peace to thy Spirit]," conjecturally dated 1803, laments in a sonnetlike structure of couplets the death of "my earliest Friend," thought to be "a boy of Lord Byron's own age, son of one of the tenants at Newstead" (from the 1832 edition, quoted in *CPW* 1:365); and two of three additional works from 1802–3—"On the Death of a Young Lady, cousin to the Author and Very Dear to Him" (Margaret Parker) and "To D[elawarr]"—are poems of rupture (*CPW* 1:124–26). The bulk of his poems on leaving the school—nearly all of the seventeen he wrote about Harrow (excluding translations, imitations, paraphrases, and such later Harrovian allusions as the complaint against Horace of *Childe Harold* 2)—come after the fact; but that so many do come suggests an acute attentiveness to the stress of departure or pressures from it, during the process or retrospectively: in some sense Byron's poetic career launched itself on a dissociative tide.

But if reluctant to leave Harrow and friends, Byron was impatient to separate from a harassing mother. Lady Randolph's opening words in *Douglas* position her ambiguously within "The court of the castle surrounded with woods," bidding adieu to the "wilds, whose melancholy gloom / Accords with my soul's sadness . . . Farewell a while." This retiring from a sympathetic turf reluctantly and temporarily, looking backward, is the attitude of Byron's school-leaving and a notably frequent posture of characters in his verse, seminal in *Childe Harold's Pilgrimage, Beppo,* and *Don Juan.*[17]

Furthermore, Lady Randolph identifies "an ancient feud / [,] Hereditary evil" as "the source / Of my misfortunes" (act 1; lines unnumbered): enmity had long divided her house and Douglas's, but her brother's unknowing rescue of Douglas's son knit the two men in eternal friendship and paved the way to her own secret union with the son of her father's foe, after which that parent forced her oath never to wed "one of Douglas's name." One of Mary Ann Chaworth's attractions for Byron was of course her blood relationship to the man fatally wounded in a duel with the boy's great uncle, the "Wicked Lord Byron." When first meeting her in 1798, Byron responded to John Hanson's tease that he had better marry so "pretty a young lady": "What—the *Capulets and Montagues* intermarry?" (Marchand 1:50). The onset of adolescence changed his mind, if indeed he was serious in such shock, and the glamour and daring of amorous connection with the historically antipathetic family, along with Mary Ann's beauty and charm, drove him back to Annesley Hall with compulsive regularity. Byron could scarcely have heard Lady Randolph's description of ancestral hostility to progenic reconciliation without relating it to his own immediate and unhappy romantic past.

Nor is that all. Lady Randolph, like Zaphira, and like Mrs. Byron in her son's view, is also threatened by a predatory rascal, one Glenalvon,[18] whose superficial resemblance to Iago only points to his clichéd villainy: he plots to kill Lord Randolph for wife and property—domains, Lady Randolph laments, that should have given her son "a Baron's title and a Baron's power" (act 1). The title is Byron's, all right, by windfall not unlike the discovery of jewels that enable the stepfather of young Douglas to migrate north and flourish for a time; but the power was problematic, given the economic prodigality of his ancestors. In a ubiquitously exasperating sense Byron, too, was a materially deprived baron, he and his property literally stripped, upon his inheriting them, of many accoutrements of the baronage.

Among the "unexpressed, dangerous emotions" that Davies finds suppressed in *Douglas* but does not himself name, incest is the most obvious, for certainly before and possibly after discovery that "Norval" is really her son Douglas, Lady Randolph views the young man with a more than maternal interest, in fact naming him "my knight" (act 1) to guard the life of her husband. Bent on securing her for himself, Glenalvon is jealous of Lady Randolph's love of Norval. In the fantasy that her dead son might have resembled Norval, Lady Randolph confesses, "A spark of fancy fell" on her melancholy heart, "and kindled up a fondness / For this young stranger" (act 2). Contemporaneous press notices left room for, if falling just short of encouraging, vicious construals of insinuations under layered sentiment: here is the *Courier's* ripe appreciation of two scenes:

> The scene between him [Norval] and his mother, where he is made acquainted with his birth, was one of the most affecting pieces of stage representation ever witnessed. He afterwards ran to her embrace, and buried his head in her bosom with such an effusion of tenderness as deeply to affect every heart that had ever received pleasure from maternal engagement.... But the dying scene exhibited powers even beyond what our most sanguine admiration could prompt us to expect.... He then falls repeating the words "My Mother? O my mother!" with his expiring breath, and in a tone that touched the inmost fibre of every heart, and drew down torrents of tears from the eyes of every parent and every child. (5 December 1804)[19]

By citing these references I do not suggest that Byron is already plotting the seduction of his half sister or finds in them encouragement to do so. But as others have pointed out, all of Byron's early (female) loves belonged to his extended family. More important, in Lady Randolph's concentrated focus upon her son, Byron might have seen a cleansed, transformed, idealized version of the maternal possessiveness which both flattered and annoyed him, and which in the ferocity it inspired on both sides almost certainly included a sexual constituent. At the same time, however, it is not insignificant that Byron's epistolary relations with his half sister began and intensified during a maternally vexed adolescence, or that they developed in almost inverse proportion to the deterioration of his relations with Mrs. Byron.[20]

It is also conceivable that Byron found intriguing a description of Norval offered by Glenalvon, especially with the femininity of Master Betty in view to prove it. Not knowing Norval's parentage, Glenalvon attributes to him "that alluring look, / 'Twixt man and woman, which I have observ'd / To charm the nicer and fantastic dames, / Who are, like Lady Randolph, full of virtue" (act 2). He proposes to excite Lord Randolph's jealousy by pointing to the wife's admiration of Norval, although that Glenalvon would himself notice and so characterize the "alluring look" is surely an equally interesting self-disclosure. To be sure, the lines may mean that Norval's "alluring look" has passed between himself and Lady Randolph, a glance of typical male flirtation. But the grammar favors description of an androgynous creature who charms but does not really threaten the virtue of proper ladies. That is, Norval by his countenance occupies some middle space between definitive masculinity and femininity, and therefore cannot subvert Glenalvon's own designs on Lady Randolph but may be used to advance them. The description, in short, tends to neuter Norval, and to an interested ear like Byron's might associate him with those pubescent and early adolescent nonthreatening friends at Harrow to whose "alluring looks" Byron was not immune. The possibility of such interpretation in any event enhances the forbidden attraction of a passage in which the potential for incest is already implicit.

In an act 4 interview between Glenalvon and the still disguised (as Norval) Douglas, the villain advises circumspect demeanor among the troops, who may take amiss his preferment. Norval accepts such counsel but deeply resents the accompanying insult to his "birth obscure," and, genuinely baffled, asks, "Why slur my power / With such contemptuous terms?" The reply forwards Glenalvon's plot to engage Norval in a quarrel, which he promptly fuels with a snobbish sneer at the feebleness of "shepherd's scorn." Aroused by this line of attack, Glenalvon pursues it, calling Norval "a peasant's son, a wand'ring beggar-boy, / At best no more." "Thou'rt all a lie," he concludes, "and false as hell / Is the vainglorious tale" of himself that he has related to Lord Randolph (act 4). Calling the aristocratic scion a peasant's son and a beggar boy is near enough to naming him "blackguard" for Byron, wounded by a similar insult, to have made the connection instantly to his own provoking past with Mark Drury, who, affronting his rank and ridiculing his fortune, in effect accused him of baronial counterfeit. Then, too, Byron's bewilderment over Mark's impudence, loosely replicative of Norval's here, increased its vexatiousness. And the literal age of the boy on the stage suffering these indignities would have fostered any process of Byron's identification invited by the recited lines.

THESE, THEN, are my conjectural explanations for Byron's apparent interest in the London stage while anticipating his second Speech Day performance at Harrow. But before turning to the text he elected to recite on that day and speculating on its possible meanings for him, I should first acknowledge the possibility that an inspiration for his choice of Zanga's speech may be more distantly rooted, in the 3 June 1802 Harrow Speech Day recitation of Henry Hinxman (Speech Bill, Harrow Archives). It must be said, however, that unlike the Virgil colloquy and most other Speech Day offerings during Byron's Harrow years, Young's character appears very rarely, indeed, only once in existing school records before Byron's performance of it. I suspect that if Hinxman gave Byron the idea, Young and the London stage provided the incentive, for the play provides peculiarly apt and touching reasons for Byron's attraction to it.

Besides, he appears to have known the history of the role he chose. He did in any event know it a year later, when writing "On a Distant View of the Village and School, of Harrow, on the Hill":

> I once more view the room, with spectators surrounded,
>   Where, as Zanga, I trod on Alonzo o'erthrown;
> While, to swell my young pride, such applauses resounded,
>   I fancied that Mossop himself was outshone.

Byron's note identifies "Mossop, a contemporary of Garrick, known for his performance of Zanga, in Young's tragedy of the Revenge" (*CPW* 1:379). Indeed, after an early struggle, Henry Mossop (1729?–74) scored his breakthrough dramatic success, at twenty, in 1749, as Zanga. Conceivably, of course, Byron had learned about Mossop from Cambridge pals; but it seems to me more probable that prior knowledge of the actor's celebrated portrayal, combined with his own partiality for impassioned speech and his (assumed) presence at Hinxman's attempt, informed and encouraged his selection of the part.

Moreover, for all of its self-deprecating irony, the quatrain quoted above admits the competitive motive in Byron's Speech Day participation, an urgent rivalry that ranges well beyond, I believe, his nearest challengers Lloyd and Long on the Harrow program, to the London stage itself, that site of spectacular recent success and acceptance by an(other) "different" boy. But for some of the same excellent psychological, sociological, and aesthetic reasons that shaped Byron's cool appraisal of Master Betty's acting, he could not afford to associate himself, especially in grubby competition, with the freakish "Phenomenon." His lyric reaches back in time, then, for the established, respected, authentic, cultural icon as the star to outshine. If Roscius could be (and beat) Garrick, why might not Byron be (and beat) Mossop? In its historical and theatrical contexts, Byron's line claims equivalency less with Mossop, an actor dead thirty-odd years, than with the live boy three years younger, for whom Mossop is venerable cover. Finally, if Byron knew anything at all of Mossop's history as Zanga, he almost certainly knew it in context, as part of the larger dramatic unit of the whole play, not merely with reference to a speech from it memorized for the occasion.

From its premier at Drury Lane on 18 April 1722 and its initial run of six performances, *The Revenge* steadily gained in popularity and by the end of the century had become a standard repertory piece,[21] having recruited most of the leading actors of the day into its major roles. John Mills, Thomas Elrington, and Henry Mossop all scored successes as the villain Zanga, and Kemble possibly played it, speculates Marchand, to Byron's viewing before the boy's performance on 6 June.[22] And as I have said, Young Roscius appeared in the play during the 1805–6 London season. If well known, the role of Zanga also appealed to Byron's taste, identified months back by Dr. Drury, for emotionally tempestuous speech; Prothero writes that "for his subjects Byron chose passages expressive of vehement passion" (1:29); and Byron himself remembers Drury's prophecy of oratorical distinction based upon the boy's "turbulence . . . my capaciousness of declamation" (Moore 20).[23] Zanga is indisputably a passionately driven character, but the "vehemence" and turbulence of his expression are *not* best illustrated in the "speech over the body of Alonzo" (as Prothero 1:20 and Marchand 1:96 and n identify the lines Byron recited), which virtually closes the play. These thirteen lines, hardly challenging to a retentive memory, amount to an anticlimactic recantation of Zanga's enmity toward Alonzo and a brief eulogy of his victim. Although in emotional complexity probably beyond the reach of an immature actor, not to mention a teenaged schoolboy, the speech is not particularly demanding of oratorical power or dramatic force.

The modern assumption that Byron recited *only* this short passage apparently rests upon his boast in "On a Distant View": "I trod on Alonzo o'erthrown" (l. 18), which indeed Zanga does; but the verbal trampling precedes his speech over the corpse, and registers his success more emphatically than does its technical climax, which, as I argue, tends to extenuate it. Furthermore, the thirteen lines could be declaimed, even by an intentional, deliberative actor, in less than a minute, hardly time to lather up a sweat of "vehement" passion, supposing the text encouraged it, which this one does not. The speech bills are too indefinite for reliable temporal conjectures—although entries on the 6 June 1805 program like Collins's "The Passions: Ode" (recited by Thomas Leeke) and Gray's "The Bard: an Ode" (climaxing the occasion, by Lloyd) presumably indicate complete and substantial texts—118 lines in the first case, 144 in the second.[24] Byron's announcement of the schedule to Augusta notwithstanding, *The Gentleman's Magazine* reports that at both of the 1805 events, speeches began at half past noon and continued until 3 P.M.[25] A story in the same periodical about the 6 June festivity strongly suggests that the whole of "The Passions" was on tap: "One circumstance, alone, tended to depress the spirits of the masters and the young gentlemen. Mr. Leeke, who had studied Collins's very difficult *Ode on the Passions* with great care, and who had recited it repeatedly in the best manner before Dr. Butler and others the day before, was taken suddenly and alarmingly ill on the morning of the day of exhibition, with a head-ache and fever. The *Ode*, therefore, was omitted; and an adequate apology was made to the company" (vol. 75, for June 1805; p. 575). Thus Mr. Leeke's reappearance on the speech bill for 4 July, again to recite the Collins ode.

Even if speech lengths widely varied from boy to boy, one with the agenda and the determination of Byron seems to me unlikely to have settled for a mere minute in the spotlight (however long that can *feel* in the heat of performance).[26] If current practice closely follows early-nineteenth-century convention, Byron spoke longer, for of the eight boys on the 1996 program, none came in much under four minutes, and the emcee, after himself declaiming, provided introductory and transitional material between deliveries. To be sure, twice as many boys were scheduled to speak on 6 June 1805 as on 23 May 1996—fifteen, in fact, with two in a colloquy, and the odal recitations may have required a balancing brevity elsewhere. Subtracting, say, fifteen minutes of deadtime from the 150 apportioned for speechmaking, each boy would have about nine minutes to speak on 6 June 1805 (assuming that academic prizes were not, as in later years, handed out after the speeches); Lloyd would have required more, but two boys shared one slot (in colloquy); and with Leeke absent, a temporal surplus should have remained. Still, says the *Gentleman's Magazine,* "the speeches closed about 3" (575). We should not read the journalistic account too closely on this point; but a sixty-second recitation might have been anomalous—suspiciously anomalous—among much longer offerings. Nor do I believe that an avid, avenging Byron, not to mention proud, admiring parents of other performers at some trouble to make the trip, would have stood still for clipped exposure of their sons. Furthermore, to establish, as a teenager, a memorable reputation for impassioned speechmaking, one would need more than a few stage minutes spread over three public appearances. Nevertheless, if Byron was good enough—if he was in fact as extraordinary a speaker as he appears to have been and certainly thought that he was—a minute or so might do it, for reputation and for psychic healing. The autotherapeutic and image-making benefits that Byron realized through his impersonation of Zanga do not require long-windedness. In its absence, however, for meaningful psychic satisfaction, consciousness of the complete role in its full context *would* have been requisite.

My guess is that the thirteen lines in question, as Byron recited them, concluded a longer speech composed of selections from others constituting the denouement of Young's tragedy including, perhaps, his attempted suicide, and almost certainly his pledge of defiance under torture—a speech that Byron, I believe, reformulated ten years later as Manfred's address to the summoning specters (3.4.124–41) when he was, in Ward Pafford's view, seeking to exorcize that part of his own identity so successfully projected and exploited in the "heroes" of the "oriental" tales and Manfred himself.[27] Perhaps with as little conscious awareness in 1805, Byron in his declamation(s) was exorcizing another demon of sorts, born of domestic and institutional circumstances and tensions in the immediate past. Keeping in mind Byron's sensitivity, as demonstrated in his maneuvering the Virgilian roles a year earlier, to the impact upon the orator's image and reputation of the character he impersonates, I am suggesting that Byron used the Zanga persona not merely to furbish his image with schoolfellows but to settle scores with some of them and their supervisors, and to relieve himself of pressure stemming from erotic as well as fraternal associations.

This hypothesis assumes, of course, Byron's familiarity with the whole of Young's play, not merely with its conclusion, whether from text or performance does not greatly matter, although given the issues involved, his exposure to them on the stage might have had greater and more enduring impact. It is another drama about a lost father, this time the Moor Zanga's, slain in conquering battle by Alonzo, who then enslaved the son in a benign and friendly if subsidiary association. But for six years Zanga has nursed against this master a rage fired to insupportable extremes by a mortifying "blow" from Alonzo, a slap to the cheek that insults both Zanga's noble blood and the presumed integrity of his relationship with his captor. The remainder of the plot tracks the stages of Zanga's revenge, which include his orchestration of a split between best friends Alonzo and Don Carlos and the murder of the latter, brutal manipulation of Alonzo's bride Leonora and her eventual suicide, and Alonzo's own consequent self-destruction, for all of which Zanga publicly takes self-satisfied responsibility. Iago-like without that monster's subtlety (the name is probably intended to evoke his Shakespearean prototype), Zanga yet earns, the prologue instructs us, our "involuntary praise" for his sufferings.[28]

Although this sketch scarcely reveals it, much here would have engaged the young Byron, about to leave Harrow and the company of beloved and intimate companions, still smarting from heartbreak, still vexed and shamed by the perceived mistreatment of his teachers, lessee, and other adults, still shackled by physical impairment, still divided by conflicting allegiances. Well might he have found appropriate to himself Zanga's boasting acknowledgment to his victor Alonzo, "You have been much abused," and claimed as his own, when speaking it, the scoundrel's resolve to "make vengeance of calamity" (act 5), for that, I believe, is the act Byron undertakes in his choice and performance of Zanga's part on Speech Day. And the act is of such momentous psychological importance that its overdetermined temporal setting emerges fourteen years later, in *Don Juan,* as the date on which Juan and Julia first consummate their passion—a liberating initiation of another sort that also avenges adult wrongs against another boy less than a year younger than Byron on the 1805 date. I will return to this point. For the moment, a caveat: if at first glance Byron appears to have less reason for personal involvement in the Zanga persona than in dramatic roles already cited, consider whether the subtlety of the appeal might not enable rather than impede identification, for it masked to the imagination what the conscience might censor. The inexactitude, looseness, and therefore suggestibility of some of the parallels I shall draw between lived and dramatized circumstances arguably strengthen the probability that Byron seized upon the Zanga character more from psychological need than thespian desire.

Young's setting is Spain, where Zanga is doubly stigmatized as servant and as Moor (an adulteration of blood from which Don Juan—but not Donna Julia—is explicitly free [*DJ* 1.9,56]), his servility particularly degrading to one of royal line. Acknowledged as nobleman, Zanga would be Alonzo's social superior, but he continues to serve while plotting the ruin of this "master"—a term no British schoolboy could indifferently hear, certainly not Byron, given the enslavement he had felt to Henry Drury's tutelage and his agitation over release from it. Nor is the public humiliation to which Byron felt he had been subjected at Harrow by some masters—particularly Mark Drury—after early acceptance into the Drury houses, wholly unlike the daily doses of disgrace that Zanga must endure as retainer of the man who killed his father and stole his inheritance: his vassalage ever declares his shame as it does Alonzo's dominion. Like Zanga, Byron hears his rank and privilege insulted by a social inferior, and although not physically abused, suffers the blow to his pride as intensely as, because he is more vulnerable than, the character he impersonates. A nearer equivalent in long-term impact, however, is the invitation experienced as repudiation by Lord Grey, an assault the more degrading because of the assumption behind it, and at all events remembered as maddening injury. Zanga's humiliation by impoverishment may have reminded Byron of the public reproaches of Mark Drury for his narrow fortune, the verbal divestment of his barony. We remember, too, that envy in part drove Byron's hostility toward Henry Drury—envy of his sonship, favoritism, influence—a vice whose much darker version consumes Zanga—and, further, Byron attributes to envy the souring of his relationship with young Delawarr, about which more in a moment. But above all in explosive impact is Zanga's ethnic identity.

More momentously than Selim is scarred by a wound in *Barbarossa*, Zanga is marked by color as alien and estranged by nationality, unmistakably Other as Byron felt himself to be Other from the day of his matriculation at Harrow and before. No uncertainty seems to have informed public perception of Moorish "difference": a 1792 edition of the play by John Bell from the Covent Garden production includes two engravings in which Zanga is sharply distinguished, from Leonora and Alonzo respectively, by both color and apparel, his dress in one a turban, loose-fitting trousers, and a full white drapery exposing and accentuating a good deal of black upper chest. About his own "different" status Byron was ambivalent, alternately cultivating a loner image by his stints of melancholy brooding on the Harrow churchyard's Peachy Stone, and actively seeking acceptance and dependence among his fellows. He, too, was physically marked, and although Harrow enrolled other lame boys at the time—Harness, for one—disability, without compensatory activity, was an estranging handicap. But why, if maneuvering to deflect attention from his bad foot on the 1804 Speech Day, does Byron risk foregrounding it by adopting the role of Other, of Different, a year later?

For one thing, preparing to leave Harrow, he need not fear the long-term repercussions of an insensitive reception. Second, as a more mature and self-assured, established young man, he can afford to fear them less. Third, emboldened by the success of his first outing, he may willingly risk more, even, I suspect, covet the kind of identification of role with actor that would enable the satisfaction of psychic need through impersonation—a project akin to contemporary therapeutic role-playing. The unconscious pressures of resentment over abuse from various sources at least in part determine Byron's selection of Zanga's speech as a disguised vehicle for repaying them, for talking back, retaliating in the public arena where he has been both forbidden and defamed. And it is particularly germane to his choice that the most abhorrent of the offenses he requites with his impersonation is the double charge of blackguardism brought by Henry and Mark Drury. Byron would not have adopted blackface to deliver the Moor's lines, but that he would have made the linguistic as well as the ethical connection between the villain he impersonated and the villainous name he had been called seems to me all but certain. Essentially, Byron elects to become the thing he has been named in order to discredit or neutralize it—to become in the role so much more than the accusation entails as to efface by outdistancing it: by illusion to displace the reality, and by the glamour and hyperbole of the representation to detoxify it, and render it by association also illusory. While disburdening himself of anger against several instruments of mistreatment, Byron challenges by assuming the persona of monster—a bluntly aggressive, "in-your-face" dramatization that dares its audience to match moral content of actor and character, or even to remember the actor's through the portrayal. At the very least, Byron's choice of role bespeaks a tremendous leap of confidence in his performative skills: being Zanga, he can get away with villainy, and avenge it, and earn acclaim for it (to set against the sore memory of public humiliation), without being thought villainous. It is a purgative opportunity. And he rehearses it with Augusta in the 23 April letter already cited, where his claim to be a *"most treasonable Culprit"* in all likelihood alludes to his Zanga impersonation as much as to Lord Melville in the dock.

Other connections suggest themselves. Zanga is preeminently not what he appears to be, and in that posture endorses the game of illusion that Byron plays with his role. Quite other than he seems in his masquerade of villainy as friendship, or his betrayal of friendship in villainy, Zanga also hyperbolically reconfigures Byron's recent experience with Lord Grey and the Drury brothers, and possibly even the more fundamental if remote abandonment of the father. Such experiences ground the anxiety registered in Byron's epistolary appeals for assurances of

Augusta's friendship, inform his need for Delawarr and other companions, and draw him to Young's meditations on fidelity, trust, and betrayal. Moreover, as Alonzo disposed of Zanga's parent, so Grey seeks to replace Byron's in the mother's affections. And with the obsessiveness of the boy's fixation on Grey's offense, Zanga fondles recollection of the audacious "blow" that demands redress: "The blow returned forever in my dream" (act 1). Alonzo, meanwhile, finds himself trapped in an amorous triangulation constructed by his best friend Don Carlos, who from prison ill-advisedly commissions Alonzo's intercessory courtship of Leonora. Predictably, Leonora and Alonzo enchant each other, an attraction useful to Zanga and ultimately fatal for Don Carlos. Leonora's "How dreadful to be cut from what we love, / And tied to what we hate" (act 1) would have had special poignancy for the lovesick Byron, but more important is the fiendish function served by mediation in this tangle. Experientially alerted—for his rage over Henry Drury's smear campaign derived in part from the tutor's deputization of agency—Byron would have noticed that a potent instrument of disaster in *The Revenge* is the mediation of Alonzo for Carlos, and of Zanga for Alonzo: indeed, without intercession, and the crafty or inadvertent manipulation of intermediaries, both love and revenge plots fail. On such, for Byron doubtful, machinery does the play turn.

But another dimension of it would have touched Byron at a sensitive and responsive place, on an equally emotional, even visceral, and perhaps unacknowledged or uneasily acknowledged plane. I refer to the fervent declarations of friendship exchanged between Alonzo and Don Carlos. Typically, as I have argued, Byron only began to realize on the eve of leaving school the depth and power of his attachment to Harrow and his schoolmates. Whether he conceived or acknowledged it at the time to have a sexual component is improbable, in Crompton's view, although obviously I am less sure in light of his skittishness about the Grey affair and his protests, from Cambridge, about the purity of his "passion" for John Edleston, for that argument assumes awareness and displays the pressures of "impure" passions. At all events, Byron in his current psychic state would have sympathetically absorbed the impassioned declarations of affection between the two friends in Young's drama, and particularly, in his romantic disillusionment, their elevation of male relationship above erotic association with women. Indeed, at points in the play, brotherhood virtually substitutes for heterosexual engagement; and the mutual attachment of Alonzo and Don Carlos to the same woman, wooed on behalf of the one by the other, is hardly free of homoerotic implications. One might plausibly argue that without the linchpin of Alonzo's and Don Carlos's entanglement with woman, Zanga's scheme collapses. Correctly believing himself responsible for Leonora's defection from Don Carlos, Alonzo declares, "I have no other love but Carlos now" (act 2), the logical consequence of the martial embrace and pledge of the previous act, "I conquer with Don Carlos in my eye." Surrendering Leonora to Alonzo, Carlos proves the triumph of friendship over romance (ending of act 2); and even Leonora acknowledges her marginalization: to Don Carlos she pines, "Why should you wish me stay! / Your friend's arrival will bring comfort to you, / My presence none." And when Zanga's lie about a jasmine-arbored rendezvous between Leonora and Don Carlos provokes Alonzo's hysteria, the villain with mock shame sneers, "O passion for a woman!" (act 4), demeaning it and the unworthy conduct that it excites. A moment later, believing himself "wedded and undone" in a single night, Alonzo longs for Don Carlos's company, cries for his comfort, "He! My bosom friend," as the affective scales rebalance in Carlos's favor against the allegedly betraying (with Don Carlos) Leonora. So concentrated and assembled, such evidence risks misrepresentation: I am not hypothesizing an illicit sexual affair or a consciously erotic attraction between Alonzo and Don Carlos. But I am suggesting that Byron's own intense emotional entanglements with schoolmates attuned him to detect or imagine in the heated verbalizations of the Alonzo-Carlos bond evidence of the kind of male attraction to male already familiar from his reading of Greek and Latin poetry.[29] It would have interested him in the play.[30]

But such slippery guesswork aside, let us admit that Zanga is a patently juicy role, offering numerous openings for stagy exhibitionism, overstated deviltry, especially to a boy prone to and notorious for mischief-making himself. Here was Byron's chance to be bad legitimately, and to earn kudos for it. And not only that: with the authority of Young's "Prologue" behind him, Byron could feel and perhaps claim heroic representation in the part, especially the great power in earning "involuntary praise" from his audience—a condition of ambivalence curiously typical of emotional attitudes in Young's characters and of Byron himself during the 1804–5 years (another reason that the play might have found sympathy in the boy). I pause over this instruction of Young to his audience and its shaping impact on the expectations of the actor playing Zanga because it anticipates precisely an authorial aim and strategy that Byron would exploit for years. Consistently he forced his readers to like and admire against their wills, to like and desire the forbidden, to applaud the transgressive actions he lavished upon them.[31] Zanga fostered that impulse.

Further, as we have seen, Byron must have taken enormous psychological satisfaction in performing an aggressive blackguardism under the legitimating cover of Speech Day in a discourse that at last so persuasively repents of it as nearly to transform obliquity into a virtue meriting praise, even moral sanction. The part suits Byron's antiestablishment sentiments, articulates his revolutionary spirit, and projects an image of subtle, insurrectionary leadership that promotes his interests in the upcoming Harrow rebellion, and all without compromising or jeopardizing social acceptability. Finally, because the play remained a London crowd pleaser, Byron could count on basking in the celebrity radiating downward from famous performers of the role; far from intimidating, their repute would have spurred him on. Although he spoke at Harrow before Master Betty brought the play to Covent Garden and Drury Lane, Byron would have already seen in the boy and in the part those distinctive marks of difference, of strangeness and arresting anomaly that matched in various particulars his sense of himself.

Just what portions, if any, of Zanga's dialogue Byron spoke, beyond the thirteen lines already indicated, remains unknown, but for the recited selection to have made self-contained sense a context was wanted (unless the play was too well known, even among the boys, to require it). For maximum clarity, he might have begun with Zanga's confession, "Know, then, 't was I . . . I hated; I despised; and I destroy" (act 5), and continued, with suitable elisions, through the recognition (important for Byron) that language avenges physical abuse (words in exchange for "blow"); his megalomaniacal appeal for international admiration of his triumph over a prostrate Alonzo; his repossession of majesty after six indentured years; his rehearsal of his capture, while guarding his father's corpse, by a squadron after he cleaves Alonzo's crest; and his reckoning of his servant's wages as "a *blow* by Heaven, a *blow*" (act 5). Following Alonzo's damp, self-pitying complaints, Zanga contemptuously wonders whether he must despise as well as hate his foe, and favorably compares his own stoically endured sorrows with those of Priam, Alexander, Caesar, and other heroes and demigods, rebuking Alonzo for his weakness in misfortune. More than that, Zanga demands acknowledgment of the justice of his actions, although not exoneration:

> Thou seest a prince, whose father thou hast slain;
> Whose native country thou hast laid in blood;
> Whose sacred person,[32] O! Thou hast profaned;
> Whose reign extinguish'd. What was left to me
> So highly born? No kingdom but revenge;
> No treasures, but thy tortures and thy groans. (act 5)

Zanga advises Alonzo that publicly naming his conqueror will leaven scorn of his fate; and in lines suggestively anticipating Byron's 1816 verse, goes on to claim membership in that company of "supreme beings, / Souls made of fire, and children of the sun, / With whom revenge is virtue," determining to teach Alonzo how to die by dying at his own hand. Prevented by his pupil, Zanga then relishes the chance "to be a raven in thy ear" (act 5), and announces Leonora's death; and upon hearing Alonzo's order to prepare the rack for him, he delivers his Manfredian defiance (cf. *Manfred* 3.4.124–41):

> The fix'd and noble mind
> Turns all occurrence to its own advantage
> And I'll make vengeance of calamity.
> Were I not thus reduced, thou wouldst not know
> That, thus reduced, I dare defy thee still.
> Torture thou mayst; but thou shall ne'er despise me.
> The blood will follow, where the knife is driven;
> The flesh will quiver, where the pincers tear;
> And sighs and cries by nature grow on pain:
> But these are foreign to the soul. Not mine
> The groans that issue, or the tears that fall;
> They disobey me: on the rack I scorn thee,
> As when my falchion clove thy helm in battle. (act 5)

Whatever it may lack in poetic brilliance, this text recovers in rhetorical fervor. It is hard to imagine the angry young aristocrat bypassing the chance it affords to adopt so nobly and glamorously defiant a posture before mates not too old, or mothers and sisters too jaded, to shiver over the anatomical graphics. More important, those physical details on the tongue of a boy who had known the wrench and tear of a "corrective" but tormenting rack borne on his own foot might have given his audience an extra shudder. And Byron's willingness to risk bringing notice to his disability measures his maturation during the year since he publicly recited Virgil. What might most forcibly have struck Byron is Zanga's determination to preserve personal honor through unspeakable torment: call him what you will, torture him as you may, his integrity of soul remains inviolate. This from an indisputable villain, but it elegantly models honorable rejoinder to ill-use of the sort, not much scaled down, Byron felt had been visited upon him by the Drurys and others. His participation in it grants Byron a public forum for an encoded rebuke of his defamers, authorizes and channels his own revenge.

Shortly after delivering this speech, Zanga hears himself pronounced avenged by Alonzo, who then proves it by suicide, depriving his foe of instrumentality. Thus is the stage set for the passage that consensus believes the seventeen-year-old Byron declaimed. It is a valedictory:

> Good ruffians, give me leave; my blood is yours;
> The wheel's prepared, and you shall have it all,
> Let me but look one moment on the dead,
> And pay yourselves with gazing on my pangs.

Whether Byron recited these introductory lines to Zanga's speech over Alonzo's corpse is uncertain. He may have omitted them in preference for the extended passage quoted above. My guess is that he did not, and that the speeches of defiance and query constituted the text he declaimed. Zanga then continues as follows:

> Is this Alonzo? Where's the haughty mien?
> Is that the hand which smote me? Heavens, how pale!
> And art thou dead? So is my enmity:
> I war not with the dust: the great, the proud,
> The conqueror of Afric, was my foe.
> A lion preys not upon carcasses.
> This was the only method to subdue me.
> Terror and doubt fall on me: all thy good
> Now blazes: all thy guilt is in the grave [.]
> Never had man such funeral applause!
> If *I* lament thee, sure, thy worth was great.
> O Vengeance! I have follow'd thee too far,
> And to receive me Hell blows all her fires. (act 5)

There is a way—by stressing "this," "that," "me," "I," and "my foe" in lines 1–5 as quoted here, along with the already emphasized "*I*" of line 11—of making Zanga sound contemptuously arrogant, imperiously condescending in this speech. A young actor, beguiled by the glamour of Zanga's evil and seduced by the egocentrism of such a reading, might be tempted by it, especially if using the part to define or revise or polish an image of the self. Just what interpretation Byron gave the speech we can only guess. But one hopes he did not choose the easy, entirely self-serving way, or voice the lines with a wooden irony unsuitable to them. For Zanga on the one hand is never more dignified, never more princely or generous than here; and although unarguably still proud, he situates himself in what seems to be modest moral subordination to the worthy Alonzo, against whose "blazing good"[33] Zanga's "Terror and doubt" nevertheless seem more vital and admirable. Perhaps that is partly why Byron could risk appearing in the repentant, apologetic mode, if in fact he recited *only* these lines, with their ostensible eulogistic deference to an ethical superior. And yet it is apology without contrition, the posture of penitence without desire or expectation of forgiveness. The speech publicizes power rather than repents of its misuse, although cunningly seeking to camouflage its vanity in eulogistic rhetoric. If capture by so noble a foe as Alonzo ratchets up the self-esteem of the captive, it inscribes itself as contempt for the physically wrecked captor, a carcass, a collection of dust hardly meriting notice by the engineer of its destruction. But by a curious turn in his argument Zanga contends that only absence, vacancy, evacuation could neutralize his rage against Alonzo: only removal could "subdue" the avenging passion and grant him peace. Byron quotes those sentiments near the date of his permanent departure from a site, initially experienced as hostile, on which he has felt himself enslaved, stunned by verbal "blows" from persons in some degree addressed and confuted by this discourse and presumably about to become forever absent to him.

Finally, the line which measures Alonzo's worth by Zanga's reluctance to concede it—"If *I* lament thee, sure, the worth was great"—is either his noblest or his basest moment: a magnanimous recognition of superior character and sincere regret over its loss, or self-aggrandizement shamelessly built upon the virtue it has trampled. The statement, after all, is (or may be hypothetical and) ambiguous: "Inasmuch as even *I* lament thee"; or "in the event that *I* should deign to lament thee." And although Zanga's final line appears to accept the justice of his consignment to flames, his pride anticipates an exceptionally warm reception. I linger over these richly ambiguous lines not so much to urge the undecidability of Zanga's character but to posit in Young a vision of human nature and endeavor not unlike the mature Byron's sense of its immensely complex "mix" of elements "contending without end or order" that so baffles the admiring and scandalized Abbot of *Manfred*. Zanga is less than Byron's hero in all respects except possibly the exercise of dark powers; but the instinctual, forbidden, irresistible impulse to praise an apparent incarnation of evil recognizes and enacts the human complexity so resistant to easy moral categorization that Byron forcefed his readers. Whatever else he may mean to Byron, Zanga represents the possibility of justified, praiseworthy villainy.

A final observation on this play: a "Friend" delivers an epilogue which reduces the whole of it to the moral tidiness of an epigram: "Ne'er break a bargain, but first take a sample"; that is, Alonzo, a "stupid sot," unaccountably killed his bride before enjoying her. It is a mildly witty and thoroughly lighthearted closure, perhaps meant, conventionally, to relieve gloom and send the audience away smiling. But its effect complements the indeterminateness on which the play ends, reinforces the paradox of "involuntary praise," and violates exactly that aesthetic principle that in Byron's also irreverent hands so exasperated tidy-minded readers of *Don Juan,* less interested in valid representation of experience than in thematic and tonal—and to him totally unlifelike—consistency. The disjunctive shock of Young's "Epilogue" previews the ottava rima reversals and narrative discontinuities of Byron's masterpiece.[34]

The earliest portrait of Byron, at seven years of age. Courtesy of the John Murray Collection.

(Possibly) a portrait of Byron at Harrow School, 1801, signed "T.W." Whereabouts of the original unknown. Courtesy of the Ashmolean Museum, Oxford.

Catherine Gordon, Mrs. Byron, the poet's mother, by T. Stewardson. Courtesy of the John Murray Collection.

Byron, in a portrait given by the poet to the Reverend Henry Drury. By permission of Lord Lytton.

The Reverend Henry Drury, Byron's first tutor at Harrow School, by Thomas Hodgetts after Mrs. Margaret Carpenter. By the kind permission of the Keepers and Governors of Harrow School.

Byron at about the time he left Harrow. Courtesy of the National Historical Museum, Athens.

George Gordon, Sixth Lord Byron (1788–1824) [with Robert Rushton?], by George Sanders. Courtesy of The Royal Collection. Her Majesty Queen Elizabeth II.

Byron, about 1816, by H. Mayer from a drawing by G. H. Harlow.
By courtesy of the National Portrait Gallery, London.

Byron, about 1815, by H. T. Ryall after James Holmes. By courtesy of the National Portrait Gallery, London.

William Henry West Betty, "Child Actor Known as the Young Roscius," by J. Ward after H. Burch. Courtesy of the Harvard Theatre Collection, Houghton Library.

William Henry West Betty, a portrait by James Northcote.
Courtesy of the Harvard Theatre Collection, Houghton Library.

"Master Betty, The Infant Roscius as Hamlet, engraved by W. Bond from a Drawing by H. Singleton, after nature during a performance at Leicester." Courtesy of the London Theatre Museum.

Lady Caroline Lamb, dressed as a page. Devonshire Collection, Chatsworth. Reproduced by permission of the Duke of Devonshire and the Chatsworth Settlement Trustees. Photograph: courtesy of the Photographic Survey, Courtauld Institute of Art.

I. R. Cruickshank, "Fashionables of 1816 taking the air in Hyde Park." Copyright the British Museum.

I. R. Cruickshank's caricature of Byron's separation from his wife, or hers from him, in 1816, Mrs. Mardyn, the actress, on the poet's arm. Copyright the British Museum.

Second Interval

BRIEF NOTICE of certain similarities, and a major difference, between *The Revenge* and *The Wheel of Fortune,* one of two plays in which Byron performed at Southwell in October 1806, may prove instructive.[1] Richard Cumberland's sentimental drama, as well regarded in its day, says Charles H. Shattuck, as *Death of a Salesman* in ours, features Roderick Penruddock, Byron's and John Philip Kemble's role, a misanthropic recluse, explicitly marked like Cain, driven by betrayal and disappointment in love to embittered withdrawal and a lust for revenge.[2] The treacherous Woodville, formerly Penruddock's best and beloved friend, has played the blackguard through villainous mediation with the beautiful Arabella (in the present context an eerie nominal anticipation of Annabella, Lady Byron), Roderick's intended, and carried her off by the "blackest treachery." Beneficiary of a windfall, Penruddock is suddenly positioned to avenge himself mercilessly upon the now bankrupt Woodville, a reckless gambler, whose chits Roderick has inherited. Partly through the good offices of the impoverished but still lovely Mrs. Woodville, Penruddock wages (singularly light, offstage) battle with his vengeful will, conquers it, forgives his fawning foe, spreads largesse about, and retires to his rural retreat to contemplate books and nature, exiting on high-minded platitudes: "The true use of riches is to share them with the worthy; and the sole remedy for injuries, to forgive them." Shattuck thriftily summarizes: "We sense the power of benevolence overmastering a good man's bad passion for revenge."[3] It is, however, a spineless, mawkish affair, this play, useful to our purposes only because offering to Byron yet another prodigal, false-hearted father, another intense male intimacy exploded by duplicitous mediation, another betrayed love and disillusioned lover thirsting for revenge. But Penruddock is fangless, and rarely the vehicle for Zangian passion, never for Byronic "vehemence." I would propose Byron's interest in the role to be partly the consequence of his Speech Day exorcism of Zangian demons and Lear-like rage, a purging of wrath and rancor that cleared

135

room for further development of the more benign persona, still misanthropic, still reclusive, still "dark" and marked and broken, but without Penruddock's bathos, that his name would come to mean.

The other play in Byron's Southwell repertory, however, is an altogether different matter. John Till Allingham's *The Weathercock,* a "comic opera" in two acts without musical content beyond two thin lyrics and a reprise, provides Byron with an expedient vehicle for expanded practice of the oratorical and theatrical gifts displayed at Harrow. Opportunistically, his choice of role—and of play, if he assisted in its selection—permits Byron's simultaneous exhibition and spoof of his speechmaking interests, the latter partly in defense against uncertain reception by a nevertheless sympathetically predisposed audience of friends gathered in the Pigot parlor. For Tristram Fickle, the weathercock, is a colossally silly fellow whose experimentation with occupational alternatives, while reflecting every young person's search for a suitable vocation and immediately evocative of Byron's parliamentary fantasies, serves largely comic purposes, so that Byron in the part can at once conscientiously act and speak without risking scorn if theatrically unsuccessful: it is, after all, all farce, and Fickle a frivolous, capering monkey until ultimately redeemed by love.

From the modern perspective, the unstable, changeable property signed in Allingham's title, redundant in his protagonist's name and the thematic center of the play, appears to anticipate an alleged Byronic trait manifest in *Don Juan*'s quick shifts from grave to gay—*The Weathercock*'s phrase is "lightness and gravity"—and, imagined or read back into authorial character, occasioned a fair amount of bad press for the poet. Alternately hellion and phlegmatic, the young man might well have been temperamentally drawn to like inconstancy in the text of this play. Indeed, his later confession to being "every thing by turns and nothing long" (to Lady Blessington, quoted in Marchand, 3:1066), might ably serve as epigraph for *The Weathercock,* and the countless changes rung on changeableness in *Don Juan* might be seen as a sophisticated, endlessly varied extension of Allingham's characterizational signature in the one-dimensional Fickle. Tristram's vocational indecision, however, is an elaborate comic medium for interrogating his emotional, affectional stability and steadfastness—questions of importance for Byron in 1804–6—which turn out to be sound enough toward Variella the love interest, who, knowing her prey, vows to assume "more forms than Proteus . . . to please him, and change as oft as his inconstant mind" (act 1) in an effort "to learn whether his declaration [of eternal devotion, passed at a masquerade, both of them masked] was merely the caprice of the moment, or the offering of a heart capable of feeling as mine does" (act 2). If we have correctly interpreted Byron's guarded poetic and epistolary allusions to Newstead incidents of late December 1803, he could not have heard these lines without recalling the Grey event and the relational "caprice" consequently assigned to his tenant. But undependability in attachments had spacious range in Byron's past, as we have seen, and from the fall of 1806 would have included Harrow and Annesley and Burgage Manor, centrally, and perhaps reached back to Holles Street in London and Queen Street in Aberdeen.

However helpful in accounting for Byron's interest in *The Weathercock*, these conjectures are ancillary to the main point, which is Fickle's penchant for oratory, newly discovered as the play opens. To be sure, he also, in the course of it and before, "becomes," in his colorful imagination, by turns an actor, a musician, a philosopher, a soldier, a gardener, a Quaker, and ultimately a "buck." But he is first and longest a lawyer, qualified for that profession solely because "convinced that I possess great powers of oratory" (act 1) fitting him to argue in Westminster Hall, although without his having disturbed the "twelve square feet of [law] books" (act 1) recently installed in his apartment. He has summoned his barber to shave half of his head in imitation of "Demosthenes, the aethenian orator" (act 1), a vision of whom inspires this panegyric:

> I see him now, awaking the dormant patriotism of his countrymen: lightning in his eye, and thunder in his voice, he pours forth a torrent of eloquence resistless in its force. The throne of Philip trembles while he speaks; he denounces, and indignation fills the bosoms of his hearers. He exposes the impending danger, and in his words everyone sees impending ruin. He threatens the tyrant, they grasp their swords. He calls for vengeance; their thirsty weapons glitter in the air, and thousands reverberate the cry.—One soul animates a nation, and that soul is the soul of an orator. (act 1)

A heady concept, this last sentence, for an eighteen-year-old with oratorical triumphs in his pocket and his eye on the House of Lords— and perhaps difficult for him to ironize in delivery. But Fickle's foolishness helps. He mimes the orator's role while others speak, fancying himself before a jury, and surrounds himself with the accessories of the profession, including a bust of Cicero—first victim, by slashing sword, of Tristram's switch from lawyering to soldiering. Earlier, however, Cicero for Fickle is "a great man [who] raised himself by his eloquence, and why should not I—I have a mouth—[and Cicero] A tongue, and every organ of speech . . . I'll imitate Cicero" (act 1). But that very mouth, in the lengthy development of Fickle's mock "cause" against coal, becomes through pollution a "dust-hole"—Allingham's clever figure for the corrupt legal profession, and perhaps as well an ironic, self-reflexive judgment against the windy speechmaking that the image climaxes. Such irony is lost, however, upon Tristram and his friend Sneer, who thinks the speech convincing evidence "that you are able to confound all the judges and jurors that ever sat in Westminster-Hall" (act 1). And for his part, Tristram finds blessing in the dustman's careless collection, for blinding coal dust precipitated his "discovery of my talents for the bar" in the eloquence of his speech against "coals." The tonal pitch is very different, but one wonders if Byron might have made the connection between Tristram's feigned denunciation of an offensive element and his own rage against an offensive epithet, displaced into formal discourse. Whether or not "coal" and "blackguardism" linked in his mind, the step from orating to acting, and the association of the two, is as short and clear for Fickle as for Byron, so that when the thought of a stage career dawns, he at once prepares to soliloquize (as Romeo). Fearful of his father's threat to disinherit so unsteady a son, Tristram considers "turn[ing] parson" (act 2)—with fluency still a desideratum—but, imagining himself before his beloved, he "want[s] words to express" himself (act 2). And yet, even in his last assumed role, as Quaker, he never, until finding his pleasure "unutterable" upon meeting his beloved, falls silent or becomes as laconic as his father's friend Briefwit, who speaks only Latin phrases or English monosyllables.

Light, shallow fare, Allingham's comedy is nevertheless a well-nigh perfect vehicle for Byron's continuing exploration of his performative aptitude, for testing the seriousness and endurance of his own interest in oratory and stagecraft, while measuring the effect of these skills on an audience likely to flatter and encourage them. With the Speech Day successes almost certainly, proudly, present in the Pigots' domestic conversation, the boy could count on spectators' particular attentiveness to his largely parodic ventures into *Weathercockian* oratory. But if he performed it well, Byron could also depend upon awareness of his Harrow achievements to overcome the foolishness of Tristram Fickle and both validiate and enhance his standing, especially with the Pigot women, as an accomplished declaimer with a future. If not quite a win-win opportunity, Byron couldn't lose either: if he botched Fickle, it was all frivolous amusement anyhow, inconsequential and without impact on his Speech Day fortunes; if he scored, he gained credibility as both orator and actor. Either way, and transcending both in importance, he participated as principal spokesperson in an ironic, self-reflexive mockery of a rhetorical form, a satiric send-up of the mode shaping its own expression. One can imagine the fun a scamp like Byron would have had with the light-headed, high-spirited Tristram, but he learned something of satiric representation from Allingham, just as he would have been touched by his figuration of inconstancy too.[4]

5: Shakespearean King: *4 July 1805*

WRITING TO AUGUSTA on the day before he declaimed Zanga's speech at Harrow festivities, Byron dropped a possible clue to his plan for delivery, and mentioned a number of concerns replicating or closely touching upon Young's in the play: "My dearest Augusta.—At last you have had a *decent* specimen of the dowagers talents for epistles in the *furioso* style." The description discloses not only his rehearsed declamatory manner but also a model and motive for it—and perhaps, given the letter's expectations of another sort of deliverance, an end which it is partly designed to accomplish?

> You are now freed from the *shackles* of her correspondence, and when I revisit her, I shall be bored with long stories of your *ingratitude* & &. She is as I have before declared certainly mad, (to say she was in her senses, would be condemning her as a Criminal), her conduct is a *happy* compound of derangement and Folly. I had the other day an epistle from her . . . [which has] given the finishing stroke to *filial,* which now gives way to *fraternal* duty. Believe me, dearest Augusta, not ten thousand *such* mothers, or indeed any mothers, Could induce me to give you up . . . and nothing now Can influence your *pretty sort of brother,* (bad as he is) to forget that he is your *Brother.* Our first Speech day will be over ere this reaches you, but against the 2d you shall have timely notice.—(*BLJ* 1:68–69)

A grim irony now shades this pledge of solidarity with Augusta, for a maternal madness of sorts did effectuate the parting of these siblings forever in 1816. But mad as is Mrs. Byron, and bad as he is, both conditions illustrate the principle of moral mixture—or "compound"— noticed above in *The Revenge.* Byron is as quick to exonerate his mother of criminality as to qualify his own prettiness with moral culpability, and if both remarks are wittily edged, they express Byron's mature attitude shared with Young's Alvarez and treated with humor in *Don Juan* that in the heart of every human a Zanga impatiently abides. Moreover, the letter firmly prioritizes brotherhood not merely over filial bonds but over any challenges whatsoever. Speaking out of a drama that tracks the tragedy of betrayed brotherhood, at a time when separation from comrades is imminent, the loss of an older companion still raw, and the (partly) substitutive gain of blood brotherhood still exhilarating, Byron reveals in this passage a heightened sensitivity to the fraternal dimension of Young's play, which may in fact inspire his reflections on the subject. In any case, he immediately mentions the next day's ceremony, for the only time in the letter, essentially deferring the subject to July.

But he is far from done on the issue: the remainder of the letter capriciously chides Augusta for indulging herself in an illness brought on by disappointment in her postponed marriage. "[Marrying later,] . . . you will no doubt say that I am a *wise man,* and that the later, one makes one's self miserable, with the matrimonial clog, the better" (*BLJ* 1:69). It is a maxim one might draw from the amorous tribulations of Alonzo and Don Carlos; but Byron's statement in its context also eclipses marriage with literal brotherhood, implicitly reserving Augusta for himself against bonding with a legal mate. And in a humorous allusion to his 25 April refusal to bestow a *"profane blessing"* on Augusta and her friend, he does grant "my *patriarchal blessing,"* which in effect doubles his familial claim upon her, secures her from another angle as brace for himself.

Byron's next surviving letter, dated 27 June, three weeks after Speech Day, promises John Hanson in London a visit on Saturday, but "it is absolutely necessary for me to return to Harrow on Tuesday or Wednesday, as Thursday is our 2d Speechday, and Butler says he cannot dispense with my absence [presence?] on that Day" (*BLJ* 1:69). Dr. Joseph Drury having stepped down at Easter, the Reverend George Butler now presided over the school, despite the protests, open rebellion, and surreptitious objections of the many boys favoring Mark Drury, his rival for the post. We have already noted that Byron took leadership of the resisting faction as the price of his active support. It is a curious turnabout, this swing from a bitter and presumably well-known dislike to election campaign chairman for the tutor once believed his vulgar foe, and it reflects most notably a ripening desire for the spotlight in this formerly retiring lad but perhaps also a seasoning of his judgment—a maturing willingness to weigh and balance evidence, responsibility, and long-range goals against narrow, short-term personal satisfactions: possibly a lesson learned from—certainly one illustrated by—his experience with the Young play. He would also appear to occupy the conservative position in supporting tradition and solidarity with the Drury family against the Cambridge interloper. At the same time, however, I do not wish to underestimate the appeal to Byron of the fight itself. It would probably not be unfair to say that he welcomed the contest for the headmastership as an opportunity for self-promotion; and his satiric attacks on Butler, circulated through the school, would also have brought him attention and notoriety. But these almost certainly appeared after the second Speech Day, in July, when Byron was essentially an ex-student, and, if immune from administrative reprisal, positioned to benefit the school as a memorable and perhaps generous alumnus. The resistance which he spearheaded probably took place between the March institution of the Reverend Butler and the first Speech Day in June.

Byron's letter to Hanson may, of course, offer his Speech Day assignment as an excuse for foreshortening an unwanted visit with the Hansons, but it seems to me rather a proud announcement of his essential part in the festival and of his coziness with the headmaster, although if the Hansons are privy to Byron's opposition to Butler's appointment, the pleasant irony of this letter would not be lost upon them. On the other hand, no very clear reason presents itself for why Byron would *need* to return on Tuesday or Wednesday for a Thursday performance unless, indeed, rehearsals were scheduled, in which case mention of them would have strengthened his excuse for truncating the visit, and reinforced the sense of his importance at Harrow. As we have seen in a report of the *Gentleman's Magazine* (June 1805) and elsewhere, rehearsals with the headmaster were routine, at least on the day before public delivery. Perhaps Byron's need to attend such a rehearsal would have been clear to Hanson without explanation.

The fascinating slip in Byron's substitution of "absence" for (presumably) "presence," however, is the letter's most curious feature. Marchand's bracketed guess presents the obvious probability of what Butler said, but other possibilities range from his having said exactly what Byron reports (with the consequent collapse of Byron's argumentative logic) to his having said nothing at all, the line then becoming Byron's fabrication to furbish his reputation with the Hansons, and the slip marking his anxiety in the lie (as he clearly lies to his mother, and admits to Hanson, in an 8 July letter [*BLJ* 1:70]). But given the tensions at the moment between the stiff-necked headmaster and the refractory boy, it is entirely possible that Butler should wish Byron absent on Speech Day, and even likelier that Byron knew he had given Butler every reason to wish it. Alternatively, the error may encode the boy's own wish for *Butler's* absence, on Speech Day and beyond, his evacuation of office, for toward the achievement of that end Byron will continue to exert himself. Or the wish-fulfilling line may express Byron's desire for authoritative permission to miss Speech Day: "Butler *can* dispense with my presence . . . ," although such interpretation challenges Byron's anticipatory logic and tone in this and neighboring letters. Further, the succession of negatives in the sentence—"cannot dispense . . . absence"—in combination with the misstep, suggests cover-up of some sort, and at the very least a mutual desire of the two parties to be as absent from each other as institutional obligations and expectations would permit. And if true, such felt antipathy would aggravate whatever stress Byron might have experienced as Speech Day approached.

The anxiety is more palpable five days later in a letter to Augusta, where its object is interestingly displaced. Byron writes on Tuesday, 2 July, presumably from Harrow, where he has just arrived from enrolling at Trinity College, Cambridge, on the earliest of the two days proposed to Hanson for returning to Harrow (so the London sojourn was short). But what one would suppose so signal an event as his matriculation gets no further notice in this letter.[1]

Byron turns immediately to the event now two days off: "Thursday is our Speechday at Harrow, and as I forgot to remind you of its approach, previous to our first declamation. [*sic*] I have given you *timely* notice this time" (*BLJ* 1:69). If so, probably in correspondence now lost: had Byron posted his letter early enough on Tuesday, it might have received same-day delivery, given the frequency of mail coaches to and from the city, but likelihood favors Augusta's receipt on Wednesday, the day before the event—hardly a "*timely* notice," given the boy's expectations about to be laid out. Of course, Byron may be joking at his own expense; but the remainder of the letter is so earnest, even self-important, that I suspect seriousness, urgency, and something close to aggrieved chastisement in his remark. The letter continues with Byron's construction, his orchestration of the performance he expects to stage. Here is the young lord at his theatrically directive best:

> If you intend doing me the *honour* of attending, I would recommend you not to come without a Gentleman [an assumption that she has an escort standing by, on call!], as I shall be too much engaged all morning to take

care of you, and I should not imagine you would admire *stalking* about by yourself. You had better be there [here?] by 12 o'clock as we begin at 1, and I should like to procure you a good place; Harrow is 11 miles from town, it will make a *comfortable* morning's drive for you. I don't know how you are to come, but for *Godsake* bring as few women with you as possible, I would wish you to Write me an answer immediately, that I may know on Thursday morning, whether you will drive over or not, and I will arrange my other engagements accordingly. I *beg Madam* you may make your appearance in one of his Lordship's most *dashing* carriages, as our Harrow *etiquette,* admits of nothing but the most *superb* vehicles, on our Grand *Festivals.* In the mean time, believe me dearest Augusta your affectionate Brother, Byron.

Temporally, the boy is cutting it very close, on Augusta's schedule and his own, but his excitement is patent, as is his anxiety about the impression Augusta may make upon Harrow, conditioned as he was to dread disaster by Mrs. Byron's embarrassing visits to Dulwich. Such anxiety, even if displaced, bespeaks Byron's establishment of an image at Harrow—or of his continuing efforts to do so—of social consequence that he does not want compromised by inappropriate appearances, although the penultimate sentence recognizes the slight absurdity of his concern and gently mocks without withdrawing it.[2]

Further, his solicitude for Augusta's well-being sounds the typical relational rhythms of Byron's later personal and textual dealings with others, as do indeed the temporal challenges he sets for her. On the one hand he is too busy to escort her touring (and he, if not also she, wants his sibling spared the indignity of appearing unattended on the Harrow lawns); and on the other hand he is eager to settle her honorably, or at any rate with a good view of the speakers. Byron is at once both absent and present to his sister—more absent than present if many women accompany her. Is this warning a plea for undivided attention? Is it dread of social embarrassment by a maidenly troupe, whereas parents and (perhaps younger?) siblings would represent other boys? Would his association with a party of unescorted women, perhaps excessive in their coddling, further stigmatize him? Is he fearful that Augusta's friends will not meet in appearance and conduct the Harrow standard of etiquette touted in his next sentence? Are these all the dicta of snobbery? Or would his plans to recite the ravings of a man driven mad by women have prompted the discouragement of female attendants? Byron's recent experience with *King Lear* may have fueled an animosity toward the manipulative, abusive female developed over the years in her son by Mrs. Byron, May Gray, and others. Whatever the contributing factors, Byron is at least as concerned about the *image* that Augusta will bring to and leave behind at Harrow as with seeing his sister, and, perhaps, being seen by her. His colorful, high-spirited stipulation of vehicular transport is also a firm, instructive imperative: there *is* a Harrow etiquette: honor it—this from one best familiar with it in the breach. If nothing else, such consciousness of the protocol observed on Speech Day as this letter throughout registers measures Byron's emotional investment in the affair. Something—much—is at stake for him. One wonders how Augusta's absence affected his performance. Would it, for example, have energized or devitalized his delivery of Lear's famous address to the storm?

We cannot know. But the excitement of Byron's expectations in the invitation, and his month-long silence to Augusta following the event (or so surviving correspondence indicates), suggests disappointment at best, perhaps anger and hurt.[3] Whether such emotions fortuitously empowered Byron's representation of the king's great grief is uncertain, and in any case, if aroused only by Augusta, obviously would not have influenced his choice of a text for declamation. But as responses to Mrs. Byron's long ill-usage, they may have done. Indeed, Shakespeare's text dramatizes domestic discord, the tensions racking parental relations with offspring and siblings with each other. Byron's most persistent epistolary complaint for many months prior to the event inverts the principal crisis of *Lear* between parent and child—that is, the abuse of the parent by the child.[4] Just as interesting is his frequent reference to Mrs. Byron's complaints of his own and of Augusta's *ingratitude*, exactly Lear's grievance against his progeny. As early as October 1804 Byron speaks to Augusta of Mrs. Byron's "monstrous pet with you for not writing," and two weeks later of her upbraiding him "as if I was the most undutiful wretch in existence" (*BLJ* 1:53, 56). Within another week, he strikes the same note: "she complains that you are negligent and do not care about her" (*BLJ* 1:59), and he repeatedly sets against his vexation with her his "gratitude" to Lord Carlisle,[5] Augusta herself, and Dr. Joseph Drury, recipient of "a memorial [of silver plate worth 330 guineas] of our Gratitude for his long service" as Harrow headmaster (*BLJ* 1:63). On the eve of the first 1805 Speech Day Byron imagines for Augusta his next visit to Burgage Manor, where "I shall be bored with long stories of your *ingratitude*" from one whose "conduct is a *happy* compound of derangement and Folly" (*BLJ* 1:68)—this, three lines after declaring his mother "certainly mad." Assuming the irony of the italicized adjective, the diagnosis admirably suits the king whose most famous utterance Byron would declaim a month later.[6]

Not long after delivering that speech, he writes again of Mrs. Byron "pouring forth compliments against your [Augusta's] ingratitude" (*BLJ* 1:72); and then on 18 August, verbal echoes of the speech emerge in an elaborate metaphorical structure adapted from Shakespeare:

> The more I see of her [Mrs. Byron] the more my dislike augments, nor can I so entirely conquer the appearance of it, as to prevent her from perceiving my opinion, this so far from calming the Gale, blows it into a *hurricane,* which threatens to destroy every thing, till exhausted by its own violence, it is lulled into a sullen torpor, which after a short period, is again roused into fresh and renewed phrenzy, to me most terrible, and to every other Spectator astonishing. She then declares that she plainly sees I hate her, that I am leagued with her bitter enemies viz. Yourself, Ld. C[arlisle] and Mr H[anson] and . . . we are all *honoured* with a multiplicity of epithets, too *numerous,* and some of them too *gross,* to be repeated. (*BLJ* 1:75–76)

It is as though Byron houses Shakespeare's tempest in his mother's lungs and directs it swarming toward himself and her other "enemies," with whom he is allegedly "leagued"—in a possible reminiscence of the collusion of Lear's opponents. But Byron's motives are not merely informative. By recasting and intertextualizing parts of the speech he has recently recited, and parts of the plot from which it is excerpted, Byron forces Augusta to hear the declamation she had disappointed him by missing: something in Lear's lines, something in Byron's feelings about them, demand Augusta's attention. I suspect that it is no other than the parent's abuse of the child for abusing the parent, the child's need to speak passionately against it, and its urgent desire not to be alone in that victimization.

BUT LET US RETURN to the 4 July Speech Day and Byron's preparations for it. While it would be useful to know the exact date of the notorious Harrow "rebellion" that Byron allegedly led—or, if Tyerman is right, that at worst Byron merely engaged in a series of schoolboy pranks meant to harass rather than harm Dr. Butler, when they took place in relation to Speech Day—it is probably fair to speculate that the boy's needling of the new headmaster commenced upon his arrival in March and extended through the summer term, perhaps increasing in aggravation as spirits became friskier with the approach of the holiday. If we can trust Byron's dating, he composed the first of his satiric attacks on Butler at Harrow in the month of his second Speech Day performance. "On a Change of Masters at a Great Public School" grounds itself in the *ubi sunt* convention that quickly yields to an acidic attack upon Butler as the barbarian invading Harrow's Rome, he as Pomposus to Drury's Probus, with the collapse of the culture the inescapable result. "Childish Recollections," written, says McGann, "late in 1806 for printing" in *Poems on Various Occasions* and revised early in 1807 for *Hours of Idleness* (1807), famously includes an additional caricature of Butler, but it is certainly possible that the lines on Pomposus, including those excised from the published version of the poem, freely circulated at Harrow during the spring and summer of 1805 and, if reaching Butler's hands, at least partially account for his antipathy toward Byron until a reconciliation was affected (by Henry Drury) three years later. (See *CPW* 1:132, 157–75, 378, 382–84; also *BLJ* 1:110–11; 144–45; 153–54). As Byron remembered it, keen enmity quickened both sides. Writing to William Bankes, a Trinity College friend whom Byron labeled "the father of all mischiefs" (letter to Murray, 19 November 1820, *BLJ* 7:231), Byron explained: "The portrait of Pomposus" in *Childish Recollections* "was drawn at Harrow after a *long Sitting,* this accounts for the Resemblance or rather the *Caricatura,* he is *your* friend, he *never was mine,* for both our sakes [Butler's and mine?], I shall now be silent on this head" (*BLJ* 1:111).

Surviving records suggest that his discretion lasted ten months. In correspondence with Henry Drury on 20 February 1808, however, after the two had patched up their Harrow divisions but a month before Byron's reconciliation with Butler,[7] Byron's old anger at the headmaster boiled over in snarling ironies:

> As for my worthy preceptor Dr. B[utler] our encounter [for which Henry Drury lobbies] would by no means prevent the *mutual endearments* he and I were wont to lavish on each other, we have only spoken once, since my departure from H—in 1805 and then he politely told Tattersall, I was not a proper associate for his pupils, this was long before my strictures in verse, but in plain *prose* had I been some years older, I should have held my tongue on his perfections.—(*BLJ* 1:145)

Relocated to Butler, here is the familiar complaint against defamation earlier directed to other school officials, with whom Butler is now collectively associated in Byron's grievance with the Harrow staff for perpetuating the tradition of Byron bashing. Remarkably, Butler commits the infuriating offenses of Henry and Mark Drury in damning Byron to one of his peers, without providing the accused an opportunity for explanation or defense: it is a craven, surreptitious attack that insults and degrades the young man who must have begun to think it standard operating procedure. And the psychological amassing of former detractors who held positions of authority is germane to Byron's performance on 4 July. But he seems oblivious to his own replication of the Butlerian defamation, if so it was, in the lampoons smearing the headmaster handed round the School.[8]

He continues to Henry: "But being laid on my back when that Schoolboy thing was written, or rather dictated, expecting to rise no more, my Physician having taken his 16th fee, and I his prescription, I could not quit this earth without leaving a memento of my constant attachment to Butler, in gratitude for his manifold good offices" (*BLJ* 1:145). The sarcasm of the previous lines yields here to wittier fare, but the excuses of illness (cf. *BLJ* 1:111, the letter to Bankes of 6 March 1807, responding to Bankes's critique of *Poems on Various Occasions*) and dictation apologize not for animus toward Butler but for inferior verse, and if anything wish for better to mock the man. Moreover, by comically casting "Childish Recollections," that "Schoolboy thing," as a last testament, urgently articulated from the edge of the grave, Byron restores and reinforces whatever authority in his dislike of Butler is challenged by his belittling epithet. Then, in what sounds very like "defence" despite Byron's later disclaimer, he "*explains*" his sensitivity to the impact of *Hours of Idleness* (or even *Poems on Various Occasions*) at Harrow, particularly his satiric portrait of Pomposus in "Childish Recollections":

> I meant to have been down [to Harrow] in July [of 1807], but thinking my appearance immediately after the publication would be construed into an Insult, I directed my steps elsewhere [to nearby London, in fact, where, he bragged to Elizabeth Pigot, "I am here in a perpetual vortex of dissipation (very pleasant for all that.)" (*BLJ* 1:126; letter of 13 July 1807)],—besides I heard that some of the Boys had got hold of my Libellus [i.e., "small book," with the pun on its possibly slanderous contents], contrary to my wishes certainly, for though requested by two or three, I never transmitted

a single copy till October, when I gave one to a Boy since gone, after repeated importunities.—You will I trust pardon this Egotism,—as you had touched on the subject, I thought some explanation necessary, defence I shall not attempt. (*BLJ* 1:145)

One wonders whether, in its posture of moral nicety, this is the send-up it appears to be by the former scapegrace of the Harrow schoolyard, or a roundabout apology to the one-time tutor for earlier misconduct, or a fair representation of Byron's scrupulous stewardship of Butler's local reputation. That it is the first may be supported by Byron's coda, a partial quotation of Horatian lines recently recited by Francis Calvert when acquitted of a rape charge: "Be this your wall of brass, to have no guilty secrets, no wrong-doing that makes you turn pale" (*BLJ* 1:145 and n). If he confesses and begs pardon for "Egotism," Byron lets stand his attack on the egotistical Pomposus and its circulation among the boys, of which, given his reputation and the doubtlessly awed recipient of the volume, he is certainly assured. In short, this part of the letter constitutes another defiance of Harrow authority directed *to* Harrow authority. More important, the gift of the "Libellus" executes a mediated attack upon the man who has maligned him and displaced his mentor, and upon the office implicated in much earlier personal calumny. The book, that is, retaliates for the mediated insults Byron believed heaped upon him by the very man (and his brother) to whom he now announces the fact. His current affection for the Drurys notwithstanding, he adopts the offensive strategy of the former foe to avenge the insults of the successor, and in that maneuver reminds Henry Drury that the rascally rebel thrives.

But Byron has not finished with Butler. On 7 February 1808, a month after sending the previous letter and shortly after his "late interview" with Henry, he writes again, now with undoubted seriousness, responding to Henry's "hints" of Butler's willingness to bury the hatchet. The equivocation of his opening is noteworthy: "I ought perhaps to apologize for troubling you . . ." not only does not apologize but highlights the absence of apology and the doubt that it is due, and in any case "all things considered you will excuse this letter," presumably even absent the apology. The cool sting of this language typifies the tonal astringency of the whole letter, which must be extensively quoted:

If I do not mistake, you hinted to me, that you had seen the Revd. Dr. Butler, who was graciously disposed to pass an act of grace in my unworthy favour, and to remit the many and repeated denunciations of his wrath against me on former occasions, in short, to consign the past to oblivion, and laugh at the absurdities on both sides of the Question.—So far, so good. (*BLJ* 1:153)

Indeed, since "So far" all the passing and remittance and consignment and laughter are Butler's. "I confess to you fairly, reflection will *probably* [my italics] cause me to expunge any opinion I may have expressed of Butler in my *funereal* couplets." Curiously, perhaps strategically, Byron reserves the option of retaining whatever view, if any, of Butler he might have but did not necessarily articulate in his dismal "Childish Recollections." It is conceivable, of course, that such slippery phrasing means to protect Byron from legal action, but more likely he is rather frostily declining to recant, and declaring that he has as yet discovered no reason to do so. The language thaws only a little as he goes on:

> And as his character had it not been for my interference would have rested among "things unattempted yet in Prose or Rhyme," I am to blame for two reasons, in the first place for permitting Resentment to appear (contrary to the precepts of Philosophy and *Religion*) and in the second place for adhering to the *Truth* without trusting to my own *Imagination* (contrary to the precepts of *poetry*, and the privileges of Parnassus)— (*BLJ* 1:153)

The ironies of this "confession" reach farther than the future author of that showcase of resentments, *English Bards and Scotch Reviewers*, could have conceived; and long before the Swiss pilgrimage found print, Byron here links himself to the conquerer whose downfall he there attributes to a reckless flaunting of contempt for perceived inferiors (*Childe Harold's Pilgrimage* 3.40). On two grounds Byron finds himself blameworthy, neither of them false representations of Butler, both of them ironically self-serving, both of them also indicting Butler, who has, if Byron's following accusations are factual, vaunted his resentments and treacherously imagined Byron's recent failures, with total disregard of truth. For his part Byron acquits himself of the hypocrisy favored by school and church, but admits a kind of blasphemous violation of the artistic covenant by profaning fancy with truth—which is indirectly to charge Butler with guile, mendacity, and libel. Then follows this brief softening before the bill of particulars cascades torrentially in a rhetorical tour de force:

> I know that during the time I was under his dominion, I gave him cause for offence, I acted like a turbulent Schoolboy, as *you* know me always to have been, what then? a man of liberal mind would have passed over the pranks of a Tyro, at least after his departure, but how did Butler proceed? why thus—he not only libelled me in every company he entered, but encouraged a report that I had been *expelled,* this most diabolical falsehood I know from undoubted authority, was if not *sanctioned*. certainly not contradicted by him, he treated me with a degree of *personal* contempt, which nothing but the respect I bear to his Situation would have prevented me from *personally* meeting [rather than textually?], and on my afterwards remonstrating with him by Letter, for I dare not trust my temper in conversation with him, he returned not the slightest answer, though I declare upon my honour, the two Letters I addressed to him were couched in terms far more respectful than his conduct deserved, and I do not hesitate to say, any man of a disposition not totally dead to feeling and generosity would have made some atonement for the manner of my reception. (*BLJ* 1:153)

For all intents and purposes, this is one massive linguistic unit, fueled by its own momentum into a tumbling, accelerating flood of incrimination, as though released from long suppression, not merely against Butler but in its indifference to syntactical structure also against the tutor responsible for teaching Byron proper writing style. One imagines much of Mrs. Byron in it. More important, it recycles precisely the complaints familiar from Byron's early Harrow years, when he felt himself maligned by other authorities. The rumor of expulsion not only reformulates Dr. Drury's encouragement of Byron to leave Harrow in 1804 and so remembers the sense of dispensability and unwantedness accompanying it; it also degrades the character by imputing to it conduct deserving such extreme discipline. That is, the rumor of expulsion inflates the crime by maximizing the punishment. And the punishment forcefully articulates Byron's unworthiness to remain at school. Butler's tale-bearing, in short, literalizes the earlier plan to send Byron home, and amounts to his erasure from the Harrow scene. The boy has suffered such imputations on various grounds since arriving at the school, from masters and tutors, as we have seen;[9] but to know himself contemned and libeled as he achieved his greatest Harrow fame, and by its headmaster, could not have been countenanced (or later, either, as his literary reputation grew).[10]

But surely Henry Drury of all persons would have *known* the rumor spurious; he would not require telling. Part of Byron's rage here is directed *at* Henry for not authoritatively quashing the rumor of expulsion. At the least, Henry may need informing of the "*personal* contempt" that has nearly led Byron to call Butler out in a confrontational accounting. It is the impulse of the egregiously insulted gentleman, the respectable citizen named and spurned as "blackguard." Indeed, although he does not repeat the schoolboy epithet, Byron's complaints virtually place it on Butler's lips and are in any case haunted by ghosts of the prior insult, memories of which doubtless feed the epistolary indignation of 1808. Additionally, there is the discourtesy of the unanswered letters, and the disagreeable reception, presumably by Butler at Harrow, insufficiently honoring the alumnus already self-regarded as distinguished, for which gaffe Butler owes "atonement." In short, Byron has barricaded himself behind a history of "mean, supercilious, and inveterate" behavior from Butler, against Henry's hopes for a reconciliation; but, remarkably, he surrenders the decision to Henry on whether to act. It is a telling moment in the letter. For despite, or perhaps because of all Byron's raving, the trusting to Henry's "Judgment," after the apparent inflexibility of Byron's own, amounts to an invitation to proceed with arrangements for a meeting. Astonishingly, it took place four days later and was successful.

But that is another story. I have passed beyond the historical parameters of this essay, and possibly beyond useful psychological boundaries as well, in order to map the depth, intensity, and endurance of the anger Byron cultivated against Harrow authority. I am aware that some of the grievances chronicled in the letter just examined postdate Speech Day 1805. But as I have tried to suggest, they are continuous and consistent with—in some instances identical to or reconstitutions of—abuses that Byron believed himself the victim of from the day of his Harrow enrollment. Although his participation in the 4 July Speech Day 1805 took partial shape from anger suppressed or subversively rechanneled, the performance failed entirely to exorcize it.

ASSUMING NO UNRECOVERED CORRESPONDENCE between Byron and Augusta for the period, the boy let a month elapse between his final Speech Day and his resumption of contact with his sister, whether in disappointment over her absence is unclear, although his letter of 6 August is without rancor. Augusta, however, has written at least once since Speech Day, commenting upon it, and to her observation and/or queries he responds after rehearsing for her his domestic situation at Burgage Manor, where discourse follows a familiar model not unrelated to Byron's recent recitation:

> I am at this moment vis a vis and Tete a tete with that amiable personage [Mrs. Byron], who is, whilst I am writing, pouring forth compliments against your *ingratitude,* giving me many oblique hints that I ought not to correspond with you, and concluding with an interdiction that if you ever after the expiration of my minority are invited to my residence, *she* will no longer condescend to grace it with her *Imperial* presence. (*BLJ* 1:72)

Here in the subtle intertextualization of Shakespeare is figurative royalty ranting of filial ingratitude, discouraging contact with disloyal blood, threatening abandonment of the child, declining to perch in a family nest fouled by ungrateful relations.

In a wry ironization of this divisive interview, Byron develops "for your [Augusta's] amusement" a family portrait of the sort that might grace modern Christmas cards, absent, of course, the father: "My solemn countenance on the occasion, and the *meek Lamblike* demeanor of her Ladyship, which contrasted with my *saintlike visage,* forms a *striking family painting,* whilst in the background, the portraits of my Great Grandfather and Grandmother suspended in their frames, seem to look with an eye of pity on their *unfortunate descendant,* whose *worth* and *accomplishments* deserve a milder fate. I am to remain in this *Garden of Eden* one month" (*BLJ* 1:72). While the contrast between "lamblike demeanor" and "saintlike visage" may be difficult to fathom, especially as attributed to *these* persons, the epistolary portrait, despite the irony, situates this late teen securely in a restored, multigenerational family unit, where the sanity, serenity, and compassion of the elders temporarily overcome the madness, turbulence, and selfishness of the mother—those realities masked by the wishful irony of the son—and yet acknowledge the son's adversity and his entitlement to a better portion. Indeed, his *"worth"*—exactly that quality so frequently interrogated at Harrow now ancestrally authenticated—and his *"accomplishments"*—including, surely, successful negotiation through Harrow to Cambridge as well as the signal triumph on the July Speech Day, of which we are about to hear—these traits and achievements warrant his admission into a domestic paradise. Transfiguring the Burgage Manor sitting room, Byron's fantasy is also informed, I believe, by the fractured, warring, noble family whose mad patriarch he has just impersonated. In fact, in a smooth segue to reflections on that subject, Byron briefly drops back into the role, reckoning that Augusta's "*sympathetic* correspondence must be some alleviation to my *sorrows*" (*BLJ* 1:72); but instantly sensing the absurdity of the posture, he waves away such afflictions as "ludicrous" only to reclaim them as "*really* more *uncomfortable* than *amusing*" (*BLJ* 1:72). The suffering is real, his need genuine.

Augusta had written her brother about press coverage of the 4 July event, which, as Byron now explains, took a curious turn:

> I perceive you were rather surprised not to see my *consequential* name in the papers amongst the orators of our 2nd speechday, but unfortunately [does Byron number this one among the misfortunes his great grandparents' pity?] some wit who had formerly been at Harrow, suppressed the *merits* of [Edward Noel] Long, [Thomas] Farrer and myself, who were always supposed to take the Lead in Harrow eloquence, and by way of a *hoax* thought proper to insert a panegyric on those speakers who were really and truly allowed to have rather disgraced than distinguished themselves, of course for the *wit* of the thing, the best were left out and the worst inserted, which accounts for the *Gothic omission* of my *superior talents*. (*BLJ* 1:72–73)

He may here refer to a notice in the Morning Post of 9 July 1805, which reproduces the Harrow speech bill and goes on to lament the absence of "Captain Lloyd" (John Arthur Lloyd, a monitor in 1804, head of school in 1805, Hamlet's Ghost in the July 1804 speeches, and sharer with Byron of kudos for superior recitation then), now of Cambridge, whose "mantle and honourable station" are said to have settled upon one William (?) Franks, representing Shakespeare's Wolsey on the recent program. The senior Franks had appeared on the 1804 bill, but Wolsey is evidently his brother's first attempt. The notice continues: "Harrington and Wildman, senior, spoke best; but all were animated, articulate, and correct. Drury, senior, the nephew of Dr. Drury, (the last Headmaster), and Thomas Erskine senior, the son of Hon. Thomas Erskine, (the Barrister) were fated '*partes ferre secundas*' in the applauses of the audience . . ."—that is, to play or bear second roles, or to take second (i.e., an inferior) place in audience appreciation (the phrase is a metaphor from the theater meaning "to be accounted to be in second place," and sometimes refers to the function of an understudy. It is in any event an unflattering designation).[11]

Now, this is hardly a "panegyric," but it does cite boys heretofore not known for oratorical distinction, omits mention of those who were so known, and credits one (perhaps two) with lesser merit than his connections and oratorical history would appear to entitle him. The *Morning Post* of 8 June had in fact favorably reviewed Harrow's foremost rhetors: "The speeches commenced soon after one, and closed at three. They consisted of interesting selections from English and Latin authors; Sallust appeared the favourite. No French or Greek was spoken. Lord Byron and Mr. Lloyd, sen. were very successful in their respective parts. The later Gentleman is *Captain* of Harrow [cricket]." (The article goes on to compliment young Drury, the former headmaster's nephew, also praised in the July review, which may question my identification of it as the parodic story. But the citations of both Drury and Erskine in the later notice, as sons of distinguished fathers, have a political and vaguely sycophantic air about them and may not reflect sound judgment of oratorical skill.) The omission of Byron's name, however, by the paper mentioning him first a month ago, and the bestowal of the Lloyd cloak upon the unheralded Franks rather than himself, must have stung even as it amused, particularly since it suggested a falling-off from his achievement of June.[12]

It is in any case a prank worthy of Byron himself (one wonders whether he suspected Butler of masterminding it), and for its "wit" earns his generous delight and admiration, although the fivefold emphasis in the letter upon his own oratorical superiority suggests not only disappointment in the omission but eagerness to ensure Augusta's awareness of his achievement. But to one level of consciousness the irony of "*Gothic*" does not penetrate, for it *was* a barbaric substitution of failure for merit in the columns of journalistic appraisal, and, given Byron's psychological investment in the project, public acknowledgment of success would have agreeably multiplied his returns. Indeed, one might say that Byron's principal audience for his speech was only partially present; the absentee needed to hear it acclaimed. Thus his self-congratulation to Augusta is an inoffensive mode of self-promotion: Byron can admire the wit of his elision in the confidence of being unchallenged by it. For perception of the wit depends entirely upon the prior perception of Byron's and his mates' elocutionary superiority. The better they are seen to be, the wittier the paper's irony. So it is a strategic advantage to Byron to report his journalistic displacement as a comic success, especially since the way is thus opened for explanations of it citing his eloquence. Possibly sensing the egotism in the argument, however, Byron backs away, a little:

> Perhaps it was done with a view to weaken our vanity, which might be too much raised, by the flattering paragraphs [?] bestowed on our performance the 1st speechday, be that as it may, we were omitted in the account to the astonishment of all Harrow. These are *disappointments* we *great men* are liable to, and we must learn to bear them with philosophy, especially when they arise from attempts at wit. (BLJ 1:73)

The proof of weakened or chastened vanity cannot be found in this announcement which in effect discredits that excuse for the newspaper's witty substitution of disgraceful for distinguished speakers; rather, Byron's statement critiques the displacement while also reminding Augusta of his prior triumph and its public recognition. Here is the future author/performer hypersensitive to press review, and already adept at disputing censure. But his coup de grace now follows: to be a local sensation may be preferable to widespread recognition; the heat of the Harrow spotlight may feel better than the warmth of diffused celebrity. The successful speakers become more vividly present in their absence from the account than their textualized repute would have rendered them, so that for once Byron shapes out of abandonment, even of betrayal, an occasion of personal and corporate fame perhaps as satisfying as success in the event. No wonder, then, that he can counsel philosophical fortitude in the teeth of disappointment, since his own has been so fortuitously—and wittily—compensated.

But however rewarding such developments, his performance might (or might not) have more deeply affected him: "I was indeed very ill at that time [Does the "indeed" respond to Augusta's inquiry or suggestion, or merely intensify?], and after I had finished my speech was so overcome by the exertion that I was obliged to quit the room. I had caught cold by sleeping in damp sheets which was the cause of my indisposition." Does this seek to excuse a handicapped delivery that under maximum health conditions would have demanded straightforward, not ironic, journalistic notice? Or does it tout success amidst and despite adversity and indeed register satisfaction in having capitalized upon indisposition? A flushed, feverish Byron, congested and hoarse, might have made a more convincing Lear than the ruddy chap about to bat against Eton in the final match of the season. More interesting, however, is Byron's coverage, so to speak, of the effect of his performance on himself. Without accusing him of stratagem and expedience, we might merely observe the melodramatic impact of an agitated, staggering exit by a Lear concluding his speech. My inclination, however, is to suppose Byron primarily "overcome" by the passion of his delivery, by his "acting" the enraged, hurt old man (the mature poet often thought of and represented himself as older than he was) with greater energy than his malady allowed him easily to sustain. His was not a perfunctory recitation. That he strenuously entered into the role, physically and verbally, is clear, even at some risk of an ignominious finish on his knees. (Despite Byron's tempting invitation, I do not suggest that he prepared for enacting the storm scene by sleeping on wet sheets!)

Here then are the familiar lines he declaimed on 4 July 1805, without the accompaniment of special effects or the Fool, or the benefits of makeup or costume:

> Blow, winds, and crack your cheeks! rage! blow!
> You cataracts and hurricanoes, spout
> Till you have drench'd our steeples, drown'd the cocks!
> You sulphurous and thought-executing fires,
> Vaunt-couriers to oak-cleaving thunderbolts,
> Singe my white head! And thou, all-shaking thunder,
> Strike flat the thick rotundity of the world!
> Crack nature's molds, all germens spill at once
> That make ingrateful man!
> . . . .
> Rumble thy bellyful! Spit, fire! spout, rain!
> Nor rain, wind, thunder, fire, are my daughters:
> I tax not you, you elements, with unkindness;
> I never gave you kingdom, call'd you children,
> You owe me no subscription: then, let fall
> Your horrible pleasure; here I stand, your slave,
> A poor, infirm, weak, and despis'd old man.
> But yet I call you servile ministers,
> That have with two pernicious daughters join'd
> Your high-engender'd battles 'gainst a head
> So old and white as this. O! O! 'tis foul. (3.2.1–23)

Notable among the curiosities shaped by this Byronic choice is the advance in self-assurance it marks over the boy's vulnerability, a year earlier, to inspection of his body. Having then traded a Virgilian role to avoid such attention, now he thrusts physicality into the forefront of audience consciousness, a dwarfed, even puny physique against the enormity and power of the storm, and an admittedly "poor, infirm, weak, and despis'd" one at that, with, for Byron's schoolboy auditors, the economic resonances of "poor," and the memories of his unpopularity evoked by "despised," combined with the peculiar application of "infirm" and "weak," likely to revive the ridicule of his lameness, poverty, and marginalization. Add to the mix the probability of irreverent chortles erupting upon a seventeen-year-old's reference to his old white head, and the risk to Byron's dignity mounts. But something, over and above his confidence in his self-command, his respect among the boys and masters, and his oratorical gifts, compelled him to take it.

Lear, of course, utters these mighty lines out of domestic catastrophe and national peril, in enraged madness, and in an awesomely imperative mood, the precariousness and slippage of his regality traceable in the modulations of the rhetoric downward toward self-pity. But he is still, in name at least, *King* Lear, and as English royalty the eponymous hero of a Shakespearean tragedy widely known he would have had a certain allure for the young aristocrat earlier immobilized and colorless in another kingly role. Moral considerations aside, Lear is Latinus with Zanga's gusto—Latinus reclaimed and momentarily energized. Despite his psychological instability, moreover, Lear appears majestic in delivering this speech, particularly if it is excerpted from context and uninterrupted by the Fool's puncturing commentary. The part offers to Byron the chance to grandstand, in short, to look and sound every inch a king; and if discernibly lame, acceptably so in the role of the injured monarch.

Injured monarchy had of course saturated British consciousness for some years, to such an extent that public performances of *King Lear* had been suspended out of deference to King George III's observable but not yet officially conceded mental and emotional impairment. That circumstance alone—the absence of *Lear* from the stage out of (feigned?) respect for an authority figure manifestly incapacitated and discredited—might well have encouraged the rebel in Byron, particularly aroused just now by local events, once more to defy current practice and decorum by bringing royal madness into the Harrow spotlight. If so, the act was political, and freighted political implications for school government too, with the headmastership still destabilized and factionalism from the election unresolved. Byron's impersonation of Lear challenges both the mad occupancy of the English throne and those who defend its continuance.

But it also—in wonderful and important paradox—challenges impairment as disabling defect, in both performing boy and performed king. For Lear is also a king commanding, demanding—orchestrating the elemental havoc of which he is simultaneously victim. On the Harrow dancing school floor, however, much as on Shakespeare's stage, the absence of sound effects or other corroborations of the tempest would have enhanced the illusion of demonic power at the disposal of an actor sufficiently forceful in his delivery of the lines. Although admittedly the enslaved object of the terrors he invokes, Lear presents a courageous if recklessly bold and defiant stature against them, and flings into their tumultuous midst his indicting insults. The passage inscribes a king in two modalities, from two fused perspectives: as weak, beaten, cast off, and yet tough, daring, potent, enduring. The young Byron in the role can acknowledge a physical infirmity that becomes both empowering as a measure of injustice, and inconsequential against compensatory strengths, including the mastery of dazzling verbal pyrotechnics. One can imagine drawing from Byron's performance a sense of the boy's thrill in appearing to challenge, overcome, and direct the forces conspiring and unjustly mounted against him, and for the duration of the scene remaining impervious to them (excerpting the text advantageously narrows and focuses interpretive options). His is a posture of majestic supervision and fiercely defiant invulnerability that, done right, would impress power-conscious young men with this lord-actor's own fire, stamina, and gutsy courage. To the extent that his choices of texts and performance are about Byron himself—as I have argued them substantially to be—this one too asserts the boy's virility and potency, despite the admission of age and enfeeblement in the character; for nothing otherwise in the speech—particularly in its performance by a seventeen-year-old—would suggest anything but great power and irrepressible fortitude. The role for Byron is less about kingliness than power, rage, and revenge. It offers him a ritual of passage whereby he can claim a robust manhood that has been in part forged by his vanquishment of perceived injustices at Harrow, here analogically evoked and again symbolically overcome. Indeed, I would argue that the Harrow quest and passage are remembered and partially rewritten in the *Pilgrimage* of the character whose name is a virtual homophone of the school's.

The character he impersonates and introjects is also, of course, driven by rage; and here, I think, we come even nearer to the perhaps unconscious reasons for Byron's attraction to the role, and perhaps to a way of understanding the appeal of "vehemence" for him. For years the target of his mother's displaced fury at her abandoning spouse—notorious, by the way, for his ingratitude for the munificence which he squandered—more recently a surrogate for her tirades against Augusta's unfaithfulness and ingratitude, and ever the object of her wrath earned by refractory conduct, Byron here in a kind of *imitatio matrix* that yet recoils against the mother adopts the *furioso* manner of the parent to vent, harmlessly but importantly to an *attentive,* even captive, audience of peers and their parents, suppressed anger against relentless agencies of unmerited torment. But Mrs. Byron shares the targeted space with institutional authority presumably present in the audience—Henry, Mark, and particularly Dr. Butler, supervisor and creator of a mighty Harrow storm to which Byron added unique punch: Butler, who had deemed essential Byron's presence on Speech Day, now subversively become a treacherous, punitive, conspiratorial assailant. One reason driving Byron's wish for Augusta's presence was his need to feel validated in his anger by a similarly abused and provoked child, just as such validation could be inferred from an audience of boys oppressed (perhaps less severely than Byron imagined himself to have been) by school authority. But the most traumatic because unspeakable assault belonged to Lord Grey, and because so cathected and so long suppressed—or rather so precariously contained just at the edge of disclosure—it may rise to stoke Byron's expression of rage against ungrateful, betraying mistreatment.

Fundamental to what Byron regarded as shabby management by all of these parties was his sense of *impugned worth*. Losing one's knights is hardly equivalent to losing one's father, or trusted ally, or respected tutor, but by all such divestments is self-esteem shaken. Similarly, blackguardism is worthlessness. And further, to be verbally (and perhaps in earlier days physically) brutalized as a deformity, and doubly and repeatedly used as a surrogate—depended upon and repudiated by an embarrassing mother—constantly destabilizes and erodes self-respect, and in a lad of natural spirit will generate a will to retaliate, indirectly if no less energetically for that, against exactly those persons shielded by cultural convention from attacks by subordinates. In the disenfranchised, deprived Lear, Byron finds a kindred victim, whose angry utterance reflects the storm he curses, and lashes through it at those who have so grievously dishonored his rank and his humanity. A man in the eye of the storm, the focus of its wrath, is a man to be reckoned with. The speech in Lear's and Byron's hands is a cry not merely for attention, though it is that, and from agents of significance; it asserts the self, its history, its judgment, its integrity, as worthy of notice, as a weight of value, an individuality meriting respect in the world.

But a more immediate if equally encoded end served by Byron's selection and delivery of the Shakespearean text developed from contemporaneous circumstances at Harrow. I refer again to the unexpected, voluntary retirement of Dr. Joseph Drury, the imminence of which, as we have seen, Byron had known—confidentially, probably as privileged student—since November 1804, and about which, as we have also seen, he remained deeply unhappy. For reasons perhaps not entirely capable of understanding by admiring boys to whom adult domestic responsibilities and retirement seem unfathomable and impossibly remote prospects, especially when their own interests are sacrificed thereunto, the much-loved and respected Drury, despite such love, resigned his kingdom, which, even under new management, continued to feel the shock of his departure for some months after the event, into the summer term of the July 1805 Speech Day and beyond. Of the three contenders for the headmastership, two came from within—one the child of the abandoning "father," the other effectively another "son" by long and close association as master with Harrow and the Drury family—while the third, an alien trespasser, hailed from Cambridge. These three vie for the evacuated throne, the beloved son finally losing, by an act of the authoritative church, to the foreigner.

One could not even by a stretch call these circumstances parallel to Lear's, but a rough, broad similarity might have encouraged Byron's selection of the Shakespearean role that provided him a platform for denouncing not merely the successful "heir" but also the figure who prematurely opened the way to succession. By adopting the role of the disappointing "father" (Lear and Drury), Byron can appear to protect that authority from his wrath, in any event largely displaced onto Butler: the traduced son replaces the offending authority, at once redeeming and by elimination condemning him. At the same time, "being Lear" also lets Byron honor the headmaster now effectively cast out, if by his own hand, in a personal tribute perhaps more meaningful to him than participation in the gift of plate; for the speaking, the act itself, validates and celebrates the oratorical gift that Dr. Drury was the first, more than a year earlier, to identify in the boy, and that now appeared to prophesy parliamentary distinction. These psychological dynamics are indeed complex, but I believe that as the disenfranchised king, Byron simultaneously enacts a sympathy with his plight, a chagrin against his irresponsible and neglectful resignation, and resentment against any who would take advantage of it. Moreover, inasmuch as Lear dictates to the elements, enjoins and reproaches them not unlike an exasperated master might harangue a class of refractory boys, this speech in an irreverent Byron's hands might turn into a kind of parody of the proper Butler's institutional and disciplinary style. It seems a profanation to so speculate, but such mockery is well within Byron's imagination and range; and he might have been tempted to it by Butler's rigid insistence on his participation in Speech Day and his deep antipathy for the man.

More certain, however, is the appeal to Byron of another component of the scene, however absent in his representation of it. Indeed, the persistence of this element in the play would have resonated with and reinforced a strain in Byron that found its supreme expression many years later but is traceable from the beginning of the career. I refer to the counterpointing presence of the Fool at Lear's side on the storm-wracked heath and to his two deflating observations on the king's rodomontade. That this presence would have been elided in Byron's recitation is supported by its documented absence in professional productions of *King Lear* at the time. As we have seen, the madness of King George III kept the play off the stage for many years, and when it was produced, the Tate version persisted. Only with McCready's 1838 production did the Fool reappear. Byron surely knew the original, even as a schoolboy, but it is unlikely that either he in choosing his text or his audience in hearing it would have expected inclusion of the Fool's lines. Coleridge in his Shakespearean criticism says nothing of the Fool; Lamb, whose own prose shares the tonal range I am here highlighting, when arguing in "The Tragedies of Shakespeare" that they cannot be acted (*Lear* is too solemn and sublime for representation), says nothing of the complex counterpointing lost in the acting version of the play. And yet I suspect that the Fool's contributions to it helped to excite Byron's interest by feeding—encouraging, endorsing—an instinct for puncturing pretense that marked even his schoolboy verses and distinguished his masterworks.

Byron the mouthpiece for Lear's language would not, I think, even at seventeen, have deceived Byron the reader of *King Lear* into accepting as truth the vision of the perorating monarch without the sanative balancing commentary of his retainer. Writing of "the grotesque" in the play, Susan Snyder points out Shakespeare's positioning of "tragic stature and suffering in uneasy proximity with the laughable, the irrelevant, the reductive": "Cataracts and hurricanes unexpectedly shrink into the prosaic 'rain-water out o' door' [in the Fool's remark]. However magnificent Lear's words and actions here, we cannot shut out another sense of him as an impotent old man comically at odds with reality," thanks to the Fool, who draws "the grandly remote down to the physical and near.... Lear reasons largely with the elements about kingdoms and moral obligations, while the Fool reflects on codpieces, lice, and corns" (162).[13] So reviewed, it is difficult for the student of Byron not to hear anticipated in *King Lear* the normative incongruities and discontinuities that so shocked readers of *Don Juan*, where not merely the dualities but multiplicities of perspective define epic vision—where grand passions rise from trivialities, epic verse from "common things." No less than *Lear,* although with different results, *Don Juan* proceeds from domestic bickering (Snyder, about *King Lear*, p. 166), just as does Byron's choice of an oration that recapitulates, extends, and retaliates for it. I do not propose *Lear* as a source for Byron's masterpiece, but I do suggest that the countervailing, often deflating reversals of *Don Juan* insist upon the perceptival capaciousness, even the abrupt shifts from sublime to pathetic, illustrated in the dialogue between King and Fool in the passage at hand and elsewhere in the drama, these two emblematic of the (in)compatibilities that Byron thought vitalizing as well as amusing in human life. The "grotesquerie" of Shakespeare's juxtapositions becomes Byron's comic blood. And our double sense of Byron the brooding melancholic and inveterate mischief maker at Harrow suggests his sensitivity to a text linking highs and lows in complementary association.

Two notes may close this discussion of *King Lear*. In August 1805, Mary Ann Chaworth wed John Musters, nuptials inspiring Byron's "Fragment Written Shortly after the Marriage of Miss Chaworth," whose literary source McGann locates in Richard Gall's "Farewell to Ayrshire," thought at the time to be Robert Burns's (*CPW* 1:356). But the imagery and action of Byron's first quatrain arise from residual memory of the passage he had proclaimed a month before:

> Hills of Annesley, bleak and barren
>   Where my thoughtless childhood stray'd,
> How the northern tempests, warring,
>   Howl above thy tufted shade!

The two stanzas lament a paradise lost, if not by his choice, nevertheless transforming his world and depriving him of a second home.

The second instance arises directly from the Speech Day experience. A cooling, Cambridge year's remove from his performance of the *Lear* text enabled the detachment and self-mockery of the following quatrain from Byron's "On a Distant View of the Village and School, of Harrow, on the Hill":

> Or, as Lear, I pour'd forth the deep imprecation,
>   By my daughters, of kingdom and reason depriv'd;
> Till, fir'd by loud plaudits, and self-adoration,
>   I regarded myself, as a Garrick reviv'd.

Its irony notwithstanding, the last line frankly purloins the epithet journalistically assigned to William Betty, as indeed the previous one might just as aptly describe Byron as the boy star. Master Betty's subtextual presence in these lines, together with the allusion to Mossop already examined, affirms the probability of Byron's rivalry with him a year earlier, for here no cover disguises, no Mossop masks it; the line usurps Betty's title and his fame, and helps to reinstate the gravity of a Speech Day recitation otherwise challenged by the hint of tonal scoff. Indeed, that Byron's recollection and inscription of his July performance prompts a tempered jeer may defend arguments for the personal claims of Lear's address upon him.[14]

Epilogue : "*The Sixth of June*"

"I LIKE TO BE PARTICULAR IN DATES," Byron writes in designating "the sixth of June" as the evening, between 6:30 and 7 P.M., of Julia's capitulation to the Juanistic addresses she has so adroitly elicited, although eighteen stanzas later *Don Juan* is less scrupulous about the day of the lovers' exposure (". . . we'll say / 'Twas in November, but I'm not so sure / About the day—the era's more obscure" [*DJ* 1.121]). Byron's specificity about the one and indifference to the other dating, while typifying the vaunted inconsistency of *Juan*'s narrator, also privileges the earlier event, grants it greater historical and commemorative status, for no very obvious reason except that, psychologically speaking, the ending signified by the November dustup, like all endings for Byron, freighted pain whose sting might be lessened by temporal imprecision. Or with the indefinitely dated terminus of the five-month affair, he may remind us that for all the unremembered dates of our countless separations, there is no forgetting—or repeating—our first sexual union: the one is indelibly etched, whereas the others are dim and become in some sort interchangeable, sharing a universal commonness anathema to the uniqueness of our sixths of June. But such arguments do not address the *particular* particularity of Byron's dateline for the onset of Juan's and Julia's intrigue. Insofar as I can determine, no contemporaneous historical, political, or social event of that date carried any special significance for Byron; in his personal life up to 1819 (the composition date of *Don Juan* I), insofar as I can with hazard conjecture, only one (other) recorded 6 June occurrence might have registered on Byron's mind with sufficient force and overdetermination to draw the date into the *Juan* text as the occasion for his lovers' summertime tryst.[1] For one thing, inasmuch as particular dates are for Byron pivotal turning points "where the Fates / Change horses, making history change its tune" (*DJ* 1.103), *this* specific date, 6 June, is more crucially a "fatal day" for the poet, for "without [its] epoch my poetic skill . . . would all be thrown away" (*DJ* 1.121): on this precise date and its unique occurrences rests the author's livelihood—perhaps an ironic inflation reminiscent of an investment in Speech Day and its attendant anxieties.

For another thing, *Don Juan* 1.126 very nearly *names the site* of that early investment: "and dear the schoolboy spot / We ne'er forget, though there we are forgot" (with unconscious, subtextual resonances of mnenomic anxiety on Speech Days). Climactically positioned in Byron's long catalog of "sweets," this reference to Harrow immediately neighbors, and even provides transition to, his return to the central subject off which the others have spun—"first and passionate love"—and against which all other sweetness abates. That is, between recollection of Harrow and the subject of the fabliau narrative there is literally, and I suspect mentally, no space.

For a third, the liaison between Julia and Juan launches them on a duplicitous course ending in a declamation—a deliberately, self-consciously performative speech act by which Julia assumes a role, feigns, with spectacular success, an identity not her own: she acts a part. Precisely in her speech she counterfeits, in a setting of general masquerade, her physically virtuous self abandoned five months earlier; indeed, as fabliau, the entire bedroom episode has the tenor, climate, and artificiality of stage—staged—farce. That Julia's harangue is usually thought to recollect Mrs. Byron's diatribes to her son strengthens, I think, the possibility of its connection to Byron's Speech Day participation, given the interweaving of these subjects in his consciousness as disclosed in contemporaneous letters. More important, however, is the highly rhetorical structure of Julia's philippic: much of it is built upon the formula—from Thomson, Burke, Milton, Pope, Ariosto, Virgil, and Homer—that furnished Wordsworth with his query opening the 1799 *Prelude*.[2] "It was for this that I became a bride," Julia imperiously asks (in what will sound to modern ears a distinctly Yiddish accent!), and, turning the phrase into an interrogatory ("Is it . . . ," or "Was it . . . ?"), repeats the formula six more times, and assumes it in the remaining lines numbering her suitors (*DJ* 1.145–51).

Despite the dramatic circumstances of its inspiration, Julia's harangue is a set-piece,[3] its first half in particular a stylized, formalized, constructed affair, for Byron parodies both his mother's rebukes and classical and modern literary sources (indeed, in rhythms and rhetoric, Julia's speech at points echoes parts of Byron's 1 November 1804 letter to Augusta: "Am I to call this woman mother?" [*BLJ* 1:56])—for us emotionally and circumstantially traceable to Byron's role in the Harrow summer festivities of 1804 and 1805. It is perhaps also worth mentioning that Julia delivers the entirety of her speech from bed, possibly from a supine posture, a fact that helps baffled students understand Alfonso's failure to search the sheets: if that narrative requirement explains Byron's positioning of Julia in the scene, we should nevertheless remember his early preference for a Speech Day role requiring little or no mobility. And the evidence ultimately exposing Juan's presence in the bedroom is a pair of shoes that textually reconfigure the boot that betrayed young Byron's anomaly in the Harrow school yard.

Various features of Byron's narrative of and editorializing upon the 6 June rendezvous also indicate latent Speech Day content in his text. Stanza 104 honors Thomas Moore—Anacreon—(blasted in *English Bards*) with "lyre and laurels" and "all the trophies of triumphant song" he has "won" for linguistic achievement in the public arena, and 1.126 admits, "'Tis sweet to win, no matter how, one's laurels / By blood or ink." The entire section might be said to debate the wisdom and usefulness of speaking and speechmaking by this unstoppably garrulous narrator: even were he privy to arrangements for the Juan/Julia interview, for example, "People should hold their tongues in any case" (1.105). In stanza 108 speech scolds, provokes dread, especially when *recited* by performing poets. Upon receiving Juan's timid kiss, Julia "strove to speak but held her tongue" (echoing the narrator's doctrine of 1.105), "her voice had grown so weak" (1.102)—a physiologically interesting tension, and a condition curiously difficult of determination! Like the narrator's voice, which prudently fails at the critical moment—"I can't go on," he cries—"Julia's voice was lost, except in sighs" until uttering, in whispers, the nonconsenting consent, which itself interrogates speechmaking in its lie: her four denying and surrendering words—"I will ne'er consent"—constitute a miniature version of her thirteen-stanza declamation, and are an encapsulated lie enacting its own prevarication, once more calling into question the act of speech. Likewise, stirred by Alfonso's interrogative lash, "Julia's tongue was not asleep" (1.146), and triumphantly avenges itself on her bumbling spouse.

The narrator has long since warned us about the "silence . . . [and] stillness" in the hour of Juan's and Julia's rendezvous, an ominous space for losing self-control (1.114), and in neat follow-up he himself falls silent not only on the moment of consummation but on the months thereafter, presumably because they offer nothing of comparable interest to the 6 June event. Finally, as Byron reviews revolutionary and innovative phenomena of his day (possibly incorporating remembrance of the flap over Butler's ascendancy at Harrow: *DJ* 1.129–30), he exclaims, "What wondrous new machines have late been spinning," an allusion to the spinning jennies which, McGann notes, "ignited England's notorious frame-breaking riots,"⁴ in sympathy with which Byron spoke in the House of Lords on 27 February 1812. Although he would speak again before his peers, that inaugural appearance, judged by himself to have been "loud & fluent enough . . . [but] perhaps a little theatrical" (*BLJ* 2:167; 5 March 1812), also climaxed the parliamentary career encouraged by Byron's participation in Harrow Speech Days 1805. But the performative penchant and genius there displayed became, ere long and for a lifetime, exhibitions on the international stage.

Notes

Prologue

1. My thinking about the life and works of Lord Byron has been significantly reshaped by Jerome Christensen's majesterial *Lord Byron's Strength* (Baltimore: Johns Hopkins University Press, 1993). Differing in a few particulars, we agree, I believe, about the general if fluid contours of the poet's identity. I locate the genesis and emergence of that identity in performative occasions of Byron's adolescence, and partially ascribe its development to the boy's reactive and proactive manipulation of his associates and environment. I accept Christensen's conclusion that our subject achieves Lord Byron's strength, but I see the lad beginning his workouts, practicing his exercise regimen, at Harrow School, in London, and in related precincts of his 1804–5 tenancy. Further, Christensen and I agree on who Byron was in the process of becoming who "Byron" is, although we focus on different phases of the "career," or the career making, which in my view commences at school, before the powerful forces astutely charted by Christensen collaborated in self-interested labor to produce the lucrative stardom of "Byron." Nothing that I claim about the boy seems to me fundamentally incompatible with Christensen's reading of the mature(ing) poet, and much of it foresees the culturally authored phenomenon whom he features.

2. P. H. M. Bryant, *Harrow* (London: Blackie and Son, 1936), 30. Here is the official explanation, from the "articles subjoined to the Statutes" of the school in the introduction to the bound collection of Harrow speech bills from the headmasterships of Dr. Joseph Drury (1780–1805) and Dr. Samuel Butler (1805–29), dated 1848. "The reasons which induced him [Dr. Heath] to abandon this ancient custom [practiced since the establishment of the school] was dignified and just: they are stated to have been the frequent exceptions from the regular business of school,—which they, who practised [*sic*] as Competitors for the prize, claimed *as a privilege, not to be infringed upon!*—as well as the band of profligate and disorderly persons, whom this exhibition brought down into the village, by reason of its vicinity to the metropolis [eleven miles]. These encroachments and annoyances had at length become so injurious to *discipline and morals,* as, after some vain attempts at correction of the evil, to call for the total abolition of the usage." Elimination of the contests appears to have represented a bold departure from a longstanding recreational emphasis at Harrow, for the

school's founder, John Lyon, had at the outset instructed boys' parents "to allow your child at all times *bowshafts, bowstrings,* and a *bracer* to exercise shooting" (ibid.). A legend current in Byron's time held that "the accidental shooting of a spectator" occasioned Dr. Heath's suppression of the archery contest (*Harrow School,* ed. Edmund W. Hawson and George Townsend Warner [London, 1898], 201; hereafter Hawson and Warner).

3. E. D. Laborde, *Harrow School Yesterday and Today* (London: Winchester Publications, 1948), 85.

4. Hawson and Warner, 199.

5. Quoted in Hawson and Warner, 201. The costume is anomalous. Speech Day participants at Harrow have rarely dressed to the role, and when doing so, only in minimalist and symbolic fashion. Whether Sheridan's example is responsible for such restraint remains uncertain.

6. Mr. Alex Ward, a participant in the 1998 Harrow Speech Day, has told me that a qualifying credential for speaking continues to be successful experience in debating societies and theatrical productions.

7. *Boswell for the Defence 1769–1774,* ed. W. K. Wimsatt and F. A. Pottle (New York: McGraw-Hill, 1959), 162.

8. H. C. Maxwell Lyte, *A History of Eton College, 1440–1884* (London: Macmillan, 1889), 369.

9. Anonymous, *Merchant Taylors' School* (Oxford: Blackwell, 1929), 58.

10. B. P. Lacelles in Hawson and Warner, 203–4.

11. Lawrence E. Tanner, *Westminster School* (London: Country Life Ltd., 1934), 65. For the following account of speechmaking at Westminster School, I am most gratefully indebted to Mr. Peter Holmes, the school archivist, for a letter of 15 January 1999: "Oral competitions, in the form of recitations, took place at the School until recently: such contests were originally held in the presence of the entire student body, being later scaled down to performance of these Orations (as they were called) by members of the Fifth Form (the youngest year group) in front of their peers. They were generally light-hearted and sometimes quite rowdy—and therefore much enjoyed by the pupils. The current rigor of the curriculum has led to their discontinuance.

"Nowadays, such customs are recalled chiefly by the recitation of the Prooemium and Epigrams at the Election Dinner. The Prooemium is declaimed by three Queen's Scholars of the Second Election (the next-to-the-youngest year group): the text is written by the Head Master, and in it he traditionally refers to eminent guests, such as the Prince of Wales at last year's dinner [1998]. The text is shared out among the . . . Scholars . . . at the end of term. Epigrams are recited and songs sung by the pupils as a further part of the entertainment, celebrating personalities and satirizing current events, as the selection may indicate. Each year two themes are chosen, one in Greek and the other in Latin, and the resulting epigrams in both the classical languages and modern ones, with concealed jokes, are composed by Common Room members, and accompanied by an English version."

12. James Sabben-Clare, current Winchester headmaster, in *Winchester College after 606 Years, 1382–1988* (Winchester: P and G Wells, 1989), 154, 156. See also Herbert Chitty, *Medal Speaking at Winchester College, 1761–1815* (Winchester: Wykehamist Society, Jacob and Johnson, 1905).

13. The following record, if describing an Eton election unusual in one respect, also captures the color, flair, and festivity of the traditional event:

> The election of 1778 was remarkable for the number of distinguished visitors who came to Eton to hear the speeches on the Monday. The royal children arrived about noon in three carriages, preceded by twelve running footmen. The King and Queen followed "in their own postchariot" and drove into the School-Yard, where they were received by two of the Fellows, and the Head-Master and Usher, the Provost being laid up with an attack of the gout. The Archbishop of Canterbury, Lord North, and other distinguished persons were assembled in the Upper School, and no time was lost in proceeding to the business of the day. Lord Wellesley, one of the senior Oppidans, enjoyed the exceptional honour of making two recitations, the latter of which, Lord Strafford's last speech [Thomas Wentworth, first Earl of Strafford (1593–1641) and favorite lieutenant of Charles I until caught in the religio-political fallout of the Scottish Rebellion, whose speech on the scaffold before execution for treason is among the most eloquently stirring farewells in British history. See the *DNB* 20:1179–94], he delivered with such pathos as to draw tears from the whole audience. The Prince of Wales and the Bishop of Osnaburg, we are told, "took most affectionate notice of all the speakers, shaking hands with them several times." The Royal Party proceeded from the Upper School to the Church and thence to the Long Chamber, where every Scholar stood by his own bedside.... After the speeches the Archbishop of Canterbury took Lord Wellesley with him to spend part of the summer holidays at Lambeth, and on the way they called on David Garrick at Hampton. "Your Lordship," said the great tragedian to Lord Wellesley, "has done what I never could accomplish—made the King weep." "That," replied the hero of the morning with equal courtesy, "is because you never spoke before him in the character of a fallen favourite." (Lyte, *A History of Eton College, 1440–1884*, 322–23)

See also p. 300 on the Eton schedule of speeches and declamations during the academic year, and on their Greek and Latin sources.

14. By the early nineteenth century at Merchant Taylors', recitation of original epigrams in Latin, Greek, and English accompanied Election Day. Some boys resorted to ghost writers, among whom Charles Lamb may be the best known today. In 1830, Lamb on request supplied two epigrams, one in English and one in Latin, for the sons of James Augustus Hessey, one of them later Archdeacon Hessey. But in 1803 Lamb had expressed to William Godwin

his difficulty in writing verses to order several times for Merchant Taylors' schoolboys at a guinea apiece. See E. V. Lucas, ed., *The Works of Charles and Mary Lamb* (London: Methuen, 1903), 5:339–40.

15. The Honorable Gilbert Coleridge, *Eton in the 'Seventies* (London: Smith, Elder, 1912), 126–30.

16. Quoted in Laborde, 87–88.

17. G. W. Fisher, *Annals of Shrewsbury School* (London, 1899), 318.

18. But not rapidly enough, evidently, to suit some. The *Eton Chronicle* prints the following letter from "Ophelia" in its edition of 27 October 1864: "Sir: It strikes me that the Histrionic Interests of the school are neglected. It is true that isolated houses perform plays, and it is also true that at Mr. Tarver's a few plays were enacted last *March,* but nothing at all equivalent to the world-renowned, and never-to-be-forgotten, celebrity of the 'Westminster Play,' an institution looked forward to by many every year. . . . Let a play worthy of the school and the occasion be enacted. Why should Etonians be content with broad farces and miserable comedies 'from the French?' Let Etonians aim higher; Shakespeare is a worthy subject to try upon. Let present Etonians form a Histrionic Club, and on the boards of the Mathematical School act Hamlet, or some such light and easy subject . . ."—to which recommendation the editor sensibly responds, "We think she is out of her reckoning when she proposes Hamlet, as a 'light and easy subject' to begin with" (116).

19. Judith Pascoe, *Romantic Theatricality: Gender, Poetry, and Spectatorship* (Ithaca: Cornell University Press, 1997), 7. See also, for example: Jonathan Bate, *Shakespearean Constitutions: Politics, Theatre, Criticism, 1730–1830* (Oxford: Oxford University Press, 1989); Paula R. Backschieder, *Spectacular Politics: Theatrical Power and Mass Culture in Early Modern England* (Baltimore: Johns Hopkins University Press, 1993); Marc Baer, *Theatre and Disorder in Late Georgian London* (Oxford: Clarendon, 1992); Julie A. Carlson, *In the Theatre of Romanticism: Coleridge, Nationalism, Women* (New York: Cambridge University Press, 1994): Marilyn Gaul, "Romantic Theatre," *Wordsworth Circle* 14 (1983), 255–63; Andrea K. Henderson, *Romantic Identities: Varieties of Subjectivity 1774–1830* (Cambridge: Cambridge University Press, 1996); Mary Jacobus, " 'That Great Stage Where Senators Perform': *Macbeth* and the Politics of Romantic Theatre," in *Romanticism, Writing, and Sexual Difference: Essays on "The Prelude"* (Oxford: Clarendon, 1989), 33–68; Alan Richardson, *A Mental Theatre: Poetic Drama and Consciousness in the Romantic Age* (University Park: Pennsylvania State University Press, 1988); Sybil Rosenfeld, *Temples of Thespis: Some Private Theatres and Theatricals in England and Wales, 1700–1820* (London: Society for Theatre Research, 1978); Gillian Russell, *The Theatres of War: Performance, Politics, and Society, 1793–1815* (Oxford: Clarendon, 1995); Timothy Webb, "The Romantic Poet and the Stage: A Short, Sad History," in *The Romantic Theatre: An International Symposium,* ed. Richard Allen Cave (Totowa, N.J.: Barnes and Noble, 1986), 9–46.

20. Pascoe, *Romantic Theatricality,* 13.

1. Tutor and Tenant

1. It is germane to the argument below that one of two very early surviving portraits of Byron (by John Kaye of Edinburgh) shows him as a surprisingly mature, slight, and feminized seven-year-old, poised with bow and arrow before a middle-distanced target, with a leafy fern discreetly obscuring—while also drawing attention to—part of the right foot. If aware of the provenance of Harrow Speech Day, Byron might well have been eager to declaim in part because of the event's birth in an athletic competition that was, unlike most others at the school, open to him. As we shall see, he aims his speeches at human targets otherwise shielded from his avenging ire.

2. No fewer than thirteen years after his death, "Byron" was heard again on Harrow Speech Day, in a performance, by one Ommanney (a first class in examinations that year), of a selection from *Marino Faliero*. On the two "bills" for 1838, *Manfred* appears twice and *Marino Faliero* once. For comparative purposes, it may be noted that the 1996 speeches celebrated the 250th anniversary of the birth of Sir William Jones, Harrow alumnus (1763) and famed orientalist, linguist, and jurist; seven of the speeches, including one in French, were excerpted from Sir William's works, the eighth from an elegy on his death. The 1999 speeches, headlined "Good Sports and Honest Games," honored the retiring headmaster, Mr. N. R. Bomford, and his spouse; arranged by category—hunting, hawking, fowling, and fishing—the nine speeches represented authors from Izaak Walton to S. T. Coleridge to A. A. Milne to Ted Hughes.

3. *King Lear* is very rarely a selection and Zanga makes no appearance on speech day programs that I have seen from other institutions.

4. E. C. Mayne, *Byron* (London: Methuen, 1924), 23.

5. When Byron and his mother first occupied Newstead Abbey, the inherited estate, Mrs. Byron's annual income was £122. Facing medical and educational expenses, with the attorney John Hanson's assistance and the Earl of Carlisle's endorsement, she petitioned the king, and subsequently on Pitt's instructions received "a provision of £300 a year" from the Civil List (Marchand 1:56). But the pension was reduced to £200 (and erratically paid) when Byron received a grant of £500 from the Court of Chancery expressly for his education (Marchand 1:68). Without such assistance, Harrow schooling would have been impossible for the young lord; thanks to his extravagance, it was a stretch in any case. That Byron's impecunious state relative to his title remained a conscious consideration of the Harrow staff is clear in Dr. Joseph Drury's allusion to it ("Deficiencies of fortune") in a letter to John Hanson of 4 February 1803 (Prothero 1:13); and see below.

6. Pryse Lockhart Gordon, *Personal Memoirs*, 2 vols. (London, 1830), 2:320.

7. But it should be remarked here that within a year the salutary discipline and social obligations of the school had begun to effect agreeable changes. Pryse Gordon, an acquaintance of Mrs. Byron who saw the boy often in London on

school holidays, remembered him at fourteen as "a fine, lively, restless lad, full of fire and energy, and passionately fond of riding" (*Personal Memoirs*, 2:332).

8. Henry Drury was twenty-three and recently graduated from Cambridge when delivered into Byron's hands, and the thirteen-year-old into his. He is remembered (not by Byron) as "a big, stalwart man" particularly effective in disciplining by intimidation; "often idle and capricious himself, he had the art of constantly keeping his boys in terror of his vigilance & of managing a whole class while his attention was necessarily fixed on one at a time" (quoted in Benita Eisler, *Byron: Child of Passion, Fool of Fame* [New York: Knopf, 1999], 51, from J. G. Cotton Minchin, *Old Harrow Days* [London: Methuen, 1898], 193, although I have been unable to locate the passage in Minchin's volume as cited by Eisler). That Byron is willing to take on, if indirectly, so formidable a presence witnesses not only a kind of reckless courage along with the petulance but also conviction in the justice of the principles he defends in so doing. The charge of "capriciousness" in Minchin's characterization links Henry with a habit of behavior seen in Byron himself; more important, it is one of Byron's most potent articulated charges against Lord Grey, who shares both Henry Drury's age and name. See below.

Responding to his own question, "Was the Rev. Harry Drury the kind of tutor for an extremely sensitive, erratic, and impressionable boy of genius?" Minchin writes, "After reading Trollope and Gambier one is tempted to think that to the list of Byron's unfortunate connections—father, mother and wife—may be added still one more, that of his tutor" (228). The first allusion is to Thomas Adolphus Trollope's *What I Remember*, a generally dyspeptic recollection of the author's Harrow years. S. J. Gambier's presumably similar unfavorable review of Henry Drury is unpublished, but Minchin reports its claim that by 1832 Drury was "completely past work": "He used to eat fruit in class" (196).

9. See "On the Death of a Young Lady, Cousin to the Author and Very Dear to Him," identified as his "first Essay," composed when he was fourteen; but McGann says that another poem to Parker, now lost, was his earliest (*CPW* 1:125).

10. Mrs. Byron had written to Hanson on her son's behalf: "Byron wishes you would write to Mr. Evans not to be prejudiced against him by H. Drury" (Willis W. Pratt, *Byron at Southwell: The Making of a Poet* [Austin: University of Texas Byron Monographs, No. 1, 1948], 6).

11. Byron's capitalizations are erratic but this one may be telling: Henry's offense is less the reprimand itself than the publicity of it—the currency made of it.

12. Probably as native proclivity and gift, Byron's theatricality exercised itself at Harrow even before given a platform, and with an actor's instinct for upstaging the competition. Newton Hanson with his father John Hanson, the Byrons' attorney, attended a Harrow Speech Day prior to Byron's participation in the event, where the young man "either to regale or shock his visitors, had

got on Dr. Drury's hat. The little boys, who ran to tell him of the Hansons' coming, laughed most heartily. It was much too large for his small head. The arch cock of his eye at the hat and then at his solicitor was unforgettable. He wore it during all the day," almost certainly diverting attention from the main events by this deviltry, and possibly distracting and irritating the headmaster on his most important public relations day. (Inasmuch as Newton Hanson's manuscript has been unavailable to me in the temporarily closed Murray archives, I take this account from Dora Neill Raymond's *The Political Career of Lord Byron* [New York: Henry Holt, 1924], 6–7).

13. Byron's affection for Harrow and comfort with its protocols grew in proportion to the success of his endeavors and their attraction of admiration. The intensity of "hate" at the beginning turned over into ardent love by the end, as he advanced in stature and favor. The academic slovenliness of his early months should not be extrapolated to cover the Harrow career. He read vastly, if mostly to his own taste. But he must also have bent to the discipline, in due course, for J. G. Cotton Minchin reports that in the 1803 and 1805 bill books, "Byron's name occurs as top of the fifth form [1803] and in the latter case [1805] as a monitor and third boy in the School" (*Old Harrow Days* [London: Methuen, 1898], 310).

14. Eric Partridge, *A Dictionary of Slang,* 8th ed. (London: Routledge and Kegan Paul, 1984), 88. See also Hugh Rawson, *Wicked Words* (New York: Crown, 1989), 45, citing the 13th edition of *Encyclopedia Britannica* (1926): "George IV's tutor, Bishop Richard Hurd, said of him when he was fifteen years old that he would be 'either the most polished gentleman or the most accomplished blackguard in Europe—possibly both, and the latter prediction was only too fully justified.'"

15. For this observation, I am indebted to my student Lisa Nevarez, an astute Byronist. Bernard Blackstone calls "Blackguard" "a favourite word with Byron," and posits its correspondence to the "banausic" of Plato's *Republic,* "the third order of men," but out of which category "highly gifted spirits could ascend to the two orders of the Guardians. . . . a [A] 'blackguard' belongs to the plebs, to the workers, indeed—and most disgustingly—to *trade*" ("Byron and the *Republic:* The Platonic Background to Byron's Political Ideas," in *Byron: Poetry and Politics,* ed. Erwin A. Sturzl and James Hogg [Salzburg: Institut für Anglistik und Amerikanistik Universitat Salzburg, 1981], 14n, 31). I have not found an entry for *blackguard* in any of the glossaries or dictionaries of public school parlance made available to me, but interestingly enough the word occurs eight times by my count in Thomas Hughes's *Tom Brown's Schooldays* (1857), about Rugby life in the 1830s, on each occasion with meanings approximating those just described. Here is a sampling: Tom's new-found friend East "begins hectoring two or three long loafing fellows, half porter half stableman, with a strong touch of the blackguard; and in the end arranges with one of them—to carry Tom's luggage up to the School house for sixpence" (*Tom Brown's Schooldays* [London: Oxford World's Classics, 1989], 90); from "Pater" Brook's part-

ing speech: "There was the good old custom of taking the linchpins out of the farmers' and bagmens' gigs at the fairs, and a cowardly blackguard custom it was" (124); "Every school, indeed, has its own traditional standard of right and wrong, which cannot be transgressed with impunity, marking certain things as low and blackguard, and certain others as lawful and right" (168). Personally, the epithet is associated with the bully Flashman, "who never speaks to one without a kick or an oath" (171), and who freely applies the term to any, including Tom, perceived to be foes (e.g., 183 and 191); but Tom also uses the term against a keeper of the property adjacent to the school, when caught illegally fishing, and again against one of the "miserable little pretty white-haired curly-headed boys, petted and pampered by some of the big fellows" who attempt to recruit him and East as fags for his "protector" (233–34). That the term *blackguard* persisted as a commonplace of disrepute on the school ground may also be witnessed by Mary McCarthy's use of it as title for the chapter in *Memories of a Catholic Girlhood* in which Mary rapturously embraces the epithet when accused by a teacher of being "a blackguard—just like Byron."

16. Charles Drury's "Memoir" praises Dr. Drury's percipience in taking "early note" of Byron's "genius," for "indications he gave of it while a school-boy were perceptible to few besides"; but it identifies Byron as one of the "favourite scholars" whom the headmaster regretted to leave behind upon quitting Harrow, in 1806, in retirement (14 and 16).

17. I have elsewhere studied the recurrent phenomenon of the "farewell event" in Byron's poetry, and the biographical circumstances and psychological imperatives that drove it. Subsequent notes identify specific essays relevant to arguments advanced below. The end of Byron's Harrow career ranks high among traumatic separations that troubled his early years and helped to fashion the disjunctive moment as a major trope in the canon.

18. Blackstone believes Harrow "the true city-state for Byron. Life here reflected the *Republic* values of 'justice'—every individual doing his own thing for the good of the whole (*Republic* IV 433)—and 'wisdom,' the guiding function of the Guardians" (12–13).

19. The lonely insecurity driving the urgency of the couplet concluding my quotation contributes to the construction of frequent figures of outstretched hands in Byron's verse; see, for example, the end of *Childe Harold's Pilgrimage,* canto 4 and of *Manfred.*

20. Byron may, of course, mean "justify your charge" rather than "explain what it means." But in any event he is asking for an explanation and justification of his alleged "blackguardism," clearly in his view a misinformed, irrational use of the language by the tutor who teaches and judges it.

21. I have confirmed with Melissa Bakewell, coauthor with Michael Bakewell of a forthcoming biography of Augusta Leigh, that no letters from his half sister to Byron during his school years have survived, save those noticed by Prothero: "Augusta," said Ms. Bakewell, "had other fish to fry; her young brother was not high on her list of priorities at the time." I am grateful to

Ms. Bakewell for most graciously taking an unexpected telephone call on a Saturday morning, and to Professor Charles Robinson for putting me in contact with her.

22. Citing Thomas Moore's phrase "an intimacy . . . soon sprung up between Byron and his noble tenant [Lord Grey]," Phyllis Grosskurth in her recent biography *Byron: The Flawed Angel* [Boston: Houghton Mifflin, 1997] speculates that by *intimacy* "Moore probably means kissing and caressing, which would fall within Byron's view of 'pure relationship'—that is, one that did not progress to full sexual relations" (40). John Cam Hobhouse's marginalia from his copy of the Moore biography—"A circumstance occurred during [this] intimacy which certainly had much effect on his future morals"—leads her to concur with the conventional conjecture: "This would suggest that Grey had attempted to sodomise him" (40).

23. I am indebted to Peter Manning for the reading of "even intimacy" offered in this paragraph.

24. See Marchand, *BLJ* 1:45n, and Doris Langley Moore, *Lord Byron: Accounts Rendered* (London: John Murray, 1974), 77ff. Louis Crompton, however, disagrees; see pp. 82–85 of *Byron and Greek Love* (Berkeley: University of California Press, 1985).

25. *Byron* (London: Thames and Hudson, 1982), 13–14. And compare Eisler: "Byron's reports of May [Gray] brutalizing him and his determination to have her fired point to shame at his complicity, as well as desire for revenge; the rage of a boy, between latency and adolescence, whose first lover and surrogate mother tortures him with her infidelities" (40).

26. That abused children often become abusers is of course a cliché of contemporary culture. Whether Byron's harsh treatment of many women reflects his own misuse by Grey and others, the psychiatrists must determine.

27. Under English law at the time, Lord Grey's life might be imperiled and his reputation certainly ruined by exposure of his homosexual conduct, or publicity of suspicions suggesting it: see Crompton, 14–18 et passim. Homosexuality remained a capital offense in England, and if executions were relatively rare, the public pillorying of offenders was not.

28. Crompton, 79–80. Stored in the John Murray archives, a collection of 1804–6 letters to Byron from his Harrow schoolmates has enabled Benita Eisler to hypothesize a startling picture of carnal activity and its sometimes lethal consequences at Harrow, and perhaps more predictably at Cambridge, during the years of Byron's attendance. These letters—from John Cecil Tattersall, Edward Noel Long, William Peel, and others—leave little doubt that heterosexual traffic and homosexual passion were nearly commonplace, if in the latter case linguistically subdued or encoded, at both institutions. I am grateful to Ms. Eisler for providing me with her transcripts of selections from these documents. John Chandos (*Boys Together: English Public Schools, 1800–1864* [New Haven: Yale University Press, 1984]) is helpful in this connection, particularly with his chapter "A Demon Hovering" (284–319), which takes an extended look at

"immorality" in the public school system. Records were few and oblique, especially on homosexual activity, until John Addington Symonds arrived at Harrow in the spring of 1854, and at age fourteen began a diary. Largely from this account, Chandos constructs his portrait of illicit sexuality at Harrow shortly after the turn of the century. "The category of homosexual," he writes, "was not recognized in Symonds's youth. . . . Previously, love between men had of course been recognized and celebrated with approval in literature and art. The occurrence of sexual lust between males was treated not as an abnormal alternative to heterosexual relations, but as a supplement to normal sexual intercourse, indulged in by profligate sensualists in quest of increased variety. A sodomite was identified by his acts, not by the nature which caused them. The boy Symonds [having homosexual tendencies] was thus to find himself a mystery to himself; for he feared and was repelled in its physical reality by what excited and disturbed his imagination, and he did not at school perform the forbidden acts, which others did out of sheer animal exuberance, but his mind dwelt on them with a mixture of revulsion and fascination" (303–4). Here is Symonds in his manuscript autobiography:

> Every boy of good looks had a female name and was recognized either as a public prostitute or as some bigger fellow's bitch. Bitch was the word in common usage to indicate a boy who yielded his person to another. The talk in the studies and dormitories was incredibly obscene. One could not avoid seeing acts of onanism, mutual masturbation and the sport of naked boys in bed together. There was no refinement, no sentiment, no passion, nothing but animal lust in these occurrences. They filled me with disgust and loathing. (quoted in Chandos, 307–8)

"They also," adds Chandos, "filled him with a curious feeling of fascination, even for the acts and players whom he most protested to loath" (308).

It would be unwise to read these conditions, recorded by an unattractive, unhappy, and unstable personality, back into 1804–5 conditions at Harrow (Chandos remarks that "the scene might equally well have been of Eton or Winchester, or any of the other public schools" [317]); but at the same time it is difficult to imagine their sudden emergence. They may have worsened over the years, but one would suppose the Regency climate more favorable than mid-century Victorianism to tolerance of—or blindness to—such misconduct. (See addendum, p. 205.) I suspect that Byron's experience of Harrow sexuality may have differed in degree but not much in kind from Symonds's, and that he too found these behaviors objectionable precisely because lacking "refinement . . . sentiment . . . passion"—because unredeemed by the intense, thrilling *emotion* of boy-love he himself felt for several school companions. It is worth noting that Symonds eventually, from Cambridge, through his father, brought down the great Harrow headmaster Dr. Charles Vaughan for homosexual relations with a fellow student, one Alfred Pretor, to whom the headmaster had declared himself in writing. Vaughan avoided a public scandal but vacated the headmastership after fifteen distinguished years, declining a number of attractive appointments, including three bishoprics, for which actions he became, "in the eyes of the world, a noble exemplar of Christian humility and disinterestedness in a Church of preferment-hungry prelates" (315).

29. The remaining possibility, of course, is that Byron did not decline Lord Grey, and now, unable to face or speak his shame, turns viciously against the older man in deeply guilty self-hatred. In such a scenario, the phrase in question would mean, "I never will *again*. . . ."

30. Hobhouse evidently believed Byron to have been homoerotically experienced before coming under the influence of Cambridge libertinism. Against Moore's charge that university companions corrupted Byron, Hobhouse confided to his diary: "Certainly Byron had nothing to learn in the way of depravity either of mind or body when he came from Harrow. . . . He [Moore] little knows the ground he treads" [15 January 1830; quoted in Doris Langley Moore, *The Late Lord Byron: Posthumous Dramas*, rev. ed. [New York: Harper and Row, 1977], 291).

31. Manuscript letter in the Meyer Davis Collection, University of Pennsylvania Library.

32. Although none of the frequent letters from Lord Grey to John Hanson during 1803 betrays any hint of trouble between the Newstead owner and tenant, the gap in surviving correspondence between tenant and attorney from 24 August 1803 to April 1804, the period including the hypothesized sexual encounter, may appear extraordinary enough to be suspicious, given the usual rate of letter exchanges between the two, although it must be said that a five-month hiatus follows the brief April 1804 resumption of contact.

33. Eisler argues that Byron's awareness of the criminal consequences of homosexual acts accounts for the "atmosphere of terror" inscribed in the "hysterical tone" of his epistolary references to Grey: "The intensity of his fear, moreover, points to an earlier complicity, followed by a guilty need to exonerate himself. On the other hand, "in tone and substance, Lord Grey's words reveal a dignified young man of deep feelings, unlikely to have imposed himself sexually on an unwilling partner. . . . Who seduced whom? At fifteen, Byron was already a charmer bent on conquest. . . . [I]t seems likely that he led his host on, believing he could be flirtatious and seductive with Lord Grey, as he was with his Harrow friends, while still retaining control. Byron may never have imagined that Lord Grey, a simpler, less sophisticated fellow, took him seriously and assumed, in the romantic solitude of Newstead, that if his guest behaved seductively, he wanted to be seduced" (73–74).

2. Virgilian King

1. But not his first entertainment of oratory as an aristocratic entitlement. Moore reports the now famous episode: "In the winter of 1797, his mother having chanced, one day, to read part of a speech spoken in the House of Commons, a friend who was present said to the boy, 'We shall have the pleasure,

some time or other, of reading your speeches in the House of Commons.' 'I hope not,' was his answer: 'if you read any speeches of mine, it will be in the House of Lords'" (Moore 1:21).

2. Benita Eisler goes further: "[Byron] persisted in blaming his mother for the abnormality, citing her 'excess of delicacy' [Moore 1:183; but Moore's phrase is 'false delicacy'] during the period immediately preceding the delivery. This phrase has been taken to refer either to Catherine's insistence on wearing corsets in the last stages of pregnancy or to her modesty during the final obstetrical examinations. Byron's accusation seized on the most damaging charge he could find to describe the damage inflicted upon him by his mother. She had cursed, crippled, and symbolically castrated her son.... Turned inward, his rage became depression, but also something more insidious: the sense that he had a special dispensation from the moral sanctions imposed upon others and a lifetime entitlement to the forbidden" (*Byron: Child of Passion, Fool of Fame*, 13).

3. The Reverend Mark Drury sired two sons, who were both at Harrow during Byron's years there: William James Joseph and George Dominico. It is unclear which rode with his father on the day Byron recalls. Both entered the school before Byron did (1795 and 1798 respectively), and both became head of school (1807 and 1809), but after Byron had gone.

4. Modern medicine might argue that his lameness helps promote the compensatory misconduct that irritated the masters. Grosskurth wonders "what Byron did about his withered leg" at a time when schoolboys typically swam naked, for as an adult, she says, "he always wore trousers" when swimming (33). This information helps us define the dilemma Byron faced even when practicing his chief athletic skill; for to bathe naked *or* trousered in the Duck Pond within the Harrow School precincts would have called attention to his deformity; thus, perhaps, his preference for the distant pool and its less exposed situation, although transportation there on horseback would also have publicized his disability.

Lest there be any doubt about the long-term effect of his lameness on the poet, Marchand reminds us that during the 1822–23 winter, in Genoa, Byron remarked to Dr. James Alexander, an English physician, "That foot has been the bane of my life" (3:1052)—this a part of a longer narrative which included Byron's admission that he had once, probably while at Harrow in Marchand's view, sought to have the foot amputated by a London physician who, fortunately, refused the job (ibid.).

An English visitor to Byron's Genoa residence on 31 March 1822 pleasantly recalled for the poet his London celebrity. Byron wrote of the meeting to Moore on 2 April: "I have . . . seen Henry Fox, Lord Holland's son, whom I had not looked upon since I left him a pretty, mild boy . . . I always liked that boy—perhaps, in part, from some resemblance in the less fortunate part of our destinies—I mean, to avoid mistakes, his lameness. But there is this difference, that *he* appears a halting angel, who has tripped against a star; whilst I am *Le*

Diable Boiteux,—a soubriquet, which I marvel that, amongst their various *nominis umbrae,* the Orthodox have not hit upon" (3:1055–56).

5. Charles Drury, "Rev. Joseph Drury, D. D., Late Head Master of Harrow," in *Annual Biography and Obituary* (London, 1835), 5–6; hereafter Drury Memoir.

6. Of course they did not remain so. Here is the thirty-three-year-old reflecting on the road not taken: Sheridan, he remembered, "was sure from [*English Bards*] and other symptoms—that I should make an Orator if I would but take to speaking and grow a parliament man—he never ceased harping upon this to me—to the last—and I remember my old tutor Dr. Drury had the same notion when I was a *boy*—but it never was my turn of inclination to try—I spoke once or twice as all young *peers* do—as a kind of introduction into public life—but dissipation—shyness—haughty and reserved opinions—together with the short time I lived in England—after my majority (only about five years in all) prevented me from resuming the experiment—as far as it went it was not discouraging—particularly my *first* speech (I spoke three or four times in all) but just after it my poem of C[hild]e H[arol]d was published—& nobody ever thought about my *prose* afterwards, nor indeed did I—it became to me a secondary and neglected object, though I sometimes wonder to myself *if* I should have succeeded?" (*BLJ* 9:16). But much of this may be disingenuous. For a shrewd and detailed reading of Byron's parliamentary experience in personal and historical contexts, see David V. Erdman, "Lord Byron as Rinaldo," *PMLA* 57 (1942), 189–231. It is difficult, as Erdman's own prose shows, to write of Byron as speaker without recourse to theatrical metaphors: "Let us approach chronologically the questions of Byron's experiences in 1812 which were to leave him with a sense of failure concerning his career in the House of Lords. Thus far we have considered only his general ambition to become a distinguished actor on that stage. Now we must discover the particular role he has selected for himself and the set of circumstances which ultimately discouraged him from playing it" (197). And, similarly, on the same page, Erdman refers to Byron as an "orator in verse—from his lines on the death of Fox in 1806 to the political cantos of *Don Juan*" (197).

7. This has in any event always been assumed to be the case. But the normal Harrow practice of staging only the Turnus/Drances dialogue lets one ask whether Leeke might have been brought in belatedly, to join Byron and Peel, after Byron objected to the potentially offensive lines, and Latinus's role was added especially to accommodate him. One wonders, of course, what form his objection took, and with whom registered: would the proud young man have petitioned a master for reassignment, or privately proposed the trade-off to a sensitive, sympathetic mate, and in either case explained his real reason for changing roles?

8. "Peel, the orator and statesman," Byron later wrote, "was my form-fellow, and we were both at the top of our remove. . . . There were always great hopes of Peel, amongst us all . . . and he has not disappointed them. As a scholar

he was greatly my superior; as a declaimer and actor, I was reckoned at least his equal; as a schoolboy, *out* of school, I was always *in* scrapes, and *he never;* and *in school,* he *always* knew his lesson, and I rarely,—but when I knew it, I knew it nearly as well. In general information, history, &c. &c., I think I was *his* superior, as well as of most boys of my standing" (Moore 1:37). In another place, Byron slightly qualifies his judgment: "Peel—my School and form-fellow—(we sate within two of each other) strange to say I have never heard—though I often wished to do so—but from what I remember of him at Harrow—he *is* or *should be*—among the best of [modern orators]" (*BLJ* 9:14). I excerpt this passage from a much longer review of orators and reflections on British eloquence, a subject curiously recurrent in Byron's *Detached Thoughts* (*BLJ* 9:11–52).

9. But not so represented, for neither sets nor costumes or makeup was ever part of Harrow Speech Day tradition. Still, Latinus's kingship would have been known from classwork, or at any rate recognized by his privileged regal repose while others stand.

10. Harrow records do not specify the exact lines chosen by the boys for recitation, and sometimes indicate only authorship. We know more in Byron's case, but not a lot more. An unknown hand has written in pencil, after the Byron entry on the 1805 Harrow speech bill in the Harrow archives, "Aen.XI.380 foll.," but of course this is not authoritative. I take Marchand (1:84) to be more nearly so.

Here are the lines Byron recited, or from which he recited excerpts:

> 'Ante equidem summa de re statuisse, Latini,
> et uellem et fuerat melius, non tempore tali
> cogere concilium, cum muros adsidet hostis.
> bellum importunum, ciues, cum gente deorum
> inuictisque uiris gerimus, quos nulla fatigant
> proelia nec uicti possunt absistere ferro.
> spem si quam ascitis Aetolum habuistis in armis,
> ponite. spes sibi quisque; sed haec quam angusta uidetis.
> cetera qua rerum iaceant perculsa ruina,
> ante oculos interque manus sunt omnia uestras.
> nec quemquam incuso: potuit quae plurima uirtus
> esse, fuit; toto certatum est corpore regni.
> nunc adeo quae sit dubiae sententia menti,
> expediam et paucis (animos adhibete) docebo.
> est antiquus ager Tusco mihi proximus amni,
> longus in occasum, finis super usque Sicanos;
> Aurunci Rutulique serunt, et uomere duros
> exercent collis atque horum asperrima pascunt.
> haec omnis regio et celsi plaga pinea montis
> cedat amicitiae Teucrorum, et foederis aequas
> dicamus leges sociosque in regna uocemus:

considant, si tantus amor, et moenia condant.
sin alios finis aliamque capessere gentem
est animus possuntque solo decedere nostro,
bis denas Italo texamus robore nauis;
seu pluris complere ualent, iacet omnis ad undam
materies: ipsi numerumque modumque carinis
praecipiant, nos aera, manus, naualia demus.
praeterea, qui dicta ferant et foedera firment
centum oratores prima de gente Latinos
ire placet pacisque manu praetendere ramos,
munera portantis aurique eborisque talenta
et sellam regni trabeamque insignia nostri.
consulite in medium et rebus succurrite fessis.'

> *Aeneid* ll. 302–35 (in *Virgil: Aeneid, Book XI,* ed. K. W. Gransden [Cambridge: Cambridge University Press, 1991], 48–49).

"O Latins, how I wish we could have settled
this mighty matter earlier: that would
have been far better than debating now
with Trojans at our walls. My citizens,
we wage a luckless war against a nation
of gods, unconquered men; no battle can
exhaust them; if defeated, they do not
give up the sword. If you had any hope
of help from the Aetolians, forget it:
each must be his own hope, but now you know
how poor a thing that is. And for the rest,
you all can see and touch what has destroyed us.
I am not blaming you: whatever courage
could do, is done; we have fought with all the force
our kingdom has. Now listen; in few words
I shall reveal, if you will pause, what course
seems justified in my uncertain mind.
I have an ancient territory near
the Tuscan river, stretching westward even
beyond the bounds of the Sicanians.
Auruncans and Rutulians now till
those fields; their plowshares work the stubborn hills;
they use the harshest slopes for pasturing.
Let all this region, with its mountain ridges
of pines, pass to the Teucrians in friendship;
and let us strike an equal treaty with them,
invite them as allies to share our kingdom.
And they can settle there, if that is what

they think worthwhile, and build their towns. But if
they long for other boundaries, another
nation, if they are free to leave our soil,
then let us build out of Italian oak
twice-ten ships for the Trojans—even more,
if they can fill them. All the wood we need
now lies, already hewn, along the shore;
and they can tell us both the size and number
of galleys they require; and we shall furnish
the brass and labor and their naval gear.
And in addition I should have this message
brought to them by a hundred Latin envoys,
men chosen from our nobles, to confirm
this treaty. They must carry with them gifts
of ivory, golden talents, and my chair
and robe—the emblems of my sovereignty.
Now counsel frankly, help our troubled state."
    Translated by Allen Mandelbaum

11. My language, like Byron's in the letter about Peel, has obviously collapsed distinctions between declamation and acting. Boleslaw Taborski has pointed out that "Renaissance rhetoric was still maintained in English schools at the turn of the XIX Century, and . . . there was no essential difference between oratory and acting. Declaiming was acting" (*Byron and the Theatre*, Salzburg Studies in English Literature, ed. James Hogg (Salzburg, 1972), 21.

12. *The Aeneid of Virgil*, translated in verse by Allen Mandelbaum (New York: Bantam, 1961), 286; ll. 444–45 in Mandelbaum; or, in R. D. Williams's text, "Stung with jealousy half-hidden and goaded with bitter torments" (*The Aeneid of Virgil, Books 7–12* [London: Macmillan, 1973]).

13. *Byron and His Fictions* (Detroit: Wayne State University Press, 1978), 177–99.

14. *Harrow Gazette,* July 1855. A photograph in my collection from the 1996 program shows one young speaker, mid-sentence, his left arm tucked behind his back, waist-high, his right arm at full stretch, angling upward and outward, pulling him onto his toes: the body is fully engaged in delivery.

15. For whatever it may be worth, speakers at the 1998 Harrow Speech Day, chosen for their proven skill in debating societies and as actors in house and school plays, received training from a tutor at two sessions with texts in hand, then at three sessions without them, and again at a dress rehearsal the evening before the performance. My source for this information is Mr. Alex Ward, currently a monitor at Harrow and a speaker at the 1998 event, in an interview conducted at the school in March 1999.

16. "Keate was a great master of oratory, and the hints which he gave to sixth form boys when they were rehearsing their speeches to him in private

proved invaluable to them in their subsequent careers as statesmen, or preachers, or as pleaders in the courts of law. An English speech was seldom tolerated in his day, and all the speeches, whether in Latin, Greek or English, were real orations, not mere recitations of poetry. It was generally remarked that the best speeches and declamations in the Upper School were those delivered by the members of the different dramatic companies, which from time to time were organized among the boys," although eventually suppressed by Dr. Keate as too distracting and time consuming (Lyte, *A History of Eton College, 1404–1884,* 369–71.

17. J. B. Oldham, *History of Shrewsbury School* (Shrewsbury, 1952), 87–88.

18. Fisher, *Annals of Shrewsbury School,* 327.

19. Dr. Butler may have been guided in designing these instructions by familiarity with eighteenth-century handbooks for actors, many of which classified emotions and described the gestures appropriate to their representation on stage. The minutely particular and elaborate guidelines are principally aimed at teaching physical gesticulation and facial expression, but the list of emotions that they are intended to project are very like Butler's: "Pride, Hope, Despair, Avarice, Wonder," and so on. See Alan S. Downer, "Players and Painted Stage: Nineteenth-Century Acting," *PMLA* 61 (1946), 522–76.

20. If not the most reliable of witnesses, and indeed a minority voice on the occasion, Robert Charles Dallas may be allowed to weigh in here with observations on Byron's rehearsals for his 1812 inaugural parliamentary address, especially because he charges its defects to public school training. Listening to Byron practice, Dallas found himself disappointed, for the young Lord's "delivery changed my opinion of his power as to eloquence, and checked my hope of his success in Parliament. He altered the natural tone of his voice, which was sweet and round, into a formal drawl, and he prepared his features for a part—it was a youth declaiming a task . . . a fault contracted in studied delivery of speeches from memory, which has been lately so much attended to in the education of boys. . . . It does not promise well; and they who fall into it are seldom prominent characters in stations where eloquence is required." But whatever the practice run may have promised, the delivery itself far surpassed, as Dallas himself conceded, in producing "a considerable effect in the House of Lords, and . . . many compliments from the Opposition Peers" (R. C. Dallas, *Recollections of the Life of Lord Byron* [Philadelphia, 1825], 1:132).

A week after the event, flushed with his success, Byron fairly gushes to Francis Hodgson: "Lds. Holland & Grenville, particularly the latter paid some high compts. in the course of their speeches as you may have seen in the papers, & Lord Eldon and Harrowby answered me.——I have had many marvelous eulogies repeated to me since in person & by proxy from divers persons *ministerial—yea ministerial!* as well as oppositionists, of them I shall only mention Sr F. Burdetts.—*He* says it is the best speech by a *Lord* since the 'Lord knows when' probably from the fellow feeling in ye. sentiments.—Ld. H[olland] tells me I shall beat them all if I persevere, & Ld. G[renville] remarked that the construction of some of my periods are very like *Burke's!!*—And so much for vanity.——I spoke very violent sentences with a sort of modest impudence, abused every thing & every body, & put the Lord Chancellor very much out of humor, & if I may believe what I hear, have not lost any character by the experiment.—As to my delivery, loud & fluent enough, perhaps a little theatrical" (*BLJ* 2:167).

The performer's ascription of theatricality to his self-representation accords with Lord Holland's private assessment, which exposes the sting beneath what Byron chose to take as the peer's praise and encouragement: "[Byron's] speech was full of fancy, wit, and invective, but not exempt from affectation nor well reasoned, nor at all suited to our common notions of Parliamentary eloquence" (quoted from Holland's *Memoirs,* 123, in *BLJ* 2:167n. See also Eisler, 325–28). It seems fair to assume in any event that Byron's Speech Day participation did not handicap his parliamentary oratory to the extent, if at all, anticipated by Dallas, and, if anything, enhanced its dramatic impact, Lord Holland's stuffy demur (in fact acknowledging its performative constituents) notwithstanding.

First Interval

1. Moore observes: "In thus personating with such success two heroes so different, the young poet displayed both that love and power of versatility by which he was afterward impelled, on a grander scale, to present himself under such opposite aspects to the world; the gloom of Penruddock, and the whim of Tristram, being types, as it were, of the two extremes, between which his own character, in after-life, so singularly vibrated" (1:65). I return to Byron's performance of these roles later in this essay. For the moment, it is useful to remember that the poet's lifelong involvement in the theater may be traced back to 1797 when, according to Moore, the nine-year-old, at the Aberdeen theater with his mother, became so caught up by a scene from *The Taming of the Shrew,* that, ever in opposition, he shouted from the audience, against Petruchio's "Nay, then, I swear it is the blessed sun," "But *I* say it is the *moon,* sir!" (Moore 1:14; my emphasis). And four years later, at about the time he entered Harrow, Byron tried his hand at writing a drama, "Ulric and Ilvina," which, he admits, "I had sense enough to burn" (Prothero 5:338). The earliest indication of his theatrical patronage is an 1804 co-sponsorship with his mother of a production in Southwell: "There is a Southwell play-bill extant," writes Moore, "dated August 8th, 1804, in which the play is announced as bespoke 'by Mrs. and Lord Byron'" (Moore 1:52).

2. According to Mary Ann's biographer, the fiancé, John Musters, was reported to be an excellent dancer. See Megan Boyers, *Queen of a Fantastic Realm: A Biography of Mary Chaworth* (Derby: Megan Boyers, 1986).

3. See my "Divided Being: The Mind in Byron's 'The Dream,'" in *The Cast of Consciousness: Concepts of the Mind in British and American Romanticism,* ed. Beverly Taylor and Robert Bain (New York: Greenwood, 1987), 104–21.

4. Dr. Ryan Lesh, Columbia University School of Medicine, in a letter to the author.

5. Byron had already translated the Nisus and Euryalus episode from *Aeneid* 9, which celebrates the heroic friendship of these two and the death of the first in the embrace of the second; see *CPW* 1:370.

6. He did, on the other hand, "compete" with Edward Noel Long without damaging their equally close relationship. Long appeared on all three of the Speech Day programs with Byron, and "Childish Recollections" is generous in remembrance: "We neither conquer'd in the classic strife: / As Speakers, each supports an equal name, / And crouds allow to both a partial fame; / To soothe a youthful Rival's early pride, / Though Cleon's candour would the palm divide, / Yet Candour's self compels me now to own, / Justice awards it to my Friend alone" (ll. 334–40). Incidentally, Byron's letter to Edward Noel Long from Southwell on 30 March 1807 thus excuses his delayed response: "Your Epistle found me in the midst of a Translation, the Episode of Nisus & Euryalus from the Aeneis, the interference of the task, prevented an immediate Reply" (*BLJ*, supplementary volume, ed. Leslie A. Marchand [Newark: University of Delaware Press, 1994], 2). The one textualized friendship interrupts the other!

7. The last sentence of this Grey quotation repeats the grammatical construction—eliding the verb "be"—observed in Byron's letter to Augusta vowing silence on his reason for refusing reconciliation with the tenant. And here once again Grey is substantively implicated. While the reappearance of the odd linguistic structure raises the possibility of idiomatic speech, the subtextual reemergence of Grey challenges it and suggests once more that pressure short-circuits normal expression. It would be extraordinary to find like irregular grammatical constructions triggered by the same anxiety, but the absence elsewhere—to my viewing—of this strange verbal elision encourages suspicion of connection between it and the Grey event.

8. That this phrase turns up in Byron's recitation of Zanga's lines from *The Revenge* may indicate his early selection of them for his second Speech Day performance, or at least his familiarity with the play and the role.

3. William Henry West Betty

1. *Daily Advertiser;* reproduced in [*Memoir of*] *Mr. W. H. W. Betty, English Roscius* . . . (London, n.d.); hereafter *Memoir*.

2. *Authentic Memoirs of that Wonderful Phenomenon The Infant Roscius* (London: W. Hodgson, n.d.), 31.

3. Herschel Baker, *John Philip Kemble: The Actor in His Theatre* (New York: Greenwood, 1942), 280.

4. By 8 December, Mrs. Byron had heard of Betty's reception and wrote to Hanson: "When he [Byron] goes to see the Young Roscius, I hope he will take care of himself in the crowd, and not go alone" (Prothero 1:64n).

5. Giles Playfair, *The Prodigy: A Study of the Strange Life of Master Betty* (London: Secker and Warburg, 1967), 73; hereafter Playfair.

6. Unidentified newspaper critique of the first performance, quoted in *Memoir,* 21.

7. Hester Lynch Thrale Piozzi, friend of Dr. Johnson and an important memoirist, wrote on 21 February 1805, "Young Roscius's premature powers attract universal attention, and I suppose that if less than an angel had told *his* parents that a bulletin of that child's health should be necessary to quiet the anxiety of a metropolis for his safety, they would not have believed the prediction" (*Life and Writings of Mrs. Piozzi* 2:263; quoted in Prothero, 1:64n).

8. John Donan, *"Their Majesties' Servants" or Annals of the English Stage from Thomas Betterton to Edmund Kean* (London: John C. Nimmo, 1912), 389–90.

9. Y. Ffrench, *Mrs. Siddons: Tragic Actress* (1936), 242; quoted in *CPW* 1:387.

10. *Critique on the First Performance of Young Roscius at Covent Garden Theatre . . . British Press* [newspaper], 3 December 1804 (London, 1804), 19; hereafter *Critique.*

11. London, 1805, p. 33; hereafter *Infant Roscius.*

12. John Genest, *Some Account of the English Stage from the Restoration in 1660 to 1830,* 10 vols. (Bath, 1832), 7:660.

13. *The Complete Works of William Hazlitt,* ed. P. P. Howe, 21 vols. (London, 1930–34), 8:294. And again on Betty in the same role: "There was a romantic sweetness in the tones of voice, and a personification of youth, of hope, and beauty in the face and figure of the Young Roscius, when he first appeared in that character [Norval] as a boy, which gave back, (more than anything we have ever seen) the image of the poet's mind" (*Works* 9:94).

14. *Life of John, Lord Campbell,* ed. by the Hon. Mrs. Hardcastle (London, 1881), 111.

15. Fox would invite Master Betty to his St. Anne's Hills estate for Easter 1806, where with Fox's son they explored the role of Edward Young's Zanga, part of Betty's repertoire for the 1805–6 season. This was, of course, the role Byron performed on his second Speech Day appearance.

16. Quoted by James Roose on the Theatre Museum Card, London.

17. *Times* obituary for Betty of 1876, unsigned.

18. *Conversations,* 32; quoted in Prothero 1:64n.

19. *TLS,* 8 June 1963, reviewing Giles Playfair's biography, 511.

20. Byron's short, coincidental meeting with Lord Clare, one of these "favourites," on the road between Imola and Bologna, Italy, in November 1821, as the two traveled in opposite directions after seven or eight years' absence from each other, inspired a reminiscence that, even if romantically misted, provides a helpful glimpse of the powerful and enduring effect upon Byron of Harrow intimacies: "This meeting annihilated for a moment all the years between the present time and the days of *Harrow*—it was a new and inexplicable feeling like rising from the grave to me.—Clare too was much agitated—more—in *appearance*—than even myself—for I could feel his heart beat to the fingers'

ends—unless indeed—it was the pulse of my own which made me think so. . . . We were but five minutes together—and in the public road—but I hardly recollect an hour of my existence which could be weighed against them. . . . Of all I have ever known . . . he has always been the least altered in every thing from the excellent qualities and kind affections which attracted me to him so strongly at School" (*BLJ* 9:49–50).

21. Dr. Annette Peach, author of a forthcoming catalog of Byron portraiture in *The Walpole Society* 62 (May 2000), has argued that this image of the young man is the product of Thomas Wood, drawing master at Harrow from 1837, possibly made from another drawing taken from life. Such an original, if it exists, is not known, and the "T.W." drawing has not been seen since 1934. I am most grateful to Dr. Peach for this information. See also her doctoral thesis, "Portraiture of Lord Byron" (University of London, 1995).

22. Stephen Gwyn, *Memorials of an Eighteenth Century Painter (James Northcote)* (London, 1898), 252.

23. Late in the development of this essay, Professor Julie A. Carlson, upon request, graciously supplied me with a copy of the galleys of her (then) forthcoming essay on Betty, subsequently appearing in SAQ 95 as "Forever Young: Master Betty and the Queer Stage of Youth in English Romanticism," a theoretically sophisticated and wide-ranging study of "Bettymania" and its lessons for Romantic theater, literature, and culture. I am grateful to Professor Carlson for an early and profitable look at her ultimately award-winning work.

4. Villain

1. Rex Warner observes that "one of the strangest phenomena of the time was the frequency of school rebellions during the closing years of the eighteenth century. These rebellions were . . . largely caused by the ferment at home and especially on the Continent; indeed, in some of them the tricolour was adopted as standard: but they are remarkable too as showing how entirely at variance had become the organisation of boys from the masters who at one time had led rather than governed them. There were four rebellions at Winchester between 1770 and 1793. Even Keate, the most notorious of disciplinarians, had several rebellions to deal with at Eton. At Harrow one revolt was led by Byron, and the independence of the boys may be judged by the fact that two Harrow rebellions were caused by the boys' insistence that they had a right to be consulted in the choice of a headmaster for the school. Indeed most, if not all of these rebellions were the result of the attempts of authority to interfere with what had become traditions among the boys. . . . In nearly all cases authority had to give in." The serious rebellion against Keate at Eton in 1818 inspired Robert Southey "to condemn the principles of insubordination" that incited it, "though he himself in his revolutionary days had been expelled from Westminster for attacking the right to flog and the authority of the masters in general" (*English Public Schools* [London: Collins, 1946], 17–20).

2. Byron's own name appears many more times on these walls than he carved it there, but eight have been authenticated as genuine. See *The Harrow Collection* (catalog by P. D. Hunter, 1994), 7.

3. Conversation of the author with Mr. Alasdair Hawkyard, former Harrow archivist, reporting on Tyerman's research of records of Harrow-on-the-Hill.

4. Admittedly, this seems an inadequate explanation for the hypochondriacal condition; one imagines a personal aggravation or grievance of some sort behind it, but determination appears impossible.

5. Hawson and Townsend, eds., *Harrow School*, 202. Mr. James Golland, a former Harrow master, whose extensive research on this subject continues, believes that the dancing school may "possibly" have occupied the present site of the Vaughan Library. I am grateful to Mr. Golland for permission to cite here his provisional findings.

6. But he had, curiously, inhabited similar spaces in earlier years. His second classroom, at five, was in an Aberdeen dancing hall, and his mother enrolled Byron in dancing classes, at seven, under one Francis Peacock, to educate him in correct courtly behavior (see Eisler, *Byron: Child of Passion, Fool of Fame*, 22 and 27. See also Megan Boyes, *My Amiable Mamma* [Megan Boyes, 1991], 41, and Pryse Lockhart Gordon, *Personal Memoirs*, 2 vols. [London: Henry Colburn and Richard Bentley, 1830], 2:321. Gordon reports: "[Byron] told me that he was desperately in love with Miss Mary Duff when he was nine years old, 'and we met,' he said, 'at the dancing school'" [2:321]). The cruelly traumatic effect of forcing the boy to attempt graceful physical negotiations of which he was almost certainly not capable, and in front of peers who were, is nearly unimaginable. But the recollection of them, if perhaps intimidating or paralyzing to a lesser spirit, might inspire one of Byron's grit and verve to reengage the space, bent upon conquest and vindication.

Dancing, however, may signify different choreographies to different times and different cultures: "Several entries in the [Harrow] school minutes speak of *the house* where dancing was taught, and it is interesting to know . . . from the lips of the late Mr. Webb, who taught him, that Lord Byron equipped himself for his London career in this then necessary particular. It is well to remember that dancing in 1804 was a somewhat stately art, and associated in our minds with the grave minuet rather than the giddy waltz" (Percy M. Thornton, *Harrow School and Its Surroundings* [London, 1885], 218–19). A note in Thornton's volume traces Mr. Webb's oral testimony through a Mr. William Winckley to the "Harrow Notes" for 2 June 1883. Witnesses to Byron's "London career," however, remain silent on his mastery of the terpsichorean art, even as articulated in the "grave minuet," whereas evidence of dancing successes by an impaired individual also the toast of the town would surely have generated significant press. Nor do other Harrow records verify Mr. Webb's recollections. But even if Byron did study dancing at Harrow, the lameness would have handicapped and compromised execution, distressed by disadvantaging the pupil, and defined as uncomfortable and disagreeable the learning environment. Among biographers it is perhaps best to let Byron's first have the final word on this issue: "In the dances of the evening . . . Miss [Mary Ann] Chaworth, of course, joined, while her lover [Lord Byron] sat looking on, solitary and mortified. It is not impossible, indeed, that the dislike which he always expressed for this amusement may have originated in some bitter pang, felt in his youth, on seeing 'the lady of his love' led out by others to the gay dance from which he was himself excluded" (Moore 1:47). For the poet's mature response, see his satire "The Waltz," a fiercely hostile view of the fashionable German import and an attack on its practitioners, including, dangerously, the Prince Regent. Among modern commentators on this strange work, see particularly Frederick L. Beaty, *Byron the Satirist* (De Kalb, Ill.: Northern Illinois University Press, 1985), 65–73, and William Childers, "Byron's *Waltz:* The Germans and Their Georges," *Keats-Shelley Journal* 18 (1969), 81–95.

7. A great deal has been made, over the years, of Byron's gritty determination to overcome his physical disadvantage by participation in Harrow athletics as he was able, particularly as cricketer. I intend no insult to his efforts, but reports may have been exaggerated. His most famous—perhaps his only—outing on the cricket field in league competition took place after he had left Harrow; the degree of his participation in intramural play is uncertain, although a letter of 22 April 1807 describing his weight-controlling exercise routines cites running and playing "at cricket" while heavily overdressed, itself perhaps an exaggeration. About the 2 August 1805 Eton match—possibly the first, certainly no later than the second in this long rivalry—in understandable pride he appears to have lied, claiming "11 notches the 1st Innings and 7 the 2d. which was more than any of our side, except [W.] Brockman and [Viscount] Ipswich, could contrive to hit" (*BLJ* 1:71). Inasmuch as this places him third on the losing team, the performance may not seem so praiseworthy; and in any event the official record book of 1805 in the Eton College Library shows him having made only nine runs (7 and 2). On the other hand, Ashley-Cooper reports that "the poet's version may well be correct, for the score which is inserted in *Scores and Biographies* was taken from a half-sheet of paper sent anonymously through Frederick Lillywhite to the Hon. Robert Grimston, who forwarded it to the editor of *Bell's Life,* for what it was worth, and from that paper it was copied in *Scores and Biographies*" (24). The anonymity of the source of this record and its circumlocutive passage to print have presumably rendered it less authoritative than the official Eton account, but at this date the issue is likely to remain contested.

Cricket Captain J. A. Lloyd, with whom Byron "competed" on Speech Day, later judged Byron's performance at cricket poor and unworthy of the team. Evidently, too, another player ran for him. (See the quotation from the reminiscence of Arthur Shakespear in F. S. Ashley-Cooper's *Eton v. Harrow at the Wicket* [London: St. Jarves Press, 1922]: "The late Lord Stratford de Redcliffe remembered seeing him [Lord Byron] playing in the match against Eton with another boy to run for him" [quoted from the *DNB* 8:133; in Ashley-Cooper, 23].) These circumstances, together with data hinting at periods of lassitude approximating sloth in the boy, except when at aquatic play, suggest the kind indulgence of his mates in allowing him to realize a dream in the match against Eton, although they would certainly have needed to conceal that sentiment from him. Such a case bespeaks peer respect for the boy, won, one imagines, in part by fine speaking and acting, as well as by scrappy belligerence, in person and in poetry, when the occasion called for it.

Here, for example, is the reply attributed to Byron following receipt, at Harrow, of this taunt from the victorious Etonians at the 1805 match. The Etonians gloated—

> Adventurous *boys* of Harrow School,
> Of cricket you've no knowledge.
> You play not cricket, but the fool,
> With *men* of Eton College.

—and got this back:

> Ye Eton wits, to play the fool
> Is not the boast of Harrow School;
> No wonder, then, at our defeat—
> Folly like yours could ne'er be beat.

8. The identification *may* indicate that Byron had seen him at Drury Lane, where he was consistently advertised as "Young Roscius," rather than at Covent Garden, which always billed him as "Master Betty." Or perhaps Byron is shy of using the alternative name to his sister, given its barely buried pun.

9. William L. Slout and Sue Rudisill, "The Enigma of the Master Betty Mania," *Journal of Popular Culture* 8 (1974), 84.

10. At an Edinburgh performance of *Douglas,* "there was [John] Home himself . . . blubbering in the boxes, and protesting that never till then had young Norvall been acted as he had conceived it. And he had seen West Digges, the original, in Edinburgh; and Spranger Barry, the original, in London!" (John Doran, *Annals of the English Stage from Thomas Betterton to Edmund Kean* [London, 1897], 388).

11. It is also conceivable, although I've found no record of it, that Betty's roles for the next season (1805–6) were announced before the end of his London run, in which case Byron's interest in him would have been piqued, for they included the scandalous Zanga whose dramatic valedictory Byron would declaim at Harrow in June.

12. Quoted in Jonathan Wordsworth's introduction to the Woodstock edition of the play, Spelsbury House, Spelsbury, Oxford, 1990; introduction pages unnumbered.

13. In dictating terms of his mother's restitution, Frederick binds himself to Agatha in language suspiciously reminiscent of marriage ritual (or perhaps

of the biblical Ruth's pledge of faithfulness to her mother-in-law Naomi): "My fate, whatever it may be, shall never part me from her. This is my firm resolution, upon all Heaven to witness. My Lord, it must be Frederick of Wildenhaim, and Agatha of Wildenhaim—or Agatha Friburg, and Frederick Friburg" (64).

14. *Lovers' Vows* reclaims Byron's attention in 1815, again through an Irish connection. During his tenure as a member of the Drury Lane Committee, that theater boasted some of the finest dramatic talent of the time, among whom was "the handsome Mrs. Mardyn," who, directly from Dublin successes, debuted in London at Drury Lane on 26 September 1815 as Amelia in *Lovers' Vows* (Marchand 2:542). What makes this fact interesting for us is the rumored liaison between Byron and Mrs. Mardyn at the time of the Separation. A Cruickshank caricature, "Fashionables of 1816 taking the air in Hyde Park," shows Mrs. Mardyn on one arm of the elegantly clad and centered poet, an unidentified woman on the other. And Byron himself told Thomas Medwin that as a consequence of his own notoriety in 1816 he could not patronize the theater, "whence the unfortunate Mrs. Mardyn had been driven with insult" because of association with him (*Medwin's Conversations of Lord Byron,* ed. Ernest J. Lovell Jr. [Princeton: Princeton University Press, 1966], 48). Reviewing the harassment of which he believed himself victim at the time of the Separation, Byron also told Medwin: "The gravest accusation that has been made against me is that of having intrigued with Mrs. Mardyn in my own house, introduced her to my own table, &c. there never was a more unfounded calumny. Being on the Committee of Drury-lane Theatre, I have no doubt that several actresses called on me; but as to Mrs. Mardyn, who was a beautiful woman, and might have been a dangerous visitress, I was scarcely acquainted (to speak) with her" (Medwin 42). Lady Byron affirmed, in this instance, her husband's claim of "unfounded calumny" (Medwin 44n). But see the 1816 I. R. Cruickshank cartoon, "The Separation, a Sketch from the private life of Lord IRON who Panegyrized his Wife, but Satirized her Confidante!!" in which Byron, with a buxom Mrs. Mardyn embraced by one arm, spouts the opening lines of "Fare Thee Well," while with the other bidding adieu to Lady Byron and their child, his wife's adviser and for Byron a viciously meddlesome busybody Mrs. Clermont strategically positioned between the couple, and selections from Byron's poetic attack on her filling up the foreground.

A month after Mrs. Mardyn's debut, Hazlitt reviewed the performance: "A young lady of the name of Mardyn has appeared in the character of Amelia Wildenhaim. Much has been said in her praise, and with a great deal of justice. Her face is handsome, and her figure is good, bordering (but not too much), on *embonpoint*. There is, also, a full luscious sweetness in her voice. . . . The whole of this play . . . of German origin, carries the romantic in sentiment and story to the extreme verge of decency as well as probability. The character of Amelia Wildenhaim is its principal charm. The open, undisguised simplicity of this character is, however, so enthusiastically extravagant, as to excite some little surprise and incredulity on an English stage. . . . Mrs. Mardyn did the part very delightfully—with great spirit, truth, and feeling. She, perhaps, gave it a greater maturity of consciousness than it is supposed to possess. Her action is, in general, graceful and easy, but her movements were, at times, too youthful and unrestrained, and too much like *waltzing*" (*Works* 5:249).

Assuming Byron's recollections of earlier experience with *Lovers' Vows*, one wonders what species of fantasy attended his theatrical engagements with Amelia, and his social diversions with her impersonator, in 1815–16.

15. Michael R. Booth, Richard Southern, Frederick and Lisa-Lone Marker, and Robertson Davies, *The Revels History of Drama, VI, 1750–1880* (London: Methuen, 1975), 154–55.

16. He appeared to remember it in any case as late as 1821 when writing from Ravenna to Douglas Kinnaird, "anxious" for word on his new play *Sardanapalus* while half through his next one, *The Two Foscari*. But he is also anxious about investments, and wonders whether Kinnaird as banker is "stirring to get me out of funds now they are *as high* as when we bought in" (*BLJ* 8:143). Then in perhaps a not entirely mocking tone, he quotes: "'Oh Douglas—Douglas—many a time & oft—['] I might continue as pathetically as Lady Randolph—& to as much purpose apparently" (*BLJ* 8:143). The quotation is evidently meant to parallel himself with Lady Randolph in futility of purpose, but in fact Lady Randolph does not speak the given lines in the 1757 Covent Garden text of *Douglas*. The phrase "many a time and oft" is fairly commonplace in poetry and drama before and during Byron's day (the Chadwyck-Healey database identifies sixteen "hits" in drama and six in verse prior to 1820, the date of this letter), and Byron himself uses it in *Childe Harold's Pilgrimage* 1.82. But it is hard to resist suspecting that he is having Kinnaird on by lifting the words from Shylock's lips (*The Merchant of Venice* 1.3.102–5). The nominal coincidence of "*Douglas*" with "Douglas Kinnaird" permits Byron to pretend quotation of John Home or conflation of two dramatic texts, but the allusive wit of the maneuver slyly chaffs the agent for financial mismanagement. Here are the relevant lines from Shylock's speech to Antonio: "many a time and oft / In the Rialto you have rated me / About my moneys and my usances: / Still have I borne it with a patient shrug / (For suff'rance is the badge of all our tribe)."

17. See my "Byron's Separation and the Endings of *Pilgrimage*," *TSSL* 37 (1995), 16–53; "Divorce Italian Style: Byron's *Beppo*," *MLQ* 46 (1985), 29–47; and "Byron and the Dissociative Imperative: The Example of *Don Juan 5*," *SP* (1993), 322–46.

18. A likely source, I suspect, for the eponymous hero of Caroline Lamb's sensational novel, *Glenarvon*, in which case Glenalvon the hated predator becomes Byron himself as Glenarvon.

19. "[Mrs. Siddons] made the play, which is famous for its touching mother-son reunion, peculiarly her own by playing the part opposite her son Henry. The line between art and life became thin enough that her son was

moved to tears in rehearsal by his mother's deathbed agonies" (Susan Staves, "Douglas's Mother," in *Brandeis Studies in Literature*, ed. John Hazel Smith [Waltham, Mass.: Brandeis University Press, 1983], 66).

20. See Peter Manning's argument to this effect in *Byron and His Fictions*, 23–25.

21. I use *Edward Young: The Complete Works, Poetry and Prose*, ed. James Nicols (London: William Tegg, 1854).

22. 1:96n. I have been unable to confirm Marchand's guess in London theater records; but Kemble did perform the role on 30 September 1805, which suggests its earlier inclusion in his repertory, during Byron's schooltime. That "Zanga" had been in the news around Easter is also likely, given Charles James Fox's entertainment of Master Betty at his estate and their perusal of Young's text there. Eisler writes that Byron "won" the role of Zanga "courted by several other boys in his form, suggesting that they had seen the play performed over the recent vacation, with the great John Kemble in the staring role" (83). No source for this information is provided.

23. Panning an unsuccessful Zanga, Hazlitt offers his own interpretation: "[Mr. Maywood] does not give sufficient scope and vehemence to [the character's] wily and malignant duplicity. Zanga's blood is on fire; it boils in his veins; it should dilate, and agitate his whole frame with the fiercest rage and revenge; and again, the suppression of his constitutional ardor, of the ungovernable passions that torment and goad on his mind, ought to be marked with a correspondent degree of artful circumspection and studied hypocrisy" (*Works* 18:253; on a performance of 2 October 1817 at Drury Lane).

But Mr. Maywood no doubt suffered from his reviewer's having experienced Mr. Kean's Zanga in May 1815, about which Hazlitt was happier: "He had all the old impetuosity of barbarous revenge, the glowing energy of the untamed children of the sun, whose blood drinks up the radiance of fiercer skies. He was like a man stung with rage, and bursting with stifled passions. His hurried motions had the restlessness of the panther's: his wily caution, his cruel eye, his quivering visage, his violent gestures, his hollow pauses, his abrupt transitions, were all in character" (*Works* 5:227–28).

If we hear a good deal of Iago in these descriptions, Byron's own early heroes (and their gothic models) are also apparent, and almost certainly influenced Hazlitt's prose and perhaps his expectations. *Manfred*, in fact, whose hero also suffers "ungovernable passions that torment and goad on his mind," appeared only three months before the Maywood critique (June 1817) and may have helped shape it.

24. Such lengths are not unheard of in speech day programs. Mrs. Hemans's "Belshazzar's Feast," for example, at 136 lines, appears on the Shrewsbury program for 1831. And recitations of above one hundred lines are not unusual.

25. In witness to the problematic length of recitations at speech day events, even for on-site institutional authorities, here are sample prognostications from the Apposition Day programs at St. Paul's School: a sentence at the

bottom of the first page of the 18 May 1847 program announces that speeches are "to commence at Three and terminate about Four o'clock." By 21 December 1854, the schedule has been revised to read, "To commence at Two o'clock, and terminate probably at Three." By 2 June 1858, in grudging but uncertain concession, speeches will "commence at Two, and terminate, probably, at Three o'clock." But by 20 December 1860, the end is no longer in sight: "Speeches to commence at Two."

26. He did, of course, like Lear, settle for just about that amount of performance time; but what the great *Lear* passage lacks in length, it more than compensates for in rhetorical genius and potential for theatrical sensation. And as autotherapy, the two speeches, in simultaneous rehearsal and performed within a month of each other, may be taken as continuous, mutually complementary, mutually completing.

27. *SIR* 1 (1962), 105–27.

28. Never content with half measures, Byron attempted the greater role some years later, and impressed at least one member of his audience. Confessing to Thomas Medwin, "I am very fond of private theatricals," he proposed that "we get up a play. My hall, which is the largest in Tuscany, would make a capital theatre." Medwin recounts that "it was accordingly agreed that we should commence with *Othello*. Lord Byron was to be Iago. . . . Perhaps Lord Byron would have made the finest actor in the world. His voice had a flexibility, a variety in its tones, a power and pathos beyond any I ever heard; and his countenance was capable of expressing the tenderest, as well as the strongest emotions. I shall never forget his reading of Iago's part in the handkerchief scene" (*Conversations of Lord Byron* [1824], 133ff).

29. See, for a striking example, his own sonnet (?) of 1811 or 1812, addressed to John Edleston ("Thyrza," dead of consumption), and modeled on Catullus, translated in *CPW* 1:459: "Beloved youth, if the name of our former love still means anything to you, I beg you to love your friend always. As often as I lament you, dearest one, and your fate, this grief of mine grows more strongly upon me. Yet how sweet, how very sweet, that grief is; and my empty love burns more sweetly still when I imagine I have held you in my arms. I am wretched; once frustrated in my prayers to have lived for you, why now have I longed in vain to die when you died? Oh how much less it means to me to go with the others seeking garlands, perfumes, and girls, than merely to remember you. What remains for me now?—only groans, or a brother's vague dreams, or else to lie awake on my bed in tears, without you. Ah Libitina [the goddess of death] come, free me from the Fates who hate me. Since our friendship is dead, let Death be my friend."

30. It is perhaps not incidental that "Alonzo" turns up a year later as the name assigned to John Wingfield in "Childish Recollections," where he is celebrated as "Friend of my heart, and foremost of the list / Of those, with whom I liv'd supremely blest" at Harrow: "our souls," Byron writes, "were

one—All, all, that brothers should be, but the name" (ll. 251–64). See my "Chasms in Connections: Byron Ending (in) *Childe Harold's Pilgrimage* 1 and 2," *ELH* 62 (1995), 121–48.

31. Thus John Wilson in his 1818 review of *Childe Harold's Pilgrimage*, canto 4, for *Blackwood's Edinburgh Magazine* (3 [May 1818], 216–24). Such impact is for Wilson the "real excellence" of Byron's poetry, giving it "power sovereign and despotical" (216). Wilson also reviewed canto 4 for the *Edinburgh Review* [30 June 1818, 87–120], his single appearance in that journal. Inasmuch as Byron had imagined the charge of blackguardism to include contempt of his physical impairment, this line would have carried the force of immediacy.

32. Compare Byron's use of this phrase in a letter to Augusta of 11 November 1804, where he argues that linguistic "ill-usage" trumps physical injury (*BLJ* 1:56–57).

33. An imagistic lapse, given the immediate evocation of hellish flames? Or a deliberate contrast, with Alonzo's blazing rectitude as hellfire for Zanga?

34. Byron's interest in *The Revenge* did not pass with his Speech Day performance. Writing from Newstead Abbey to the Reverend John Becher on 14 September 1808, he announced this plan: "I am going to get up a play here, the hall will constitute a most admirable theatre, I have settled the Dram[atis] pers[onae] and can do without the Ladies, as I have some young friends who will make tolerable substitutes for females, and we only want three male characters besides Mr. Hobhouse and myself for the play we have fixed on, which will be the Revenge" (*BLJ* 1:170). No surviving evidence witnesses this production, if it took place at all, but it seems safe to assume that Byron, eager to repeat the earlier triumph, cast himself as the glamorous villain, perhaps with friend Hobhouse as Alonzo—a pairing with provocative psychological potential. (Imagine the dynamic were they cast as Alonzo and Don Carlos!) One wonders, too, about those androgynous "young friends" for the women's roles, and whether Robert Rushton might have been recruited, with Master Betty's androgyny as authorizing precedent in mind. (Byron also quoted from *The Revenge* in a letter from Venice to Thomas Moore on 25 March 1817, and credited Young with suggesting lines 16 and 17 of *The Bride of Abydos* [see *BLJ* 5:188 and n]).

Second Interval

1. John Pigot, neighbor with his mother and sisters to Burgage Manor, wrote from Harrowgate to his sister Elizabeth of preparations for these entertainments even while he and Byron enjoyed a holiday: "How go our theatricals? Lord Byron can say *all* his part, and I *most* of mine. He certainly acts it inimitably" (Moore 1:63). A letter received by Mr. Pigot from Southwell declares Byron's centrality in the planned event: "Till Lord Byron returns, nothing can be done" (Prothero 1:118n). Highlights of the theatrical evening are summarized from a manuscript by Miss Bristoe, one of the performers, in Prothero 1:118n. Regrettably, the following delightful anecdote reported by Moore is

ruled "erroneous" by Prothero (1:118n) in all but one particular; but it is worth reproducing if only for the one authentic moment.

    The Reverend Mr. John T. Becher furnished the epilogue, to follow performances of *The Wheel of Fortune* and *The Weathercock* in the Leacrofts' converted drawing room, "for the purpose of affording Lord Byron, who was to speak it, an opportunity of displaying his power of mimicry. . . . [The epilogue] consisted of good-humored portraits of all the persons concerned in the representation." But rumors of the planned send-up so alarmed the performers that the Reverend Becher and Byron conspired to have him deliver the piece at rehearsal "in a tone as innocent and free from all point as possible . . . reserving his mimicry, in which the whole sting of the pleasantry lay, for the evening of representation." "Suspicions of waggery" allayed, the production proceeded as planned, until "all the personages of the green room . . . on hearing the audience convulsed with laughter at this same composition . . . discovered, at last, the trick which the unsuspected mimic had played on them, and . . . join[ed] in the laugh which his playful imitation of the whole dramatis personae excited" (Moore 1:65–66). But Prothero writes, "Only one word gave the opportunity for mimicry. It occurs in the lines 'Tempest becalmed forgets his blust'ring rage, / He calls Dame Dunckley "sister" off the stage.'" In pronouncing the word "sister," Byron "took off exactly the voice and manner of Mr. R. Leacroft" (Prothero 1:118n). See also George Ticknor, *Life, Letters, and Journals* (1876); after visiting Byron at Piccadilly Terrace on 26 June 1815 he records: "The conversation . . . turned on the stage. Lord Byron asked me what actors I had heard, and when I told him, imitated to me the manner of Munden, Braham, Cooke, and Kemble, with exactness, as far as I had heard them" (1:66). This emphasis on Byron's mimetic skill links him in yet another respect to Master Betty, who to some spectators was more mimic than actor.

    2. Hazlitt's review of Kemble's performance sounds the familiar Byronic notes: "The deeply rooted, mild, pensive melancholy of the character, its embittered recollections and dignified benevolence, were given by Mr. Kemble with equal truth, elegance, and feeling" (Hazlitt, *Works* 18:198).

    3. *John Philip Kemble Promptbooks*, The Folger Facsimiles, ed. Charles H. Shattuck, vol. 11 (Charlottesville: University Press of Virginia, 1974), ii.

    4. It is worth mentioning here, as a sign of Byron's maturing self-confidence, at least among the Southwell company, that he acted a role requiring the following speech, delivered as a euphoric Tristram anticipates his betrothal: "Oh! I'm so happy, I could dance and I could jump! no, I must not jump—quakers do not jump—no, verily, I must not be a jumping quaker" (act 2). The site is possibly more forgiving of "difference" than Harrow would have been; but if Byron dared to speak such lines (and a later one comparing Tristram to a dancing puppet), raising the question of physical agility, he has moved some distance toward accommodation since trading parts with Leeke in embarrassment over his lameness.

5. Shakespearean King

1. Thanks to Dr. Drury and his own Harrow experience, Byron carried with him to Cambridge an elocutionary sensitivity which ably served his satiric interest in a poem written in his first university term, "Thoughts Suggested by a College Examination":

> Such is the youth, whose scientific pate,
> Class honours, medals, fellowships, await;
> Or, even, perhaps, the declamation prize,
> If, to such glorious height, he lift his eyes,
> But, lo! No common orator can hope,
> The envied silver cup within his scope:
> Not that our heads much eloquence require,
> Th' Athenian's glowing style, or Tully's fire.
> A manner clear or warm is useless since
> We do not try, by speaking, to convince;
> Be other orators of pleasing proud,
> We speak to please ourselves, not move the crowd;
> Our gravity prefers the muttering tone,
> A proper mixture of the squeak and groan;
> No borrow'd grace of action, must be seen,
> The slightest motion would displease the dean;
> Whilst ev'ry staring graduate would prate,
> Against what he could never imitate.
>
> The man, who hopes t'obtain the promis'd cup,
> Must in one posture stand, and ne'er look up;
> Nor stop, but rattle over every word,
> No matter what, so it can *not* be heard;
> Thus let him hurry on, nor think to rest;
> Who speaks the fastest's sure to speak the best:
> Who utters most within the shortest space,
> May, safely, hope to win the wordy race. (ll. 23–48)

2. Boys' concern over the suitability of the family vehicle delivering relatives to the festivities still prevails at Harrow on Speech Day. The "splendid equippages" and "elegant equippages and carriages of every fashionable description" cited in the *Gentleman's Magazine* for June and July 1805 (75:575 and 75:768, respectively) have been replaced with Rolls Royces, Mercedeses, BMWs, Jaguars, and even the occasional helicopter; and if unaccompanied women are less an anathema than in Byron's time—indeed, boys escorting mothers, without other male accompaniment, was not an uncommon sight in 1996—the attention and expense lavished on apparel must, if anything, have

proportionately increased since 1805. But elegance of guest matches elegance of host. Twentieth-century correspondence between Harrow School officials and local caterers, musicians, parking valet companies, the police force, and other city officials, and, yes, providers of toilet units, paint an institutional picture of intense and meticulous, even perfectionist concern for the smooth and satisfying orchestration of Speech Day activities.

Orders for tea are minutely specific and luxuriously lengthy: "Egg and cress—white bread and brown bread; Cucumber—on brown bread only; Positively no tomato or cheese!" "Cottage cheese and walnut [sandwiches], coffee and chocolate eclairs, Brandy snaps, liqueur cream gateau, macaroons, Fresh Fruit tartlets, Chocolate Nut Clusters, Ginger cake, flapjacks, almond slice, spiced apple cake, India tea," and so on. Worries about crowd control and mobility, the distribution of appropriately colored tickets to selected guests, the need for "slightly increased" pressure in the garden fountain, the provision of soft drinks for young children, the desire for "extra supplies in exchange for the sausage rolls not required"—such anxieties clutter the increasingly crisp correspondence of officials as Speech Day approaches. Details of the table do not survive from the 1804–5 Harrow Speech Days, but in light of Byron's expressed concern for protocol and other records, we may safely assume that current hospitality honors and perpetuates a tradition of sumptuousness, finery, and grace at least as old as Byron's time at the school. Indeed, Arnold Lunn in *The Harrovians* (London: Methuen, 1913) has written, "Solomon in all his glory was not arrayed like a flannel at Lord's or a monitor on Speech Day" (139).

3. Interestingly, Byron replicates Augusta's absence three years later on Harrow Speech Day 1808 when his lame friend William Harness also declaimed lines from *King Lear*. "We shall meet," Byron writes to Harness, "at all events on two, [if] not three Speechdays, I feel assured from my Recollection of you as a boy you will speak well, and I have the vanity to fancy myself a Critic in Elocution, I hope you may, most sincerely, indeed I *know* you will, for in this Country, nothing is to be done at the Bar, Stage, Pulpit, or Senate, without it— Adieu, dear William" (*BLJ* 1:164; 29 March 1808). (With Tristram Fickle's multiple career choices in mind, it is hard not to hear the Weathercock's voice dubiously echoed in this lofty declaration!) And on Saturday, 4 June, after the Thursday speeches, Byron again to Harness: "I have particularly to regret the late hour of my arrival on Thursday, which prevented me the pleasure I anticipated in hearing your Lear. However I heard your *Fame,* & congratulate myself on the escape of my *Vanity,* which would have suffered severely, though the pleasure I must experience in any performance of yours would console me under the mortification of Self-Love. I was so unfortunate as not to meet you during the day, or to see you except at a distance in the Dancing Room, but on Monday I dine with H. Drury & take Harrow in my way to the Montem of the Etonians on Tuesday. I shall make my escape as soon as possible after Dinner, in the hope of seeing you" (*BLJ* 1:166; 4 June 1808).

Did ever youth receive a more elegant apology from a revered nobleman? One wonders whether residual offense and disappointment exacted such gallantry toward a favorite conceivably hurt by absence as Byron himself had been. On the other hand, Byron writes on the second day after missing William's performance, without having apologized in person, postponing a meeting for two more days and merely hoping for, not scheduling one then, if he can squeeze Harness in between other engagements. Read thus, after such warm expectation of meeting, the note might seem more damaging than the failure to appear by one who had not promised to do so. For all of its refined gentility, Byron's second letter, together with the late arrival sparing him confrontation with a rival performing "self," may requite and compensate his dashed hopes of Augusta's visit in 1805; and its jocular modesty and flattering deference may disguise an anxious pride. His two notes to his friend enact again, of course, the approach-withdrawal rhythms so frequently observed in Byron's intimacies.

But now compare the sentiments in these letters to Harness with those expressed to Edward Noel Long just over a year earlier. To that former classmate Byron writes: "I am become rather *misanthropica* & no longer feel the same romantic attachment to Harrow & my *Theban Band,* which formerly swayed my nature, my last letter to you (in verse) was it's [sic] last Effusion, the *final Spark* of enchanted Romance & boyish ⟨Fancy⟩ Enthusiasm.—I shall not visit the *Speeches,* without *you,* they would be dull indeed. I did hope we should have trod our former paths together" [*BLJ*, supplementary vol., 5]. Does this last (disappointed) anticipation foresee the lifting of "*misanthropica*" and revival of the "romantic attachment to Harrow" reflected in the Harness correspondence of 1808? Is the declared indifference to the speeches calculated flattery? Is such indifference sincere and the elaborate gesture to Harness then all charade? Dissembling in either case may seem unlikely—without a personal interest in the speakers or in an accompanying companion, Byron probably would have been bored—*unless,* of course, the 1807 program also featured a role that Byron had performed and he knew at the time of writing to Long that it would do. As it happens, the 1807 program*s* featured all *three* of "Byron's" roles: Latinus by Wroughton on 5 May, and Zanga by Drury major, Lear by Morant senior on 2 July. The evidence is slight, but especially as corroborated by his conduct toward Harness a year later, it does raise the question of Byron's reluctance to see his performing self challenged on the site and by the vehicular identities of his Speech Day triumphs. Finally: it is tempting to attribute Byron's "misanthropia" precisely to his withdrawal of romantic attachment from that "band" whose *former* influence over his "nature" he now seems to decry. Whether this intriguing statement encrypts sexual reference seems improbable in the context, but should not be ruled out.

4. Byron's recollection of Lear's domestic and political troubles is clear in Marino Faliero and Doge Foscari (from 1821), and possibly in Werner (1822) as well. The intertextualization or resonance of *Lear* need not date from the Har-

row recitation or from schooltime exposure to the play, but the impact of this third Speech Day event upon the boy, in my view, approached traumatic proportions, and might easily have required therapeutic management by later textual activity. For discussion of Shakespeare in these plays, see Richard Lansdown, *Byron's Historical Dramas* (Oxford: Oxford University Press, 1992).

5. This would, of course, soon change: *English Bards* cites Carlisle among several "Grub-street [and] Grosvenor-Place" scrawlers of strained and senseless verse, Byron's note to which lines savages his kinsman, one among "Patrician Literati," and he virtually withdraws the dedication of *Hours of Idleness* to him.

6. One can scarcely contemplate this utterance without imagining its sensitizing influence on the psyche of a man later charged with madness by his own spouse.

7. In 1822, upon the death of his illegitimate daughter Allegra, the poet wrote to Murray with instructions for arrangements. Recalling his fondness for the Peachy Stone area of the Harrow churchyard and its prospect, he nevertheless asked that Allegra be interred in the nearby St. Mary's Church, since he intended to erect a tablet in her honor, with an inscription of his composition. "And I could hope," he wrote, "that Henry Drury will, perhaps, read the service over her.—If he should decline it—it can be done by the usual Minister for the time being" (*BLJ* 9:164). The Reverend J. W. Cunningham, however, rector of the parish church, appears to have officiated at the funeral. Whether he or Henry Drury knew of Byron's preference for an officiant is unclear. The Reverend Cunningham and his warden, with the agitated backing of the community, denied permission to erect the memorial tablet, for it declared Byron's paternity. The child is buried just inside the church. Today, a cornerstone commemorates her. (See Marchand 3:1000–1; and Iris Origo, *A Measure of Love* [New York: Pantheon, 1958(?)], 78–82.)

8. Their nastiness may be gauged by this sample, whose mock modesty only shows off the arrogance of a smart aleck savoring his own thin wit:

> Says Edward to George, 'poor Pompous forgive,
> Or else in your lines his remembrance will live';
> Says George, 'it is just the reverse:
> Oblivion should ever be Pedantry's lot;
> As I wish that his name should at once be forgot
> I give it a place in my verse.'
>
> (*CPW* 1:173)

9. In one of the "[Three Poems Associated with 'Childish Recollections']," the "[Portrait of Pomposus]" that probably circulated at the school during the late spring and summer of 1805, Byron repays, I think, the economic snobbery of the Harrow faculty with this fiscal disparagement of the new headmaster:

> Just half a Pedagogue, and half a Fop,
> Not formed to grace the Pulpit, but the shop;
> The *Counter,* not the *Desk,* should be his place,
> Who deals out precepts, as if dealing lace. . . . (ll. 1–4)

10. The charge of "libel" is particularly interesting in light of the line in the already composed "Reply" (1807) admitting Byron's own libel against Butler (l. 35), and his self-counsel to forsake verse-making for more school, although the school now is Cambridge, which he had avoided for two-thirds of the year. I suspect that the audiences of the two discourses account for the difference: John Pigot in the first case is a casual pal, thoroughly out of the Harrow loop; Henry Drury, if becoming a friend, remains implicated in Byron's long grievance against Harrow authority and is in some measure tainted by Butler's sins against the boy.

11. I am indebted to Professor William Race, formerly of the Vanderbilt University Department of Classics, for this translation and information, and to our colleague Professor Susan Wiltshire for assistance with Latin elsewhere in these pages.

12. I am not myself certain that the *Post's is* the story Byron had in mind, but in the absence of another and better fit with his epistolary description, I advance its candidacy. It is not inconceivable, I suppose, that Byron doubled the spoof by inventing the newspaper's "hoax" to explain the unaccountable omission of his own and Lloyd's names from the published review, but the idea seems too clever by (at least) half.

13. Susan Snyder, *The Comic Matrix of Shakespeare's Tragedies* (Princeton: Princeton University Press, 1979), 159–60. See also Philip John Thomson's "formula" for the grotesque: "It is not just that life is now a vale of tears, now a circus . . . but that the vale and the circus are one" (*The Grotesque* [London: Methuen, 1977], quoted in Snyder, 159).

14. Although Byron would not have spoken the king's name in his declamation, a note to *Hints from Horace* provides an interesting and amusing sidelight on his prosodic understanding of the word. The relevant lines from *Hints* follow:

> To skilful writers it will much import
> Whence spring their scenes, from common life or court;
> Whether they seek applause by smile or tear,
> To draw a 'Lying Valet' or a 'Lear',
> A sage or rakish youngster wild from school,
> A wandering 'Peregrine', or plain 'John Bull'.
> (*CPW* 1:295; ll. 159–64)

And here is Byron's note to the lines: "I have Johnson's authority for making Lear a monosyllable—'Perhaps where Lear rav'd or Hamlet died / On flying cars new sorcerers may ride.'" McGann points out (*CPW* 1:433) Byron's misquotation in omitting the "has" before "rav'd"; by it, of course, Byron loses the syllable gained by pronouncing "Lear" in one.

Epilogue

1. Phyllis Grosskurth, *Byron: The Flawed Angel* (Boston: Houghton Mifflin, 1997), 336. Grosskurth suggests that *Don Juan* is "another rendering of [Byron's m]emoirs in its account of the troubled childhood and adolescence of a guileless young man who becomes a rake *malgre lui,*" and goes on to wonder whether the seduction of the sixteen-year-old Juan by the twenty-three-year-old Julia "is a veiled reference to Byron's relationship with Lord Grey, especially as it ends with a chastisement of Plato" (336).

In an early draft of this argument, I advanced 6 June *1810* as crucial to Byron's personal history, for on that day, in Constantinople, Marchand says, Byron learned from mail off a British lugger that John Edleston had been detained on charges of "indecency" (1:245) (i.e., for homosexual conduct). This circumstance tempted me to hypothesize that the shocking report, remembered nine years later, helped to shape the 6 June episode of *Don Juan* 1, which could then be seen transformatively to rewrite, sanitize, idealize, rationalize, and justify the "passion" that Byron confessed to feeling for young Edleston in 1807–8 and, despite Hobhouse's scandalized caution, in some measure thereafter. Since Edleston is implicated (at least) by way of Lord Grey in Byron's Speech Day preparations and experiences as these would be remembered in 1819, it seemed to me conceivable that the 6 June 1810 arrival of news about the former Cambridge choirboy's acting as Byron believes or imagines Grey to have acted toward himself helps bring the date into Byron's mind and text in connection with a sexual episode involving the seduction of a young man by an adult.

However convenient to my project, the argument won't fly, and I have Phyllis Grosskurth to thank for leading me to withdraw it. In some respects a disappointing book, Grosskurth's biography of Byron nevertheless, among other virtues, corrects a long-standing misapprehension based upon Marchand's misreading of Hobhouse's diary. Hers is a startling but valid claim (111). On the date in question, Hobhouse did indeed receive letters from a ship (Marchand and Grosskurth name it *Black John,* but to my eye the script looks more like *Black Jake* or possibly even *Black Joke.* In the registries of currently active English vessels provided me by the British Library, however, no ship bearing any such names turned up. The ship is identified in the diary entry for 7 June 1810). One of these letters reported that Hobhouse's recently published collection of poems had offended puritanical tastes in England. The relevant sentence in the diary reads: "the *Collection* is accused of indecency." I have now verified this reading on a microfilm of the diary manuscript (courtesy of the British Library). In mistaking "*Collection*" for "Edleston," Marchand inadvertently set in motion forty years of (sometimes prurient) speculation on young John's illicit sexual adventures and how news of them affected Byron and his retrospective view of intimacy with Edleston. In the light of Grosskurth's discovery, parts of the Byron-Edleston relationship will require reinterpretation, but I am not yet myself convinced that the restoration of the younger man's "decency" should materially affect our understanding of the homoeroticism distinguishing his undergraduate association with the poet. (It is important to add that Grosskurth mistakes the *date* of the Hobhouse diary entry. It is for 6 June 1810, not 6 July.)

2. See the Norton *Prelude,* ed. M. H. Abrams, Stephen Gill, and Jonathan Wordsworth, 1979; and *TLS,* April to September 1975.

3. Like her letter at the end of the canto; see my " 'Breaking Up Is Hard To Do': Byron's Julia and the Instabilities of Valediction," *SAR* 56 (1991), 43–57.

4. *Byron,* ed. Jerome J. McGann (Oxford: Oxford University Press, 1986), 1046.

Addendum to Page 178

A family history from 1910, recently brought to my attention in private correspondence, may corroborate Symonds's report of Harrow practices offensive to his sensibility. James Munro Macnabb (1790–1860), at Harrow School from 1798 through 1806, recalled that Byron used to call him "Lucretia" because he was "so beautiful." Family portraits are said to validate Byron's aesthetic taste. One wonders, of course, whether and in what manner his lordship may have played Tarquin to the fetching lad's Lucretia. (I am grateful to the Reverend Donald McNeile of Oxfordshire for permission to cite this clip of his great, great grandfather's schooldays, before the gentleman went on to sire ten children. The Reverend McNeile suggests that, in light of a then-current meaning of "Lucretia" as "chaste woman," Byron's sobriquet for young Macnabb may be his first known joke.)

Selected Bibliography

Books and Articles

Abrams, M. H., Stephen Gill, and Jonathan Wordsworth. *The Prelude: 1799, 1805, 1850.* New York: Norton, 1979.

Allingham, John Till. *The Weathercock.* New York: Longworth, 1806.

[Anonymous]. *Authentic Memoirs of that Wonderful Phenomenon The Infant Roscius.* London: W. Hodgson, n.d.

———. "Boy Wonder." *Theatre Arts* 38 (June 1954), 62–64, 94–95.

———. *Critique on the First Performance of Young Roscius at Covent Garden Theatre, on Saturday, Dec. 1, As it Appeared in the British Press* [newspaper] *on Monday, Dec. 3, 1804.* I. Gold for J. Kirby, 1804.

———. *[Memoir of] Mr. W. H. W. Betty, English Roscius.* London: B. D. Cousins, n.d.

———. *Merchant Taylors' School: Its Origin, History, and Present Surroundings.* Oxford: Blackwell, 1929.

———. *Mr. W. H. Betty, The English Roscius.* London: B. D. Cousins, n.d.

Arrilla, Lillian. *Catalogue of Dramatic Portraits in the Theatre Collection of the Harvard College Library.* Cambridge: Harvard University Press, 1930.

Ashley-Cooper, F. S. *Eton v. Harrow at the Wicket.* London: St. Jarves Press, 1922.

Backschieder, Paula R. *Spectacular Politics: Theatrical Power and Mass Culture in Early Modern England.* Baltimore: Johns Hopkins University Press, 1993.

Baer, Marc. *Theatre and Disorder in Late Georgian London.* Oxford: Clarendon, 1992.

Baker, Herschel. *John Philip Kemble: The Actor in His Theatre.* New York: Greenwood, 1942.

Barbary, James. *The Young Lord Byron.* New York: Roy Publishers, 1965.

Bate, Jonathan. *Shakespearean Constitutions: Politics, Theatre, Criticism, 1730–1830.* Oxford: Oxford University Press, 1989.

Beaty, Frederick L. *Byron the Satirist.* De Kalb, Ill.: Northern Illinois University Press, 1985.

Bisset, James, comp. *Critical Essays on the Young Roscius by Gentlemen of Distinguished Literary Talents and Theatrical Amateurs.* London: J. Johnson, 1805.

Blackstone, Bernard. "Byron and the *Republic:* The Platonic Background to

Byron's Political Ideas," in *Byron: Poetry and Politics.* Edited by Erwin A. Sturzl and James Hogg. Salzburg: Institut fur Anglistik und Amerikanistik Universitat Salzburg, 1981.

Blessington, Lady. *Conversations of Lord Byron.* Edited by Ernest J. Lovell Jr. Princeton: Princeton University Press, 1969.

Booth, Michael R., Richard Southern, Frederick and Lisa-Lone Marker, and Robertson Davies. *The Revels History of Drama.* 8 volumes. 6: *1750–1880.* London: Methuen, 1975.

Boyes, Megan. *My Amiable Mamma: A Biography of Mrs. Catherine Gordon Byron.* Derby: Megan Boyes, 1991.

———. *Queen of a Fantastic Realm: A Biography of Mary Chaworth.* Derby: Megan Boyes, 1986.

Brent, Peter. *Lord Byron.* London: Weidenfeld and Nicolson, 1965.

Brown, The Reverend Doctor John. *Barbarossa: A Tragedy.* London: J. Wenman, 1777.

Bryant, P. H. M. *Harrow.* London: Blackie and Son, 1936.

Cafarelli, Annette Wheller. "Byron and the Pathology of Genius," in *Rereading Byron: Essays Selected from Hofstra University's Byron Bicentennial Conference.* Edited by Alice Levine and Robert N. Keane. New York: Garland, 1993.

Carleton, John. *Westminster School.* London: Rupert Karl-Davis, 1925.

Carlson, Julie A. "Forever Young: Master Betty and the Queer Stage of Youth in English Romanticism." *South Atlantic Quarterly* 95 (Summer 1996), 575–602.

———. *In the Theatre of Romanticism: Coleridge, Nationalism, Women.* New York: Cambridge University Press, 1994.

Cave, Richard Allen, ed. *The Romantic Theatre: An International Symposium.* Totowa, N.J.: Barnes and Noble, 1986.

Chancellor, E. Beresford. *Life in Regency and Early Victorian Times: An Account of the Days of Brummel and D'Orsay.* London: B. T. Betsford, 1933.

Chandos, John. *Boys Together: English Public Schools, 1800–1864.* New Haven: Yale University Press, 1984.

Childers, William. "Byron's *Waltz:* The Germans and Their Georges." *Keats-Shelley Journal* 18 (1969), 81–95.

Chitty, Herbert. *Medal Speaking at Winchester College, 1761–1815.* Winchester: Wykehamist Society, Jacob and Johnson, 1905.

Christensen, Jerome. *Lord Byron's Strength.* Baltimore: Johns Hopkins University Press, 1993.

Clarence, Reginald, comp. *"The Stage" Cyclopaedia: A Bibliography of Plays.* London: "The Stage," 1909.

Coleridge, Arthur Duke. *Eton in the Forties, by an Old Colleger.* 2nd edition. London: Bentley and Son, 1898.

Coleridge, The Honorable Gilbert. *Eton in the 'Seventies.* London: Smith, Elder, 1912.

Cotton, J. G. Minchin. *Old Harrow Days.* London: Methuen, 1898.

Crompton, Louis. *Byron and Greek Love: Homophobia in 19th Century England.* Berkeley: University of California Press, 1985.

———. "Byron's Bisexuality: The Biographical Evidence and the Poems." In *Approaches to Teaching Byron's Poetry,* edited by Frederick W. Shilstone. New York: Modern Language Association of America, 1991. Pp. 54–58.

Cumberland, Richard. *The Wheel of Fortune, a comedy.* New York: David Longworth, 1818.

Cust, Lionel. "Notes on Pictures in the Royal Collection—XXXI." *Burlington Magazine for Connoisseurs* 27 (April to September 1915), no. 145, 3–7.

Dallas, Robert Charles. *Recollections of the Life of Lord Byron.* 2 volumes. Philadelphia, 1825.

DeSelincourt, Ernest, ed. *The Letters of William and Dorothy Wordsworth.* 2nd edition. 1. *The Early Years.* Oxford: Clarendon, 1967. Revised by Chester L. Shaver.

Doherty, F. M. "Byron and the Sense of the Dramatic." In *Byron and the Limits of Fiction,* edited by Bernard Beatty and Vincent Newey. Liverpool: Liverpool University Press, 1988.

Doran, John. *"Their Majesties' Servants" or Annals of the English Stage from Thomas Betterton to Edmund Kean.* London: John C. Nimmo, 1897.

Downer, Alan S. "Players and Painted Stage: Nineteenth-Century Acting." *PMLA* 61 (1946), 522–76.

Draper, F. W. M. *Four Centuries of Merchant Taylors School 1561–1961.* London: Oxford University Press, 1962.

Drury, Charles. "Rev. Joseph Drury, D. D., Late Head Master of Harrow." In *Annual Biography and Obituary.* London, 1835.

Du Bos, Charles. *Byron and the Need of Fatality.* Translated by Ethel Colburn Mayne. London: Putnam, 1932.

E., O. *Eton under Hornby: Some Reminiscences and Reflections.* London: A. C. Fifield, 1910.

Earland, Ada. *John Opie and His Circle.* London: Hutchinson and Company, 1911.

Eisler, Benita. *Byron: Child of Passion, Fool of Fame.* New York: Knopf, 1999.

Elfenbein, Andrew. "Byronism and the Work of Homosexual Performance in Early Victorian England." *Modern Language Quarterly* 54 (December 1993), 535–66.

Elledge, Paul. " 'Breaking Up Is Hard to Do': Byron's Julia and the Instabilities of Valediction." *SAR* 56 (1991), 43–57.

———. "Byron and the Dissociative Imperative: The Example of *Don Juan* 5." *SP* (1993), 322–46.

———. "Byron's Separation and the Endings of *Pilgrimage.*" *TSSL* 37 (1995), 16–53.

———. "Chasms in Connections: Byron Ending (in) *Childe Harold's Pilgrimage* 1 and 2." *ELH* 62 (1995), 121–48.

———. "Divorce Italian Style: Byron's *Beppo.*" *MLQ* 46 (1985), 29–47.

Erdman, David V. "Byron's Stage Fright: The History of His Ambition and Fear of Writing for the Stage." *ELH* 6 (September 1939), 219–43.

———. "Lord Byron as Rinaldo." *PMLA* 57 (1942), 189–231.

Farmer, John S., comp. and ed. *Slang and Its Analogues Past and Present.* 7 volumes. London [printed for subscribers only], 1890–94.

Ffrench, Yvonne. *Mrs. Siddons: Tragic Actress.* Revised edition. London: D. Verschoyle, 1954.

Fisher, G. W. *Annals of Shrewsbury School.* London, 1899.

Gardiner, R. B., and John Lupton, eds. *Res Paulinae: The Eighth Half-Century of St. Paul's School.* London, 1911.

Gaul, Marilyn. "Romantic Theatre." *Wordsworth Circle* 14 (1983), 255–63.

Genest, John. *Some Accounts of the English Stage, from the Restoration in 1660 to 1830.* 10 volumes. 7 and 8. Bath, 1832.

Goodman, Nigel. *Eton College.* Pitkin Pictorials, 1989.

Gordon, Pryse Lockhart. *Personal Memoirs,* 2 vols. London, 1830.

Gransden, K. W. *Virgil: Aeneid, Book XI.* Cambridge: Cambridge University Press, 1991.

Grebanier, Bernard D. *The Uninhibited Byron: An Account of His Sexual Confusion.* New York: Crown, 1970.

———. *Then Came Each Actor.* New York: David McKay, 1975.

Grosskurth, Phyllis. *Byron: The Flawed Angel.* Boston: Houghton Mifflin, 1997.

Gunn, Peter. *My Dearest Augusta.* New York: Atheneum, 1968.

Gwyn, Stephen. *Memorials of an Eighteenth Century Painter (James Northcote).* London, 1898.

Hall, Jean. "The Evolution of the Surface Self: Byron's Poetic Career." *Keats-Shelley Journal* 36 (1987), 134–57.

Hardcastle, the Honorable Mrs., ed. *Life of John, Lord Campbell, Lord High Chancellor of Great Britain.* London, 1881.

Harley, George Davis. *An Authentic Biographical Sketch of the Life, Education, and Personal Character, William Henry West Betty, The Celebrated Young Roscius.* London, 1804.

Hawson, Edmund W., and George Townsend Warner. *Harrow School.* London, 1898.

Heffernan, James A. W. "Self-Representation in Byron and Turner." *Poetics Today* 10 (Summer 1989), 209–41.

Henderson, Andrea K. *Romantic Identities: Varieties of Subjectivity 1774–1830.* Cambridge: Cambridge University Press, 1996.

His Very Self and Voice: Collected Conversations of Lord Byron. Edited by Ernest J. Lovell Jr. New York: Macmillan, 1954.

Hogg, James, ed. *Byron and the Theatre.* Salzburg Studies in *English Literature* (Salzburg, 1972).

Home, John. *The Plays of John Home.* Edited with an introduction by James S. Malek. New York: Garland, 1980.

———. *The Works of John Home, Esq.* Edited by Henry Mackenzie. 3 volumes. Edinburgh: Archibald Constable, 1822.

Hughes, Thomas. *Tom Brown's Schooldays.* London: Oxford World's Classics, 1989.

Hunter, P. D., ed. *The Harrow Collection.* Harrow-on-the-Hill: Harrow School Press, 1994.

Inchbald, Mrs. Elizabeth. *Lovers' Vows.* Woodstock Edition. Oxford: Spelsbury House, 1990.

Irving, Washington. "Letters of Washington Irving." Edited by Clara and Rudolf Kirk. Part 3: "Irving in London." *Journal of the Rutgers University Library* 10 (December 1946), 20–27.

Jackson, John. *Strictures upon the Merits of Young Roscius.* 3rd edition. London: Longman, Hurst, Reese, and Orme, 1804.

Jacobus, Mary. *Romanticism, Writing, and Sexual Difference: Essays on "The Prelude."* Oxford: Clarendon Press, 1989.

Jump, John D. *Byron.* London: Routledge and Kegan Paul, 1972.

Kelly, Linda. *The Kemble Era: John Philip Kemble, Sarah Siddons, and the London Stage.* New York: Random House, 1980.

John Philip Kemble Promptbooks. Edited by Charles H. Shattuck. 11 volumes. Folger Facsimiles, Volume 11. Charlottesville: University Press of Virginia, 1974.

Laborde, E. D. *Harrow School Yesterday and Today.* London: Winchester, 1948.

Lascelles, B. P. "Early Harrow Theatricals." *The Harrovian* 28, no. 8 (18 November 1905), page unnumbered.

Lansdown, Richard. *Byron's Historical Dramas.* Oxford: Clarendon Press, 1992.

Leaf, John. *Harrow School.* Pitkin Pictorials, 1990.

Lucas, E. V. *The Works of Charles and Mary Lamb.* 7 volumes. Volume 5. London: Methuen, 1903.

Lunn, Arnold. *The Harrovians.* London: Methuen, 1913.

Lyte, H. C. Maxwell. *A History of Eton College, 1404–1884.* London: Macmillan, 1889.

MacKenzie, Compton. *Sinister Street.* London: Martin Secker, 1923.

Mahon, Lord (Philip Henry Stanhope). *History of England from the Peace of Utrecht to the Peace of Versailles: 1713–1783.* 7 volumes. Volume 5: 1763–1774. London: John Murray, 1851.

Manning, Peter. *Byron and His Fictions.* Detroit: Wayne State University Press, 1978.

Marchand, Leslie A. *Byron: A Biography.* 3 volumes. New York, 1957.

———. *Byron: A Portrait.* Chicago: University of Chicago Press, 1970.

———, ed. *Byron's Letters and Journals.* 13 volumes. The Belknap Press of Harvard University Press, 1973–94.

———. *Byron's Poetry: A Critical Introduction.* Boston: Houghton Mifflin, 1965.

Markham, Captain F. *Recollections of a Town Boy at Westminster.* London: Edward Arnold, 1903.

Mayne, E. C. *Byron.* London: Methuen, 1924.

McCarthy, Mary. *Memories of a Catholic Girlhood.* New York: Harcourt, 1957.

McDonald, D. L. "Childhood Abuse as Romantic Reality: The Case of Byron." *Literature and Psychology* 40 (1994), 24–47.

McGann, Jerome J., ed. *Byron.* Oxford: Oxford University Press, 1986.

———, ed. *The Complete Poetical Works of Lord Byron.* 7 volumes. Oxford: Clarendon Press, 1980–93.

———. *The Poetics of Sensibility: A Revolution in Literary Style.* Oxford: Clarendon Press, 1996.

Mead, A. H. *A Miraculous Draught of Fishes: A History of St. Paul's School 1509–1990.* London: James and James, 1990.

Medwin, Thomas. *Conversations of Lord Byron.* Edited by Ernest J. Lovell Jr. Princeton: Princeton University Press, 1966.

Merrit, John. *Memoirs of the Life of Wm. Henry West Betty, Known by the Name of the Young Roscius.* London: Longman, 1804.

Milbanke, Ralph, Earl of Lovelace. *Astarte: A Fragment of the Truth Concerning George Gordon Byron, Sixth Lord Byron.* New York: Scribner's, 1921.

Miller, Carl. "Master Betty: A Gothic Tale." Unpublished play. Manuscript courtesy of the author.

Moore, Doris Langley. *Lord Byron: Accounts Rendered.* London: John Murray, 1974.

———. *The Late Lord Byron: Posthumous Dramas.* Revised edition. New York: Harper and Row, 1977.

Moore, Thomas. *The Letters and Journals of Lord Byron, with Notices of His Life.* 2 volumes. Paris: Baudry's European Library, 1833.

Murdoch, James Edward. *The Stage, or Recollections of Actors and Acting from an Experience of Fifty Years, A Series of Dramatic Sketches.* New York: Benjamin Blom, 1818; reissued 1969.

Nettleton, George Henry. *English Drama of the Restoration and Eighteenth Century (1642–1780).* New York: Cooper Square, 1968.

Nicoll, Allardyce. *A History of Early Nineteenth Century Drama 1800–1850.* 2 volumes. Volume 1. Cambridge: Cambridge University Press, 1930.

Norton, Sandra K. "William Henry West Betty: Romantic Child Actor." Ph.D. Dissertation, University of Missouri, Columbia, August 1976.

Oldham, J. B. *History of Shrewsbury School.* Shrewsbury, 1952.

Origo, Iris. *A Measure of Love.* New York: Pantheon, 1957.

Parker, Derek. *Byron and His World.* London: Thames and Hudson, 1968.

Partridge, Eric. *A Dictionary of Slang.* 8th edition. London: Routledge and Kegan Paul, 1984.

Pascoe, Judith. *Romantic Theatricality.* Ithaca: Cornell University Press, 1997.

Peach, Annette. "Controlling an Image: Two Venetian Miniatures of Byron." *Byron Journal* 26 (1998), 17–28.

Piozzi, Hester Lynch. *Autobiography, Letters, and Literary Remains of Mrs. Piozzi (Thrale)*. Edited with notes and an introductory account of her life and writings by A. Hayward. 2nd edition. New York: AMS Press, 1975.

Piper, David. *The Image of the Poet: British Poets and Their Portraits*. Oxford: Clarendon Press, 1982.

Playfair, Giles. *Kean*. New York: E. P. Dutton, 1939.

———. *The Prodigy: A Study of the Strange Life of Master Betty*. London: Secker and Warburg, 1967.

Potkay, Adam. "Beckford's Haven of Boys." *Raritan* 13 (Summer 1993), 73–86.

Pratt, Willis W. *Byron at Southwell: The Making of a Poet*. Austin: University of Texas Byron Monographs, Number 1, 1948.

Prothero, Rowland E., ed. *The Works of Lord Byron: Letters and Journals*. 6 volumes. London: John Murray, 1898–1902.

Rapf, Joanna. "Poetic Performance: Byron and the Concept of a Male Muse." In *Approaches to Teaching Byron's Poetry*, edited by Frederick W. Shilstone. New York: Modern Language Association of America, 1991.

Raphael, Frederic. *Byron*. London: Thames and Hudson, 1982.

Rawson, Hugh. *Wicked Words*. New York: Crown, 1989.

Raymond, Dora Neill. *The Political Career of Lord Byron*. New York: Henry Holt, 1924.

Raymond, Ernest. *Mr. Olim*. London: Cassell, 1961.

Richardson, Alan. *A Mental Theatre: Poetic Drama and Consciousness in the Romantic Age*. University Park: Pennsylvania State University Press, 1988.

Robinson, Charles, ed. *Lord Byron and His Contemporaries: Essays from the Sixth International Byron Seminar*. Newark: University of Delaware Press; London and Toronto: Associated University Presses, 1982.

Rosenfeld, Sybil. *Temples of Thespis: Some Private Theatres and Theatricals in England and Wales, 1700–1820*. London: Society for Theatre Research, 1978.

Russell, Gillian. *The Theatres of War: Performance, Politics, and Society, 1793–1815*. Oxford: Clarendon Press, 1995.

Russell, Lord John, ed. *Memorials and Correspondence of Charles James Fox*. AMS Press, 1990; a reprint of the 1857 edition.

Sabben-Clare, James. *Winchester College after 606 Years, 1382–1986*. Winchester: P. and G. Wells, 1989.

Slout, William L., and Sue Rudisill. "The Enigma of the Master Betty Mania." *Journal of Popular Culture* 8 (Summer 1974), 81–90.

Smiles, Samuel. *A Publisher and His Friends: Memoir and Correspondence of the Late John Murray*. 2 volumes. London: John Murray, 1881.

Snyder, Susan. *The Comic Matrix of Shakespeare's Tragedies*. Princeton: Princeton University Press, 1979.

Staves, Susan. "Douglas's Mother." In *Brandeis Studies in Literature*, edited by John Hazel Smith. Waltham, Mass.: Brandeis University Press, 1983.

St. Clair, William. "The Temptations of a Biographer: Thomas Moore and Byron." *Byron Journal* 17 (1989), 5–56.

Symon, James David. *Byron in Perspective.* New York: Frederick A. Stokes, 1925.

Taborski, Boleslaw. *Byron and the Theatre.* Salzburg Studies in English Literature, edited by James Hogg. Salzburg, 1972.

Tanner, Lawrence E. *Westminster School: A History.* London: Country Life Ltd., 1934.

Taylor, Beverly, and Robert Bain, eds. *The Cast of Consciousness: Concepts of the Mind in British and American Romanticism.* New York: Greenwood, 1987.

Taylor, Paul. "Cracked Actor." A review of Carl Miller's play "Master Betty." *The Independent,* 22 June 1990.

Thompson, Philip John. *The Grotesque.* London: Methuen, 1972.

Thornton, Percy M. *Harrow School and Its Surroundings.* London, 1885.

Tichener-Barrett, Robert. *Eton and Harrow at Lords since 1805.* London: Quiller Press, 1996.

Ticknor, George. *Life, Letters, and Journals.* 2 volumes. 5th edition. Boston: J. R. Osgood, 1876.

Trollope, Thomas Adolphus. *What I Remember.* London: Kimber, 1973.

Virgil. *The Aeneid.* Translated in verse by Allen Mandelbaum. New York: Bantam, 1961.

Walford, Geoffrey. *Life in Public Schools.* London: Methuen, 1986.

Warner, Rex. *English Public Schools.* London: Collins, 1946.

Webb, Timothy. "The Romantic Poet and the Stage: A Short, Sad History." In *The Romantic Theatre: An International Symposium,* edited by Richard Allen Cave. Totowa, N.J.: Barnes and Noble, 1986.

Williams, R. D. *The Aeneid of Virgil, Books 7–12.* London: Macmillan, 1973.

Wilson, Frances, ed. *Byromania: Portraits of the Artist in Nineteenth- and Twentieth-Century Culture.* New York: St. Martin's, 1999.

Wimsatt, W. K., and F. A. Pottle. *Boswell for the Defence 1769–1774.* New York, 1959.

Wyndham, Henry Saxe. *The Annals of Covent Garden Theatre from 1782 to 1897.* 2 volumes. London: Chatto and Windus, 1906.

Young, Edward. *The Complete Works, Poetry and Prose,* edited by James Nicols. London: William Tegg, 1854.

Periodicals

Blackwoods Edinburgh Magazine
The Daily Advertiser
The Daily Telegraph
The Edinburgh Review
The Eton College Chronicle
The Gentleman's Magazine
Harrow Gazette
Harrow Notes

The Harrovian
London *Times*
The Morning Post
The Taylorian
Times Literary Supplement
The Triumvirate [Harrow in-house paper]

Index

Addison, Joseph, 16
Adolescence, 3, 36–37
Aeneid (Virgil): Byron's recitation from, 1, 16–17, 57–63; mentioned, 11; quoted, 182 n. 10
Albert, Prince, 9–10
Alexander, Dr. James, 180 n. 4
Allingham, John Till, 64, 136–39, 198 n. 1
Ariosto, 166
Aristophanes, 8
Austen, Jane, 11, 110

Bakewell, Melissa, 176–77 n. 21
Bankes, William, 147, 148
Banti, Brigitta, 89
Barbarossa (Browne), 107–10, 126
"Bard, The: An Ode" (Gray), 122
Bath, D., 93
Becher, Rev. John T., 197 n. 34, 198 n. 1
Beckford, William, 68
Beppo (Byron), 117
Bessborough, Countess of, 95
Betty, William Henry West: Byron's criticism of, 86, 88–90, 106–8; influence on Byron, 3, 14, 94–95, 110, 119, 130; as object of male desire, 96–97, 189 n. 23; reviews of, 87–88, 91–93
Billington, Elizabeth, 89
Blackstone, Bernard, 175 n. 15, 176 n. 18
Blessington, Lady, 136
Boswell, James, 5
Bride of Abydos, The (Byron), 68, 197 n. 34
Brown, Rev. Dr. John, 107–10
Burke, Edmund, 5, 13, 166
Burns, Robert, 163
Butler, Dr. George: becomes Harrow headmaster, 99–100; mentioned, 123, 155, 160, 168; satirized by Byron, 100, 146–52, 202 n. 9, 203 n. 10

Butler, Dr. Samuel, 8, 63, 169 n. 2, 185 n. 19
Byron, Allegra, 202 n. 7
Byron, Lady Annabella, 66, 70, 116, 135, 193 n. 14
Byron, Mrs. Catherine (née Gordon): Byron's letters to, 19–27, 39–41, 46–52; mentioned, 14, 35, 59, 109, 187 n. 4; quarrels with Byron, 30–31, 64–84, 103–6, 113–14, 140–41, 145–46, 153–54, 166; relationship with Lord Grey, 64–66, 74–77, 79, 82
Byron, George Gordon, sixth Lord: affection for Augusta Leigh, 29–31, 70; aristocratic pride of, 19–22, 29, 44, 48, 56, 78, 115; athletic activities of, 13, 191–92 n. 7; on being a poet, 56–57; dismissal from Harrow, 85, 98; and Elizabeth Pigot, 69–70; entry into Harrow, 17; fascination with William Betty, 88–97, 106–8; fatherlessness of, 23–24, 28, 65, 127; feelings for Mary Duff, 66–69; feelings of betrayal, 30, 75–77, 127–28; homosexuality of, 35, 37–39, 40–41, 74, 76, 97, 120, 128–29, 179 n. 10; as King Latinus, 57, 61–63; as King Lear, 156–64; lameness of, 1, 17, 22, 28, 49, 51, 57–58, 126, 131, 158–59, 180 nn. 2, 4, 190 n. 6; melancholy of, 13, 61, 115–16, 126, 136–37; oratorical skill of, 53–54, 64, 86, 155, 159, 161, 185 n. 20; parliamentary aspirations of, 86, 104, 108–9, 136, 137, 161, 168, 179 n. 1, 181 n. 6, 185 n. 20; poverty of, 17, 28, 32, 47–49, 51, 58–59, 118, 126, 158, 173 n. 5; quarrels with mother, 30–31, 64–84, 103–6, 113–14, 140–41, 145–46, 153–54, 166; quarrel with Henry Drury, 17–28; quarrel with Mark Drury, 47–52; rebels against George Butler, 99–100, 112, 130, 141–42, 146–52, 189 n. 1;

217

Byron, George Gordon (*continued*)
rejected by Mary Ann Chaworth, 65–66; rejects role of Drances, 57–61; religious unorthodoxy of, 85; reputation for fighting, 19, 21, 60, 109; revolutionary sensibilities of, 100, 112, 115, 130; as Roderick Penruddock, 64, 135–36, 186 n. 1, 198 n. 1; satire of, 100, 142, 147, 199 n. 1, 202 nn. 8, 9, 203 n. 10; scholastic deficiency of, 17, 46, 85; self-fashioning of, 1–4; as Tristram Fickle, 64, 136–39, 186 n. 1, 197 n. 1, 198 n. 4; valedictory impulses of, 2, 62, 116–17, 132, 176 n. 17; as Zanga the Moor, 120–34, 140–41

Byron, Maria (Aunt Sophia), 72

Calthorpe, Frederick Gough, 17
Calvert, Francis, 149
Campbell, Lord, 92
Canning, George, 92
Carlisle, Lord, 78, 85, 86, 101, 109, 145, 173 n. 5, 202 n. 5
Carlson, Julie A., 189 n. 23
Catullus, 196 n. 29
Chandos, John, 177–79 n. 28
Charlotte, Princess of Wales, 101–2
Charterhouse School, 7
Chaworth, Mary Ann, 14, 29, 30, 59–60, 65–66, 68, 71, 81, 117, 118, 163, 191 n. 6
Chaworth, William, 59, 118
Childe Harold's Pilgrimage (Byron), 11, 117, 150, 159, 176 n. 19, 194 n. 16, 197 n. 31
"Childish Recollections" (Byron), 23–24, 55, 73, 74, 98, 147–48, 150, 187 n. 6, 196–97 n. 30
Child of Love (Kotzebue), 110
Christensen, Jerome, 169 n. 1
Clare, Lord, 73, 93, 188 n. 20
Claridge, George and John Thomas, 93
Coleman, John, 108
Coleridge, Samuel Taylor, 162
Collet, Dean John, 8
Collins, William, 16, 122
Crompton, Louis, 128
Cumberland, Richard, 135–36
Curzon, George Augustus William, 93

Dallas, Robert Charles, 185 n. 20
Dancing, at Harrow, 102–3, 190 n. 6

Davies, Robertson, 115–16, 118
Delawarr, Lady, 72
Delawarr, Lord George, 14, 72, 73–74, 76–77, 93, 101–3, 126, 128
Dennis, John, 4
Detached Thoughts (Byron), 54, 182 n. 8
Devonshire, Duchess of, 88
Don Juan (Byron), 3, 14, 50, 54, 71, 79, 117, 125, 134, 136, 163, 181 n. 6; significance of 6 June in, 165–68, 204 n. 1
Douglas (Home), 108–9, 115–18, 192 n. 10, 194 n. 16
"Dream, The" (Byron), 66
Drury, Charles, 55, 176 n. 16
Drury, Henry: mentioned, 32, 46, 125–28, 202 n. 7; quarrel with Byron, 14, 17–28, 30; reconciled with Byron, 100, 147–52, 203 n. 10
Drury, Dr. Joseph: as father figure to Byron, 23–25, 26, 62, 80–81, 101, 110, 161; elocutionary skill of, 54–56, 62; mentioned, 49–50; opinions about Byron, 17–19, 27–28, 46–47, 53–54, 55–56, 85; retirement of, 85, 99, 141, 145, 161
Drury, Mark: as candidate for Harrow headmastership, 99–100, 141; quarrel with Byron, 27, 47–52, 58, 71, 78, 120, 125–27
Duff, Mary, 14, 66–69, 81, 190 n. 6

"Edinburgh Ladies' Petition to Doctor Mayes, and His Reply, The" (Byron), 89–90
Edleston, John, 34, 38, 40, 93–94, 128, 196 n. 29, 204 n. 1
Eisler, Benita, 174 n. 8, 177 nn. 25, 28, 179 n. 33, 180 n. 2, 186 n. 20, 195 n. 22
Ellison, Cuthbert, 17
Elocutionary training, in public schools, 8–9, 62–63
Elrington, John, 122
English Bards and Scotch Reviewers (Byron), 89, 150, 167, 202 n. 5
Erdman, David V., 181 n. 6
Erskine, Thomas, 154, 155
Eton College, 5, 7, 8–9, 10–11, 62, 171 n. 13, 172 n. 18, 189 n. 1, 191 n. 7
Evans, Benjamin, 19, 26, 27, 47, 99, 174 n. 10

218 : Index

"Fare Thee Well" (Byron), 193 n. 14
"Farewell to Ayrshire" (Gall), 163
Farrer, Thomas, 154
Fletcher, William, 39
Fox, Charles James, 92, 188 n. 15, 195 n. 22
"Fragment Written Shortly after the Marriage of Miss Chaworth" (Byron), 163–64
Franks, William, 154, 155
Frederick, George John, 93
French Revolution, 12
Fugitive Pieces (Byron), 56

Gall, Richard, 163
Garrick, David, 86, 87, 88, 92, 107, 164
Genest, John, 94
George III, 7, 12, 158, 162
Glenarvon (Caroline Lamb), 194 n. 18
Godwin, William, 171–72 n. 14
Golland, James, 190 n. 5
Gordon, Charles David, 93
Gordon, Pryse Lockhart, 17, 173 n. 7, 190 n. 6
Gower, Lord Granville Leveson, 95
Gray, May, 33, 37, 65, 145
Gray, William, 16, 122
Grey de Ruthyn, Lord Henry: alleged sexual proposition to Byron, 32–33, 35–39, 110, 160, 177 n. 22, 179 n. 33; Byron's quarrel with, 14, 28–45, 50, 204 n. 1; marriage of, 39–40; and Owen Mealey, 41–42, 44–45; relationship with Mrs. Byron, 65–66, 74–78, 82
Grosskurth, Phyllis, 43, 177 n. 22, 180 n. 4, 204 n. 1

Hamlet (Shakespeare), 108
Hanson, Hargreaves, 27
Hanson, John, 18, 27, 28, 50, 53, 56, 62, 64, 71, 82, 83–84, 85, 86, 98–99, 101, 103, 107, 113, 118, 141–43, 173 n. 5, 174 n. 12, 187 n. 4
Harness, William, 93, 126, 200 n. 3
Harrow School Speech Day: compared with other schools', 5, 7–10, 62–63, 195 n. 25; competitive aspect of, 16, 45, 103; origins of, 4–5; performativity of, 5, 9–11, 62; program of, 5–7, 16–17, 122–23, 199 n. 2; as ritual of closure, 116–17
Hawkyard, Alasdair, 190 n. 3

Haydon, Benjamin Robert, 40
Hazlitt, William, 92, 188 n. 13, 193 n. 14, 195 n. 23, 198 n. 2
Heath, Dr. William, 4, 7, 8, 102, 169 n. 2
Hints from Horace (Byron), 203 n. 14
Hinxman, Henry, 17, 120–21
Hobhouse, John Cam, 32, 40, 177 n. 22, 179 n. 30, 197 n. 34, 204 n. 1
Hodgson, Francis, 185 n. 20
Holland, Lord, 106, 186 n.20
Holmes, Peter, 170 n. 11
Home, John, 108–9, 115–18, 192 n. 10, 194 n. 16
Homer, 49, 166
Homosexuality: in English public schools, 35, 177 n. 28; penalties for, 177 n. 27
Hough, William, 93, 97
Hours of Idleness (Byron), 56, 89–90, 147, 148, 202 n. 5
Hughes, Charles, 175 n. 15
Hume, David, 16
Hunter, Peter, 93

Incest, 65, 70, 115, 118–19, 120
Inchbald, Mrs. Elizabeth, 108, 110–15, 193 n. 14
Infant Roscius, The, 91, 92

Jackson, Dr. William, 54
Jones, Sir William, 173 n. 2

Kaye, John, 173 n. 1
Kean, Edmund, 54, 195 n. 23
Keate, Dr. John, 184 n. 16, 189 n. 1
Kemble, John Philip, 87, 91–93, 122, 195 n. 22, 198 n. 2
King Lear (Shakespeare), 1, 3, 14, 17, 71–72, 145–46, 200 n. 3; Byron's recitation from, 156–64; quoted, 157
Kinnaird, Douglas, 194 n. 16
Kotzebue, August, 108, 110

Lallah Rookh (Byron), 68
Lamb, Lady Caroline, 95, 194 n. 18
Lamb, Charles, 162, 171 n. 14
"L'Amitie Est L'Amour Sans Ailes" (Byron), 73
Lascelles, B. P., 4, 10
Lee, Nathaniel, 4
Leeke, Thomas, 57, 61, 122–23, 181 n. 7, 198 n. 4

Leigh, Augusta: Byron's letters to, 14, 29–36, 42, 44–45, 70–84, 86, 101–6, 108–9, 140–41, 143–46, 152–57, 176 n. 21, 197 n. 32; incestuous relationship with Byron, 65, 70–71, 113, 119–20
Leigh, General Charles, 71
Life of William Jones (Teignmouth), 4
Lloyd, John Arthur, 121–23, 154–55, 203 n. 12
Long, Edward Noel, 93, 154, 187 n. 6, 201 n. 3
Lovers' Vows (Inchbald), 108–9, 110–15, 193 n. 14
Lyon, John, 169 n. 2
Lyte, H. C. Maxwell, 171 n. 13

Manfred (Byron), 71, 124, 131, 134, 173 n. 2, 176 n. 19, 195 n. 23
Manning, Peter, 62
Mansfield Park (Austen), 11, 110
Marchand, Leslie A., 29, 30, 39, 42, 57, 85, 101, 107, 108, 122, 173 n. 5, 180 n. 4, 182 n. 10, 193 n. 14, 195 n. 22, 204 n. 1
Mardyn, Mrs., 193 n. 14
Marino Faliero (Byron), 173 n. 2, 201 n. 4
Matthews, Charles Skinner, 40
Matthews, Mrs. Charles, 96–97
Mayne, E. C., 17
McGann, Jerome J., 89, 117, 147, 164, 168, 174 n. 9, 204 n. 14
Mealey, Owen, 29, 32, 41, 44–45
Medwin, Thomas, 193 n. 14, 196 n. 28
Melville, Lord Henry Dundas, 103–4, 127
Merchant of Venice, The (Shakespeare), 194 n. 16
Merchant Taylors' School, 5, 7–8
Mills, John, 122
Milton, John, 16, 166
Minchin, J. G. Cotton, 174 n. 8, 175 n. 13
Molière, 8
Moore, Thomas, 1, 23, 34, 53, 64, 68, 167, 177 n. 22, 179 n. 30, 180 n. 4, 186 n. 1, 191 n. 6, 197 n. 34, 197 n. 1
Mossop, Henry, 121–22, 164
Mountaineers, The (Coleman), 108
Murray, Joe, 30, 32, 36, 39
Musters, John, 60, 163, 186 n. 2

Napoleon, 87
Nevarez, Lisa, 175 n. 15

Nietzsche, Friedrich, 22
Northcote, James, 87–88, 92–96

"Occasional Prologue, Delivered Previous to the Performance of 'The Wheel of Fortune,' An" (Byron), 88–89
"On a Change of Masters at a Great Public School" (Byron), 147
"On a Distant View of the Village" (Byron), 102, 121–22, 164
"On the Death of a Young Lady, Cousin to the Author" (Byron), 117, 174 n. 9
Osborne, Lord Sidney, 30, 36
Othello (Shakespeare), 118, 124–25, 196 n. 28

Pafford, Ward, 124
Parker, Margaret, 19, 117, 174 n. 9
Pascoe, Judith, 12
"Passions, The" (Collins), 122–23
Peach, Annette, 189 n. 21
Peel, Sir Robert, 55, 57, 61, 181 nn. 7, 8
Petty, Henry, 89
Pigot, Elizabeth, 69–70, 71, 90, 148
Pigot, John, 88, 197 n. 1, 203 n. 10
Piozzi, Hester Lynch Thrale, 188 n. 7
Pitt, William, 92
Plato, 175 n. 15, 176 n. 18
Plautus, 8
Playfair, Giles, 96–97
Poems on Various Occasions (Byron), 56, 147, 148
Pope, Alexander, 166
Prelude, The (Wordsworth), 166
Prothero, Rowland E., 122, 176 n. 21, 197 n. 1

Raphael, Frederic, 33
Raymond, Dora Neill, 174–75 n. 12
Republic, The (Plato), 175 n. 15, 176 n. 18
Revenge, The (Young), 1, 14, 101, 106; Byron's recitation of, 120–34; Zanga compared to Iago, 118, 124–25, 187 n. 8, 196 n. 28
Richard III (Shakespeare), 108
Rogers, Samuel, 92
Rushton, Robert, 39–41, 197 n. 34

St. Paul's School, 5, 8, 195 n. 25
Sanders, George, 39
Sardanapalus (Byron), 194 n. 16

Self-fashioning, Romantic, 3, 12–13
Shakespeare, William, 108, 118, 124–25, 186 n. 1, 194 n. 16, 196 n. 28; *King Lear*, 1, 3, 14, 17, 71–72, 145–46, 156–64, 200 n. 3
Shattuck, Charles H., 135
Shelley, Percy Bysshe, 13
Sheridan, Richard Brinsley, 4–5, 8, 170 n. 5
Shrewsbury School, 5, 8, 10, 62–63, 195 n. 24
Siddons, Mrs. Sarah, 91, 194 n. 19
Snyder, Susan, 159–60
Sophonisba (Lee), 4–5
Southey, Robert, 25, 86, 110, 113, 115, 189 n. 1
Summer, Dr. Robert, 54
Sutton, Thomas, 7
Symonds, John Addington, 178 n. 28

Taborski, Boleslaw, 184 n. 11
Taming of the Shrew, The (Shakespeare), 186 n. 1
Tancred and Sigismunda (Thomson), 108
Tarver, Frank, 8–9
Tattersall, John Cecil, 93, 147, 177 n. 28
Teignmouth, Lord, 4
Theatricality, Romantic, 9, 11–13
"[Then Peace to Thy Spirit]" (Byron), 117
Thomson, James, 108
Thomson, Philip John, 203 n. 13
Thornton, Percy M., 190 n. 6
"Thoughts Suggested by a College Examination" (Byron), 199 n. 1
"Thyrza" (Byron), 196 n. 29
Ticknor, George, 198 n. 1
"To an Oak in the Garden of Newstead Abbey" (Byron), 34
"To D[elawarr]" (Byron), 117
"To Emma" (Byron), 66

Tom Brown's Schooldays (Hughes), 175 n. 15
"To the Duke of D[orset]" (Byron), 52–53
Townley, James, 8
"Tragedies of Shakespeare, The" (Lamb), 162
Two Foscari, The (Byron), 194 n. 16, 201 n. 4
Tyerman, C. J., 57, 100, 146

Vathek (Beckford), 68
Vaughan, Dr. Charles, 178 n. 28
Virgil, 49, 79, 166; *Aeneid*, 1, 11, 16–17, 57–63, 182 n. 10
Vision of Judgment, The (Byron), 86, 113

"Waltz, The" (Byron), 191 n. 6
Ward, Alex, 170 n. 6, 184 n. 15
Ward, J., 94–95
Warner, Rex, 189 n. 1
Weathercock, The (Allingham), 64, 136–39, 198 n. 1
Wellesley, Marquis of, 92
Werner (Byron), 201 n. 4
Westminster School, 7, 170 n. 11
Wheel of Fortune, The (Cumberland), 135–36, 198 n. 1
Wildman, Tom, 99–100
Williams, R. D., 58
Wilson, John, 197 n. 31
Winchester College, 7, 189 n. 1
Wingfield, John, 93, 196 n. 30
Wood, Thomas, 189 n. 21
Wordsworth, William, 166

Yelverton, Henry Edward. *See* Grey de Ruthyn, Lord Henry
Young, Edward, 1, 14, 101, 106, 120–34, 187 n. 8
"Young Roscius." *See* Betty, William Henry West

Library of Congress Cataloging-in-Publication Data

Elledge, Paul.

Lord Byron at Harrow School: speaking out, talking back, acting up, bowing out / Paul Elledge.

    p. cm.

    Includes bibliographical references (p.) and index.

    ISBN 0-8018-6343-0 (acid-free paper)

    1. Byron, George Gordon Byron, Baron, 1788–1824—Childhood and youth. 2. Byron, George Gordon Byron, Baron, 1788–1824—Knowledge and learning. 3. Byron, George Gordon Byron, Baron, 1788–1824—Homes and haunts—England—London. 4. Education, Secondary—England—London—History—19th century. 5. Boarding schools—England—London—History—19th century. 6. Poets, English—19th century—Biography. 7. Harrow School—History. I. Title.

PR4382.E36 2000

821′.7—dc21

[B]   99-049394